The Prehistoric Landscapes
of the Eastern Black Mountains

Frank Olding

BAR British Series 297
2000

Published in 2016 by
BAR Publishing, Oxford

BAR British Series 297

The Prehistoric Landscapes of the Eastern Black Mountains

ISBN 978 1 84171 057 0

BAR Publishing is the trading name of British Archaeological Reports (Oxford) Ltd.
British Archaeological Reports was first incorporated in 1974 to publish the BAR
Series, International and British. In 1992 Hadrian Books Ltd became part of the BAR
group. This volume was originally published by Archaeopress in conjunction with
British Archaeological Reports (Oxford) Ltd / Hadrian Books Ltd, the Series principal
publisher, in 2000. This present volume is published by BAR Publishing, 2016.

Printed in England

BAR
PUBLISHING

BAR titles are available from:

BAR Publishing
122 Banbury Rd, Oxford, OX2 7BP, UK
EMAIL   info@barpublishing.com
PHONE   +44 (0)1865 310431
FAX   +44 (0)1865 316916
www.barpublishing.com

Er cof am fy mam-gu

Ethel Mary Evans

1909 – 1997

A chwrlid dail a churlaw – yn ubain
Anobaith eu halaw
Athrist, mor gadarn ddistaw
Yw'r graig lwyd er rhegi'r glaw.

Cover Picture: "Arthur's Stone, Dorstone" from the frontispiece to John Duncumb's
Collections towards the
History and Antiquities of Herefordshire (1804).

CONTENTS

Prologue iv
Summary v
Acknowledgements v
Presentation of Material v

1 Introduction
1.1 Geology and Topography 1
1.2 The Problem of Lithic Scatters 1

2 The Palaeolithic 4

3 The Mesolithic
3.1 Lithic Scatters and Mesolithic Settlement 4
3.2 Mesolithic Land Use and Settlement 4

4 The Neolithic
4.1 Lithic Scatters and Neolithic Settlement 10
4.2 Neolithic Land Use 10
4.3 Neolithic Settlement 12
4.4 Neolithic Ritual 20
 Chambered Tombs – Their Uses and Meanings 20
 The Black Mountains Chambered Tombs in their Landscape 20
4.5 The Later Neolithic 27

5 The Bronze Age
5.1 Early Bronze Age Lithic Scatters 32
5.2 Early Bronze Age Land Use 32
5.3 Early Bronze Age Settlement 32
5.4 Early Bronze Age Ritual 35
 Dated Early Bronze Age Burials 35
 Round Cairns and Barrows 38
 Stone Circles 42
 Ring-Banks and Ring-Cairns 42
 Standing Stones 46
 Ritual Complexes 46
5.5 Early Bronze Age Metalwork 51
5.6 The Middle and Late Bronze Age 51
5.7 Late Bronze Hill-forts 55

6 The Iron Age
6.1 Hill-forts 56
6.2 Smaller Defended Settlements 63
6.3 Population, Economy and Territory 67
6.4 Iron Age Ritual 77

7 Conclusions 78

8 Monmouthshire Gazetteer

8.1 Mesolithic Sites
 Lithic Finds: MM 1-13 86
8.2 Neolithic Sites
 Chambered Tombs: BN 1-MN 1 87
 Axes: MN 2-13 87
 Lithic Finds: MN 14-25 87
8.3 Bronze Age Sites
 Round Cairns and Barrows: MB 1-27 89
 Stone Circles and Ring-Cairns: MB 28-29 90
 Dykes: MB 30 91
 Standing Stones: MB 31-36 91
 Metalwork: MB 37-45 91
 Lithic Finds: MB 46-58 92

8.4 Iron Age Sites
Hill-forts: MI 1-7   93
Smaller Defended Settlements: MI 8-10   93
Stray Finds: MI 11-14   94

9 Herefordshire Gazetteer

9.1 Mesolithic Sites
Lithic Finds: HM 1-23   96
9.2 Neolithic Sites
Long Barrows and Cairns: HN 1-7   98
Settlement Sites: HN 8-10   99
Axes: HN 11-22   99
Lithic Finds: HN 23-54   100
9.3 Bronze Age Sites
Round Barrows and Cairns: HB 1-26   103
Ring-ditches: HB 27-32   104
Stone Circles and Ring-banks: HB 33-37   105
Standing Stones: HB 38-42   105
Settlement Sites: HB 43-46   106
Metalwork: HB 47-56   106
Lithic Finds: HB 57-79   107
9.4 Iron Age Sites
Hill-forts: HI 1-7   109
Smaller Defended Settlements: HI 8-11   109
Stray Finds: HI 12-13   110
Barrows: HI 14   110

Appendix - Aerial Photographs Consulted   111

Bibliography   111

List of Figures

Fig. 1: The Black Mountains (drawn by Eleri Lynn)   2
Fig. 2: The eastern Black Mountains   3
Fig. 3: Mesolithic Sites   5
Fig. 4: The Mesolithic Landscape   8
Fig. 5: The Earlier Neolithic Landscape   11
Fig. 6: Neolithic timber structures   13
Fig. 7: Earlier Neolithic Tombs and Settlements   14
Fig. 8: Earlier Neolithic Lithic Finds   16
Fig. 9: Neolithic Axe Finds   18
Fig. 10: Neolithic Axe Finds by Group   19
Fig. 11: Earlier Neolithic Territories   21
Fig. 12: The Black Mountains Chambered Tombs   23
Fig. 13: Mynydd Bach (HN 1) and Arthur's Stone (HN 2) Chambered Tombs   24
Fig. 14: Maes Coch-Twyn y Beddau Long Cairn (BN 1)   26
Fig. 15: Garway Hill Long Barrow (HN 5)   28
Fig. 16: Great Llanavon-Cross Lodge Long Barrow (HN 3)   29
Fig. 17: The Later Neolithic Landscape   30
Fig. 18: The Early Bronze Age Landscape   33
Fig. 19: Early Bronze Age Lithic Finds   34
Fig. 20: The Urishay Common Core Area   36
Fig. 21: Early Bronze Age Territories   37
Fig. 22: Dated Early Bronze Age Burials   39
Fig. 23: Early Bronze Age Round Cairns and Barrows   40
Fig. 24: The Poston Mound (HI 14) and Ring-Bank (HB 34)   43
Fig. 25: The Clifford Ring-Bank (HB 33) and Upper Chilstone Ring-Bank and Barrow Cemetery (HB 35)   44

Fig. 26: Standing Stones, Stone Circles, Ring-Cairns and Ring-Banks   47
Fig. 27: The Garreg Las Ring-Cairn (MB 29)   48
Fig. 28: The Garn Wen Ritual Complex   49
Fig. 29: The Garn Wen and Haterrall Hill Ritual Complexes   50
Fig. 30: Bronze Age Metalwork Finds   52
Fig. 31: The Middle and Late Bronze Age Landscape   53
Fig. 32: The Black Darren Hill-Fort (HI 4)   54
Fig. 33: Iron Age Sites and Finds   57
Fig. 34: Credenhill Hill-Fort (HI 7)   58
Fig. 35: Dorstone (HI 1), Poston (HI 2) and the Garway Hill Enclosure (HI 11)   60
Fig. 36: Eaton Camp (HI 6), Poston (HI 2), Walterstone (HI 5)   61
Fig. 37: Twyn y Gaer (MI 2)   62
Fig. 38: Pentwyn (MI 1) and Skirrid Fawr (MI 3)   64
Fig. 39: Whitton Iron Age Farmstead   65
Fig. 40: Camp Hill Iron Age Enclosure (MI 10)   66
Fig. 41: White Castle Farm Iron Age Enclosure (MI 8)   68
Fig. 42: Twyn yr Allt Iron Age Enclosure (MI 4)   69
Fig. 43: Twyn yr Allt and Cefn Coed (B-HF 63)   70
Fig. 44: Twyn yr Allt and Twyn y Gaer Phase I   71
Fig. 45: Garway Hill (HI 11) and Whitton   72
Fig. 46: Hill-Fort Territories   74
Fig. 47: Thiessen Polygons for the eastern Black Mountains   75
Fig. 48: Hill-Fort Territories for the eastern Black Mountains   76
Fig. 49: The Mesolithic and Earlier Neolithic Landscapes   79
Fig. 50: The Later Neolithic and Early Bronze Age Landscapes   80
Fig. 51: The Middle-Late Bronze Age and Iron Age Landscapes   82

Prologue

"See this layered sandstone in the short mountain grass. Place your right hand on it, palm downward. See where the summer sun rises and where it stands at noon. Direct your index finger midway between them. Spread your fingers, not widely. You now hold this place in your hand.

The six rivers rise in the plateau towards your wrist. The first river, now called Mynwy, flows at the outside edge of your thumb. The second river, now called Olchon, flows between your thumb and the first finger, to join the Mynwy at the top of your thumb. The third river, now called Honddu, flows between your first and second fingers and then curves to join the Mynwy. The fourth river, now called Grwyne Fawr, flows between your second and third fingers and then curves the other way, south, to join the fifth river, now called Grwyne Fechan, that has been flowing between your third and your outside finger. The sixth river, now called Rhiangoll, flows at the edge of your outside finger.

This is the hand of the Black Mountains, the shape first learned. Your thumb is Crib y Gath. Your first finger is Curum and Hateral. Your second finger is Ffawyddog, with Tal y Cefn and Bâl Mawr at its knuckles. Your third finger is Cadair Fawr. Your outside finger is Allt Mawr, from Llysiau to Cerrig Calch, and its nail is Crug Hywel. On the high plateau of the back of your hand are Twyn y Llech and Twmpa, Rhos Dirion, Waun Fach and Y Dâs. You hold their shapes and their names."

Raymond Williams, *People of the Black Mountains*.

Summary

The prehistoric and Roman archaeology of the Brecon Beacons and western Black Mountains has recently benefited from the publication of comprehensive Inventories for the county of Brecknock by RCAHMW. The eastern Black Mountains, however, are divided between three counties, two national governments, three planning authorities and two Royal Commissions. The Herefordshire Inventory was published in 1931 and there is no Inventory for Monmouthshire and no intention to publish one.

This study has examined the evidence for the land use, settlement, economy and ritual activities of the area during prehistory and has identified both the density and chronological depth of prehistoric human activity. It has also attempted to identify distinct Mesolithic, Neolithic, Bronze Age and Iron Age territories.

Sections 8 and 9 present gazetteers of the prehistoric sites of the eastern Black Mountains drawn from the information available in the current literature, on the SMRs for Glamorgan-Gwent, the Brecon Beacons National Park and Herefordshire, the NMR for Wales, the NMR for England and the accession records of the National Museums and Galleries of Wales, Hereford City Museum, Abergavenny Museum and Newport Museum.

Acknowledgements

This study was originally presented to the University of Bristol as an M. A. dissertation and I should to thank the university for their co-operation in its publication and especially Dr. George Nash and Dr. Mark Horton for their support and enthusiasm. I should also like to thank the following for their kind help: Dr. R. Brewer and the staff of the National Museums and Galleries of Wales, Mr. R. Trett of Newport Museum, Ms. Judy Stevenson of Hereford City Museum, Dr. Paul Graves-Brown of the Glamorgan-Gwent Archaeological Trust, Ms. Rebecca Roseff SMR Officer for Herefordshire County Council, Dr. C. S. Briggs and the staff of the Royal Commission on the Ancient and Historic Monuments of Wales, Ms. Sharon Soutar and Mr. Chris Chandler of the National Monuments Record for England, Mr. Peter Dorling of the Brecon Beacons National Park. I should also like to thank Stuart Needham, Humphrey Case and Prof. Richard Harrison for their generosity and patience. To Graham Makepeace, Neil Phillips and Jonathan Stockley I owe thanks for valuable help in the field and for buying the beer! I should especially like to thank Aidan McCooey for his enthusiastic participation in fieldwork and surveys – without his sharp eyes some of these sites would never have been recorded!

Most of all, I should like to thank my wife, Wendy, and all the staff of Abergavenny Museum for putting up with me and with this book for so long!

Frank Olding,
Abergavenny Museum,
March 2000.

Presentation of Material

The reference numbers in brackets after site names in the text (e.g. HM 11, MI 13) are the unique site numbers assigned to each site in the gazetteers included in Section 8 (Monmouthshire) and Section 9 (Herefordshire). The site numbers prefixed by the letter M refer to Monmouthshire sites, those with H to those in Herefordshire. The numbers also indicate period i.e. MM - Monmouthshire Mesolithic, MN - Monmouthshire Neolithic, MB - Monmouthshire Bronze Age, MI - Monmouthshire Iron Age, HM - Herefordshire Mesolithic etc. Site numbers prefixed by B (e.g. B-RC 100) refer to sites published in the Inventories for Brecknock (RCAHMW 1986, 1997), the second element (e.g. RC 100) being their Inventory number. Unless otherwise indicated, the contours on all maps are shown at 150m, 300m and 450m above OD.

1 - INTRODUCTION

1.1 Geology and Topography

The Black Mountains (Figs. 1, 2) are composed of strata of Old Red Sandstone with a gentle dip to the SE. The prominent NW escarpment rises to over 700m and has a NE to SW trend. The long, steep-sided river valleys of the rivers Grwyne Fawr, Grwyne Fechan, Honddu and Monnow (with its tributaries the Olchon and Escley brooks), run to the SE and dissect the massif of the mountains into narrow ridges. Throughout the area, the stepping and terracing of the tablelands and the valley sides have been caused by differential erosion of the various sandstone layers. The NW escarpment shows three major breaks of slope due to differential weathering of the capping Brownstones, lower limestones and thin sandstones. To the SW, Pen Cerrig Calch, which rises to some 800m is an eroded outlier of Carboniferous Limestone capping Old Red Sandstone. The eastern foot-hills of the massif are defined by the valleys of the Olchon, Escley, and Monnow and the broad Golden Valley through which runs the River Dore. The far eastern edge of the Black Mountains is formed by the long ridge which separates the Golden Valley from that of the River Wye. Except for in the Golden Valley, the amount of land suitable for arable agriculture in the area is very limited (RCAHMW 1986, 3).

The heavy clay soils on the Old Red Sandstone do not lend themselves as well to the recognition of sites from the air as the lighter soils of the neighbouring limestone areas and the results of extensive examination of aerial photographs have proved extremely disappointing (see Appendix).

1.2 The Problem of Lithic Scatters

As a significant proportion of the evidence for prehistoric activity in the eastern Black Mountains takes the form of scatters of flint and lithic artefacts and debitage, a general overview of lithic methodologies at this point seems not out of place. Approaches to the analysis of multi-period lithic collections range from the simply descriptive to the interpretative (Schofield 1987, 1991; Garton et. al. 1989; Brown 1991), from the enthusiastic (Mellars 1976) to the frankly pessimistic (Tingle 1987, 99). However, "settlement areas" or "possible settlement activity" are still being identified by surface lithic scatters (Clay 1998, 327). Fieldwaking in the environs of ceremonial areas in Rutland suggest nearby foci for possible settlement (ibid., 328) - a juxtaposition which occurs in other areas e.g. North Stoke, Oxon. (Ford 1987a) and Stonehenge (Richards 1990) and which is evident locally in the relationship between Arthur's Stone (HN 2) and Cross Lodge (HN 3) chambered tombs and the Dorstone Hill settlement (HN 8 - see below).

The study of artefact scatters is fraught with difficulties - even to the level of agreeing what may or may not constitute a "site" (Haselgrove 1985, 14; Schofield 1991a, 3). Even when such terminological difficulties are resolved by accepting that high density scatters do, in fact, represent "sites" i.e. "repeated occupation and the accumulation of discard in specific locations" (ibid., 5), the terms "site" and "settlement" are not synonymous. Little light seems shed when some ethnographic studies indicate that lithic discard tends to occur more frequently away from habitation areas while others seem to demonstrate that secondary "sites" contain higher artefact densities than base camps (ibid., 4).

Despite these difficulties, patterns in the distribution of artefact scatters are discernible and should be capable of meaningful interpretation. Schofield offers the hope that analysis of the contents of scatters in terms of artefact diversity as well as quantity and density may improve our understanding of what lithic scatters represent (ibid. 5).

In the past, field-walking surveys have placed a strong emphasis on a high proportion and diverse range of implements within lithic assemblages as indicators of settlement sites (Holgate 1985, 53). Indeed, in the Abingdon area, the excavation of two such concentrations produced sub-soil contexts containing Neolithic domestic debris in association with flint assemblages consistent with these criteria (ibid., 56).

Others have attempted to deal with the problem of assemblages with few or no diagnostic flints by defining sets of internal criteria by which they can be dated and their function interpreted. By reference to microwear analysis, replicative experiments and ethnography, unmodified flakes have been assigned functions (Ford 1987a, 68), while flake thickness and length:breadth ratios have been used as chronological indicators (ibid., 69).

In more recent work, domestic and industrial zones have been distinguished on the basis of correlation between specific artefact groups. High proportions of retouched artefacts are considered a feature of domestic contexts, while dense scatters with high proportions of primary waste are characteristic of industrial zones. If density and assemblage composition can be established for prehistoric settlements and industrial zones, this may enable us to assign domestic or industrial status to lithic material recovered by surface collection (Schofield 1991b, 117).

These problems inherent in the study of lithic scatters are exacerbated when the surface finds under discussion are old museum collections amassed by keen local amateurs with all that this implies in variation of documentation, provenance and identification (Gardiner 1987, 50). Even so, there is still much to be gained from studying such "unsystematic" collections (ibid., 56). Luckily, the thoroughness, detailed documentation and full and prompt publication of Herefordshire's most prolific flint collector, R. S. Gavin Robinson, mean that his data are infinitely more reliable than most (see below)

Even if the study of surface lithic scatters can only put dots the map, this is still of value in giving a generalised picture of prehistoric landscapes (Holgate 1985, 56).

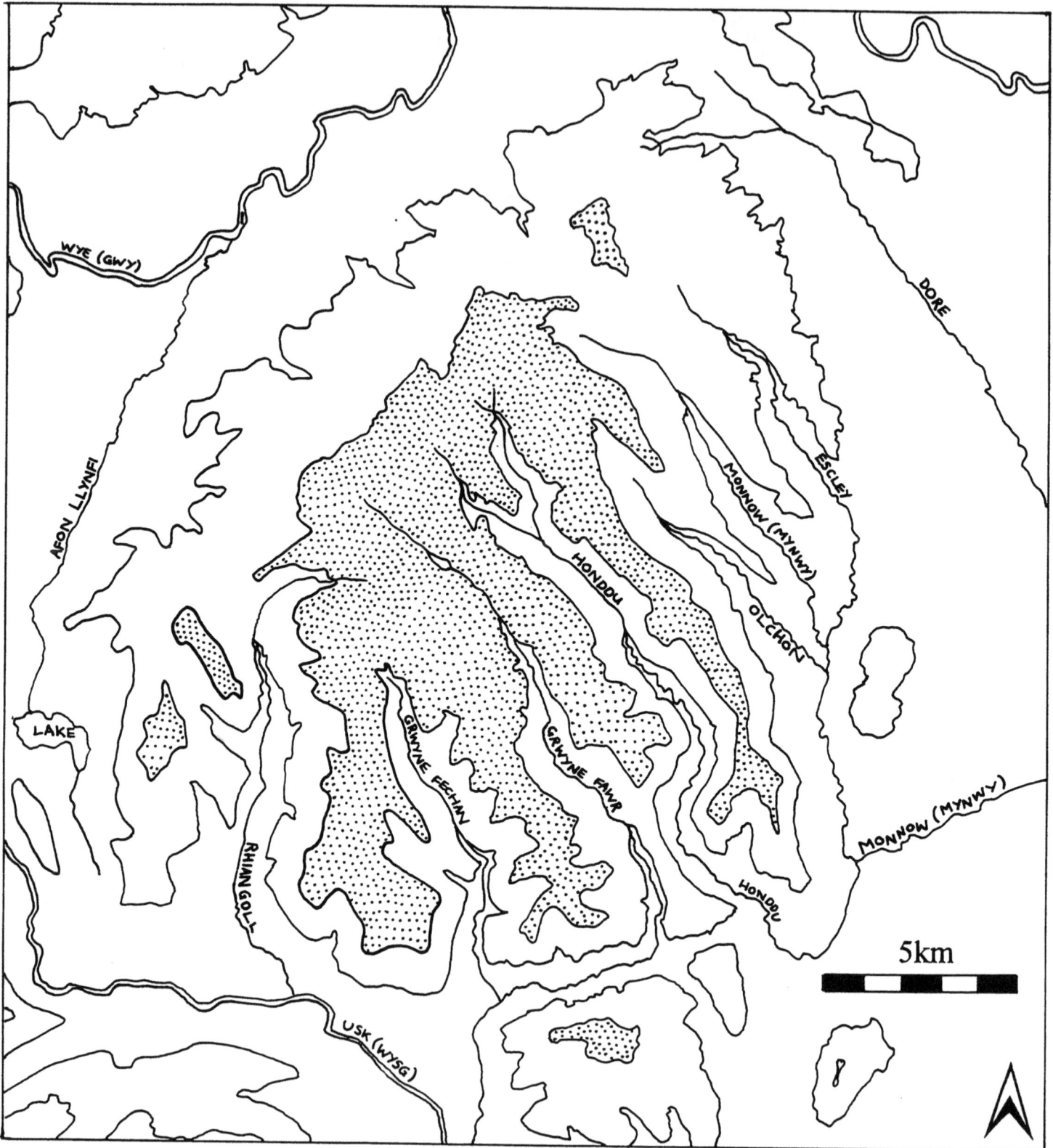

WYE (GWY)

DORE

AFON LLYNFI

ESCLEY

MONNOW (MYNWY)

HONDDU

OLCHON

LAKE

GRWYNE FECHAN

GRWYNE FAWR

MONNOW (MYNWY)

RHIANGOLL

HONDDU

5km

USK (WYSG)

Fig. 1: The Black Mountains (drawn by Eleri Lynn).

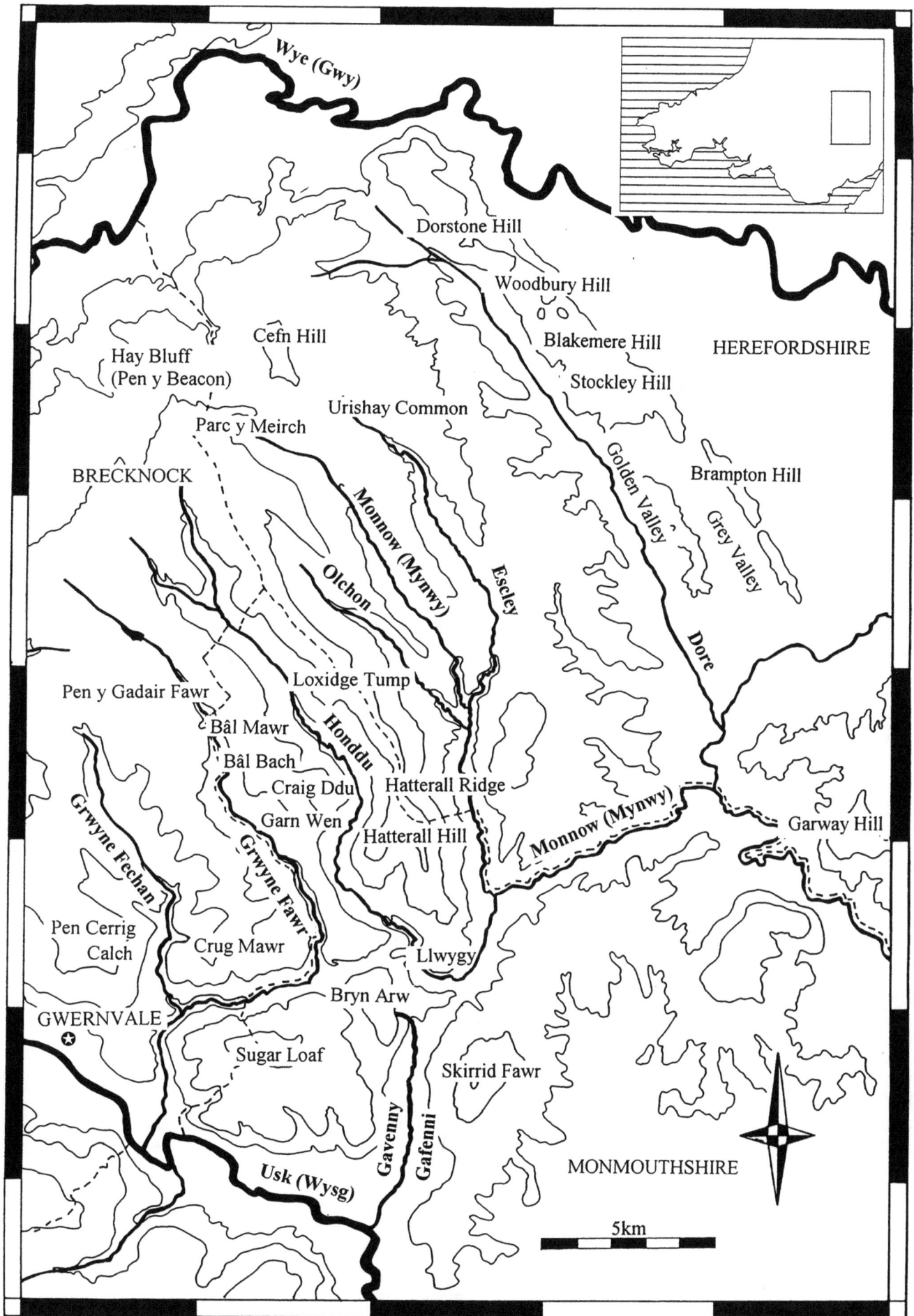

Wye (Gwy)

Dorstone Hill

Woodbury Hill

HEREFORDSHIRE

Cefn Hill

Blakemere Hill

Stockley Hill

Hay Bluff
(Pen y Beacon)

Urishay Common

Brampton Hill

Parc y Meirch

Golden Valley

Grey Valley

BRECKNOCK

Monnow (Mynwy)

Olchon

Escley

Dore

Pen y Gadair Fawr

Loxidge Tump

Bâl Mawr

Honddu

Bâl Bach

Craig Ddu

Hatterall Ridge

Garn Wen

Monnow (Mynwy)

Garway Hill

Hatterall Hill

Grwyne Fechan

Grwyne Fawr

Pen Cerrig
Calch

Crug Mawr

Llwygy

Bryn Arw

GWERNVALE

Sugar Loaf

Skirrid Fawr

Gavenny

Gafenni

MONMOUTHSHIRE

Usk (Wysg)

5km

Fig. 2: The eastern Black Mountains.

3

2 - THE PALAEOLITHIC

On the strength of seven backed, burnt flint tools, Gwernvale, the sole Palaeolithic site in the eastern Black Mountains, has also been claimed as the first Late Upper Palaeolithic open site in Wales and interpreted as playing a role in "bi-polar" settlement and hunting patterns (Britnell and Savory 1984, 136).

3 - THE MESOLITHIC

3.1 Lithic Scatters and Mesolithic Settlement

In his discussion of Mesolithic stone and flint assemblages, Paul Mellars (1976) adopts the definition of settlement as "any place occupied by one or more individuals for one or more nights, for any purpose that falls within the ordinary, expected and predictable round of activities of the society in question". Such settlements are visible in the archaeological record either as the remains of structural features (such as pits, post-holes etc.) or in the distribution of stone implements and the debris of stone tool manufacture. Although due caution must be exercised in the interpretation of lithic scatters, settlement areas identified from such evidence may be comparable to those based on the direct evidence of structural remains (*ibid.*, 377). Mellars goes on to outline three Mesolithic settlement types:

Type I - settlements which occupy a very restricted area, no more than 10-15 square metres in extent occupied by groups of very limited size.

Type II - much larger sites ranging between 44 and 210 square metres with concentrated artefact distributions over a well-defined, regular area. These may have been occupied by residential groups substantially larger than Type I (*loc. cit.*).

Type III - artefact scatters that cover an extensive area but with marked concentrations at localised points. At such "multiple-focus" sites, it is difficult to assess how many individual concentrations (interpreted by Mellars as occupation areas) were occupied at one and the same time (*ibid.*, 379).

In terms of populations, Type I seem unlikely to represent groups of more than five or six individuals, whether nuclear families or more specialised "task groups" such as male hunting parties. Types II and III are likely to represent social units of at least two or three nuclear families and sometimes more (*ibid.*, 380). Mellars goes on to define three basic types of artefact assemblage which may be present at any or all of these settlement types:

Type A - microlith-dominated assemblages with high percentages of microliths, i.e. 88-97% of the total tool inventory; low proportions of all other tool forms and extremely low percentages of flake/blade end-scrapers. Small blade-cores and microburins are usually well-represented and probably reflect the manufacture of microliths on the spot (*ibid.*, 386). The overall impression created by such assemblages is a strong bias in favour of "primary subsistence activities" (i.e. hunting) as against

"maintenance" or "domestic" activities (e.g. skin preparation, bone working etc.)(*ibid.*, 388).

The majority of such assemblages in Mellars' data base came from sites on present-day moorland, generally above the 1,000 ft (305m) contour and frequently occupying prominent exposed positions with extensive views over the surrounding countryside. All Mellars' Type A assemblages came from Type I settlements i.e. small social units (*ibid.*, 389). The majority can be characterised as short-lived summer settlements occupied by very small social groups.

Type B - "balanced" assemblages with 30-60% microliths, higher percentages of flake/blade scrapers (usually 25-50%). These suggest an emphasis not only on hunting activities but also on various "domestically oriented" tasks (*ibid.*, 391).

Type B assemblages occur in a range of environments but are particularly well represented at coastal sites. The majority of sites with "balanced" assemblages cover areas of at least 50m sg. and are likely to represent settlements of at least two or three family groups. Excavated examples also produce clearly defined traces of living structures (*ibid.*, 392). In upland areas (e.g. Deepcar, Warcock Hill), they have been seen as the summer encampments of groups who spent the winter months in adjacent areas of lowlands (*ibid.*, 393). In other areas (e.g. Star Carr, Flixton), however, their location below the 200m contour and at sites offering protection from winter weather, the widespread occurrence of hazel nut shells and the evidence for the gathering of larger social groups seem to indicate winter-season settlements (*ibid.* 395).

Type C - scraper-dominated assemblages with exceptionally high proportions of flake/blade scrapers (i.e. 82-90%) which appear to reflect a limited and specialised range of activities in which the preparation of animal skins played a dominant role. The social groups involved seem to be small and the occupations of short duration. Scraper-dominated assemblages from sites above the 305m contour (e.g. Blubberhouses Moor with its fragmentary hazel nut shells) may well have been occupied during the autumn with intensive skin working in preparation for the winter (*ibid.* 395). Lowland sites (e.g. Kettlebury I, Surrey, and Freshwater West, Pembs.) may also represent autumn or early winter settlements (*loc. cit.*).

3.2 Mesolithic Land Use and Settlement

There are three recognisable Mesolithic technologies in lowland Wales and the Marches. An Earlier Mesolithic technology characterised by simple "non-geometric" microliths and by single and double-ended, convex-edged scrapers together with burins, finely serrated blades, ground-edged pieces, punches and core adzes (often in stone). Later Mesolithic technologies are dominated by narrow microlith forms, especially scalene micro-triangles and rod-like pieces blunted down one edge. In southern Wales these are associated with deeply denticulated (as opposed to convex) scrapers, notched pieces, truncated pieces and narrow burins, though as yet there is no evidence for localised traditions or industries (Jacobi 1980, 169). Core adzes are absent, being replaced by various forms of chopper or chopping tool. In

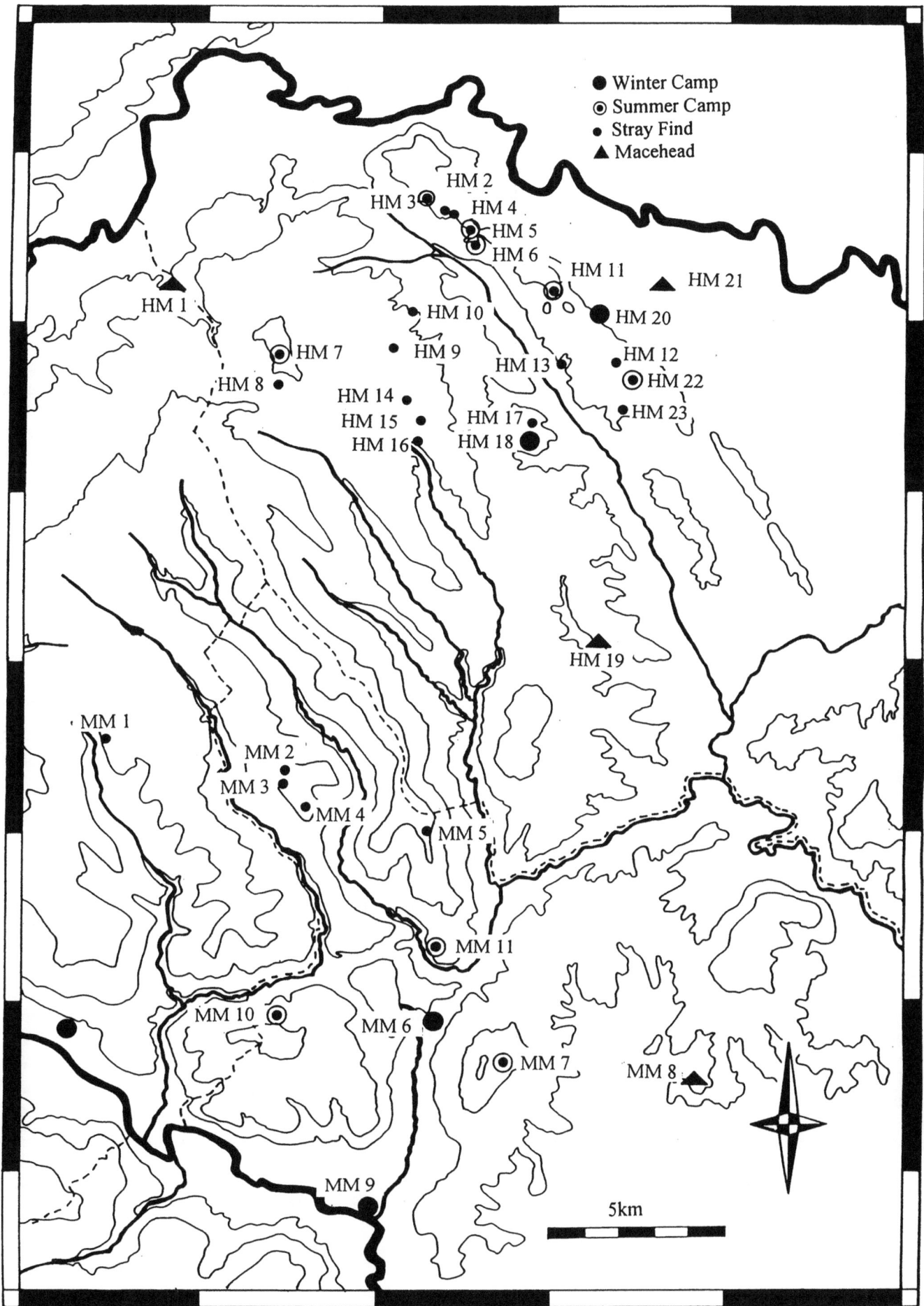

Winter Camp ●
Summer Camp ◉
Stray Find ·
Macehead ▲

HM 2
HM 3
HM 4
HM 5
HM 6
HM 11
HM 21
HM 1
HM 10
HM 20
HM 7
HM 9
HM 13
HM 12
HM 8
HM 22
HM 14
HM 17
HM 23
HM 15
HM 18
HM 16
HM 19

MM 1
MM 2
MM 3
MM 4
MM 5
MM 11
MM 10
MM 6
MM 7
MM 8
MM 9

5km

Fig. 3: Mesolithic Sites.

5

north Wales, these are replaced by small, convex-edged scrapers and steeply retouched pieces (*ibid.* 177).

The transition between the Earlier and Later Mesolithic can be assigned to the 7th millennium b. c., perhaps as early as 6800 b. c. (Pitts and Jacobi 1979, 164). This occurred at the same time as the transition from pollen zones V-VIa, the start of the replacement of birch-pine woodland by mixed deciduous forest (*ibid.*, 174).

In the period c. 9,000 B. C., the Brecon Beacons supported considerable stands of oak with elm more frequent at lower levels. By c. 6,000 B. C., lime and ash were widespread, particularly at lowland sites and mixed woodlands were probably common in both the Brecon Beacons and Black Mountains to a height of 450m or more (RCAHMW 1997, 5).

Environmental data from Waun Fignen Felen (B-MS 2) in the western Beacons (NGR: SS 825 179) suggests Mesolithic activity before 8,000 B. P. with the regular burning off of the birch woodland which may have led to the development of acid soils, heather heath and hazel copses. The microliths from this site span both the Earlier and Later Mesolithic but it was not possible to differentiate between seasonal activity or occupation on a more permanent basis (*ibid.*, 17). Similar contemporary activity may be discernible at Llyn Mire in the Wye valley (NGR: SN 00 55) (*ibid.*, 6).

Some clearances of this sort may have been aimed at the creation of new settlement sites. Other, more widespread burning was probably used to manage animal and plant resources by increasing grazing potential, as well as flushing animals from forests and increasing visibility for hunters under the canopies and from nearby ridge-tops (Webley 1976, 26; Bewley 1994, 40; RCAHMW 1997, 17). This led ultimately to podsolisation and the onset of blanket peat formation (*ibid.*, 6).

At Gwernvale (B-MS 15), pre-cairn soil levels at the E end of the cairn produced 56 microliths and microlithic fragments. Some 23 were characteristic of Earlier Mesolithic industries, 25 were scalene micro-triangles or rods assigned to Later Mesolithic traditions. The site has been interpreted as a temporary camp for the exploitation of ungulates and has been seen as forming part of a pattern of "bi-polar" settlement with its roots in the Late Upper Palaeolithic (Britnell and Savory 1984, 130). This saw seasonal movement from home-bases in the lowland coastal areas towards temporary inland encampments in pursuit of migrating herds of larger herbivores - reindeer and horse in the Late Glacial, wild ox and red deer in the Flandrian. By the Later Mesolithic and Earlier Neolithic periods, this pattern appears to have developed into coastal and inland economies dependant on transhumance. Rises in sea level throughout the Mesolithic may have led to denser and more permanent inland settlement (*ibid.*, 136).

Gwernvale's position on the margins of the uplands on a terrace overlooking the River Usk provided a convenient vantage point for the exploitation of several ecological zones. It remains difficult to assess the precise nature or permanence of settlement from lithic evidence alone, but the range and quantity of the material equipment found on the site suggests temporary settlements representing the seasonal movement of hunting parties towards the Welsh highlands from a home-base near the Bristol Channel in pursuit of game (*loc. cit.*).

With the exception of Cefn Hill (see below), Jacobi assigns all the Black Mountains sites (Fig. 3) to the Later Mesolithic tradition and notes that the greater number of find-spots in Herefordshire reflects the areas of maximum accumulated annual temperatures i.e. those areas best suited to supporting populations of grazing animals (1980, 191). Lowland sites below the 600ft (182m) contour he characterises as winter occupation sites, though suggesting that their use may occasionally have extended into the summer months. He also points out that the annual routine of Mesolithic groups in Wales was almost certainly organised to take advantage of non-ungulate food sources such as fish and hazel-nuts as well as the ungulates themselves (*ibid.*, 192).

Upland sites, he postulates, were occupied during the summer months for regular exploitation of ungulates in their summer grazing grounds and there is a great deal of evidence in the Black Mountains for the widespread repeated use of fire to encourage browse for the migratory deer populations (*loc. cit.*). Environmental evidence suggests the presence in the upland areas of productive browse woodland. Pollen diagrams emphasise the importance of deciduous woodland at all altitudes, particularly oak in southern Wales (*ibid.*, 194). The presence of oak stumps at 610m above O. D. on Y Gadair at the centre of the Black Mountains (Wheeler 1925, 58) is further evidence of the drastic changes which have taken place in the upland landscape. Spells of fine weather may have extended the summer upland hunting season into the autumn (Jacobi 1980, 194).

Linking specific upland summer camps to specific lowland winter bases is problematic but Jacobi makes a case for accepting such a relationship between the Glamorgan sites of Pen y Bont (lowland) and Craig y Llyn. Hypothetical home ranges of 6 miles (10km) for each site overlap and each site is well placed to exploit either end of the local topographical range (*ibid.*, 195). Jacobi's distribution plans of upland and lowland Later Mesolithic sites show that the Black Mountains sites are placed so as to exploit both the summer and winter ungulate grazing grounds - the former on the tops of the long ridges, the latter in the lower ground to the east of Skirrid Fawr (*ibid.*, Figs. 4.31-32). Interestingly, this striking landmark sits at the edge of both catchments (see below).

In the Later Mesolithic period, improved climatic conditions may well have encouraged similar land-use patterns between lowland and highland within inland areas (Britnell and Savory, 138). Across Wales as a whole, the Later Mesolithic sites tend to cluster very high - at over 360m OD - or on the lowest lying ground. Within red deer populations, the males will tend to graze the lowest parts of the winter range and, together with the barren females, the highest areas of summer browse, well above the levels utilised by the productive females and their young. Cropping this non-reproductive section of the herd is the most efficient use of the ungulate resource and goes some way to explaining the Mesolithic distributions (Jacobi 1980, 195).

In contrast with the Earlier Mesolithic strategy of selecting favourable places to intercept their prey (Myers 1987, 145), Later Mesolithic hunting may have been increasingly centred around small task-groups actively searching for their prey. The Later Mesolithic settlement pattern may therefore differ from that of the Earlier Mesolithic in that Later Mesolithic hunting may have involved a more general use of the landscape without the location-specific emphasis of the earlier period. The more general representation of sites for the Later Mesolithic in the eastern Black Mountains accords with the expected pattern (*ibid.*, 147). Bearing this in mind and applying Mellars' methodology to the local data, it is possible to attempt to classify the Mesolithic scatters of the eastern Black Mountains (Fig. 4).

That exploitation of the area began in the Earlier Mesolithic is attested by obliquely blunted points and isosceles triangles from a group of sites just below the 1,550 ft. (470m) above OD contour on Cefn Hill (HM 7) (Jacobi 1980, 193). Apart from Gwernvale, this is the sole Earlier Mesolithic site in the area. In Herefordshire, almost half of the Later Mesolithic sites (12 out of 22) are single finds or pairs of flints (HM2, HM14), there are also three single perforated pebbles (HM1, HM19 and HM21). Among the single finds, there are eight microliths (HM 4, 8, 10, 12-15, 17), four unretouched flakes or blades (HM 2, 3, 16, 23) and a solitary microlithic core (HM9). These should probably be regarded as casual losses on hunting-foraging expeditions and their distribution may in some measure reflect the territories of the base camps discussed below. The remaining seven sites are assemblages of surface finds:

Merbach Hill (HM3) is an upland blade/flake dominated site set on an exposed plateau at 285m above OD with excellent views over the Golden Valley. This probably represents a summer domestic/base camp.

On Arthur's Stone Ridge (HM5) is another exposed hilltop site (260m above OD) at the head of two valleys dropping down west to the Golden Valley and east to the River Wye. The assemblage is blade/flake dominated and represents another summer base/domestic camp.

Dorstone Hill (HM6) is another exposed hilltop site about 500m SE of HM5 at 270m above OD. As the site remains unpublished and the flints in private hands, it is impossible to assess the nature of the assemblage but another summer camp site seems likely. The site later became a focus for Neolithic settlement (HN 8).

Woodbury Hill (HM11) is another exposed hilltop site at 260m above OD with extensive views over both the Golden Valley and the Wye Valley. The lack of published information on the nature of the assemblage makes it impossible to characterise, but another summer camp seems possible.

Cothill Farm (HM 18) is a sheltered site at 185m above OD on the E slope of Urishay Common. The site commands two valleys running E into the Golden Valley and has extensive views to the E and SE. The assemblage consists only of five microliths but a small winter or autumn "task group" camp seems possible.

Lower Blakemere Farm (HM 20) is another sheltered, E-facing site at 110m above OD on the slopes of Blakemere Hill. The blade/flake dominated assemblage probably represents a winter domestic camp for a small group.

Hill Farm (HM 22) is an exposed site at 220m above OD at the head of a small S-E facing valley. The assemblage is the single largest in the area and is blade/flake dominated (40 blade/flakes to 1 microlith) and probably represents a summer base camp for a larger group. The site is ideally placed to observe the movement of game up the broad expanse of the Grey Valley.

It is tempting to see in the Lower Blakemere Farm site (HM 20) a potential winter base for the groups exploiting the summer camps on the eastern ridge of the Golden Valley (HM 3, 5, 6, 11, 22). All are within the sort of 5km radius postulated for potential base camp or hunting site catchment areas (Bewley 1994, 35). It is also possible to postulate a similar relationship between the Cothill Farm task-group camp (HM 18) and the single find-spots on Vagar Hill and Urishay Common (HM 9, 10, 14-16).

Estimates for Mesolithic populations on the North York Moors give an average group size of about 25 persons (*ibid.*, 38) and it has been suggested that the distribution of Mesolithic flint in the Golden Valley represents the territories of extended family groupings. It is possible, therefore, that the Later Mesolithic communities of the Golden Valley exploited two distinct territories meering along the river Dore itself.

The Mesolithic material from Monmouthshire is much scarcer and more difficult to characterise. The single flints from upland areas (MM 1-5) probably represent losses on hunting-foraging expeditions in summer grazing areas. The remaining five sites are assemblages of surface finds:

The scatter at Skirrid Fawr (MM 7) is sited at 335m above OD, but sheltered from the worst of the westerly weather by the mountain itself. The site commands the head of the SE facing valley of the Llanymynach brook and enjoys extensive views across the lowland areas to the E. It sits at the interface of the winter and summer grazing grounds proposed by Jacobi for this area (see above) and would be an excellent intercept station for the spring migration of ungulates onto the higher ground. It would be interesting to see whether more detailed re-evaluation of the lithics could assign the assemblage to the Earlier or Later Mesolithic. Its topographical position certainly fits well with known Earlier Mesolithic subsistence strategies attested at Gwernvale and Cefn Hill (see above).

The microlithic chipping floor at Abergavenny on the glacial bluff overlooking the flood-plain of the river Usk (MM 9) can also be compared in its topographical situation to Gwernvale and may have performed a similar function as a winter base-camp. Its position is in striking contrast to that of the flake-blade scatter on the exposed northern face of the Sugar Loaf at 350m above OD (MM 10) which can only be a summer habitation - possibly a base camp. The most likely route from the valley bottom at Abergavenny to the summit of the Sugar Loaf is via the valley of the Cybi Brook - the very area enclosed in the 13th century as a deer park by the

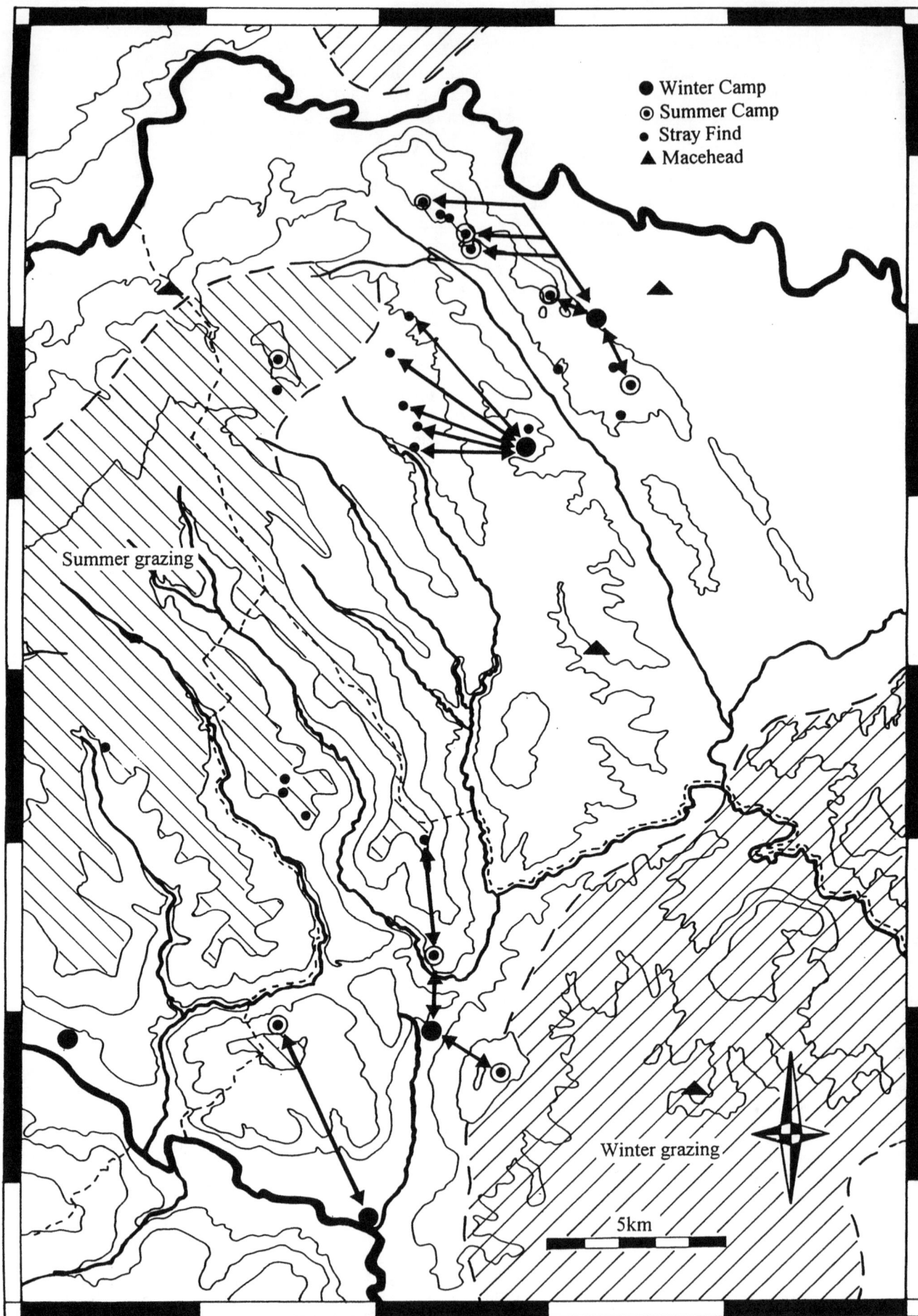

Fig. 4: The Mesolithic Landscape (possible relationships between sites arrowed).

Legend:
- ● Winter Camp
- ◉ Summer Camp
- • Stray Find
- ▲ Macehead

Summer grazing

Winter grazing

5km

lords of Abergavenny. It is tempting to see the sites as forming elements in the sort of bi-polar upland-lowland settlement pattern postulated for Gwernvale.

It is equally tempting to associate the flake scatter at 260m above OD on the NW-facing summit of the Llwygy (MM 11) with the Blaengavenny blade-flake scatter (MM 6). Blaengavenny is a sheltered site at 150m above OD on a slight knoll in the valley bottom overlooking the river Gavenny. Stretching Mellar's hypothesis to the point of attenuation, it could be characterised as a very small scale winter base camp. The Llwygy scatter is situated at an exposed NW facing spot on the natural route from the valley floor to Hatterall Ridge and could be interpreted as a summer camp. The lowest ford on the river Honddu lies between the two sites at Lower Stanton (NGR: SO 3154 2113). Pushing the available evidence to its absolute limits, the single microlith from Hatterall Hill (MM 5) could then be seen as reflecting the high uplands hunting grounds exploited from the Llwygy.

The postulated winter base-camps for Monmouthshire seem to cluster more closely in the more confined terrain of the Gavenny and Usk valleys. It is possible that the groups involved were smaller than those of their Herefordshire neighbours, or that the major food resource of the river Usk attracted more Mesolithic people to the area.

Over the eastern Black Mountains as a whole, the distribution of perforated pebble mace-heads (HM 1, 19, 21; MM 8) forms an interesting contrast with the other Mesolithic material. The find-spots for these enigmatic implements are confined to lowland river valley sites which suggests that they did not form part of the regular hunting-foraging tool-kit. With more and more evidence for Mesolithic votive deposits in natural locations (Bradley 1998, 28), it should always be borne in mind that their deposition may have been governed more by ritual than practical considerations.

Comparison of the distributions of Later Mesolithic and Earlier Neolithic flint sites shows a considerable amount of overlap and apparent continuity. Ten of the Herefordshire Mesolithic sites have also produced Earlier Neolithic material: Arthur's Stone Ridge (HM5-HN 29), Dorstone Hill (HM 6-HN 8), Cefn Hill (HM 7-HN 9), Abbey Farm (HM 8-HN 10), Woodbury (HM 11-HN 35), Stockley no. 1 (HM 12-HN 45), Pucha no. 1 (HM 14-HN 32), Pentwyn (HM 16-HN 34), Shegear no. 1 (HM 17-HN 41) and Hill Farm (HM 22-HN 50). In Monmouthshire, only the flint find spot on Hatterall Hill (MM 5-MN 18), the scatters on the Llwygy (MM 11-MN 19) and Skirrid Fawr (MM 7-MN 21) and the Flannel Street excavations at Abergavenny (MM 9-MN 24) produced material of both periods. Clearings made by hunter-gatherers for management of game may have been attractive to early farmers (Darvill 1987, 49). In southern England, hunter-gatherers probably operated alongside farmers (*ibid.*, 50), though the strong possibility that the same groups practised a combination of both subsistence strategies should be borne in mind.

The same sites obviously remained significant for many generations and this deep social, economic and ritual knowledge of the landscape may have helped to engender the sense of attachment to place which seems to figure so strongly in the Neolithic period (Children and Nash 1994, 16).

4 - THE NEOLITHIC

4.1 Lithic Scatters and Neolithic Settlement

Any regional survey must bear in mind the obvious, but all too often ignored fact that some areas are suitable for settlement and others are not. In terms of Neolithic settlement, various factors had to be taken into account - the availability of arable and grazing land, the supply of water, fuel and building materials, defence, the need to avoid flooding and natural shelter. So, for instance, south-facing slopes are more attractive to settlement than north-facing ones as offering more day-time sun and shelter from prevailing winter winds (Schofield 1991b, 118).

Settlements of a specific period will therefore tend to occur and recur in specific types of location. It was not a random process and areas of domestic activity will appear concentrated in specific zones. Schofield defines the lithic assemblage characteristics for settlement/domestic areas as: low overall density, low proportions of primary waste and high proportions of both retouched tools and cores. Industrial areas, on the other hand, are characterised by high density scatters, high proportions of primary waste but low levels of retouched tools and cores (*ibid.*, 119, Table 10.1)

On the basis of field-walking and assemblage analysis, Schofield was able to identify three distinct zones in the Neolithic landscape of the Meon Valley - area 1 was primarily industrial for the extraction and working of flint, areas 2 and 3 were settlement zones which provided greater natural protection as well as a greater variety of resource habitats. Within the settlement zones, the distribution of leaf-shaped arrowheads and flint axes suggested that the higher ground was used for hunting and timber extraction (*ibid.*, 127/8).

Even if the results of fieldwalking contain an in-built bias against the recognition of material from the Earlier Neolithic (Healy 1987, 15) and even if many of the sites identified by lithic scatters never had any significant structure which may have left earth-bound sub-soil features, they still represent the only evidence for the core of the prehistoric settlement pattern (Haselgrove 1985, 17).

The results of extensive field-walking in Oxfordshire and Berkshire indicated that Earlier Neolithic settlements were, on the whole, small in area and short lived in occupancy and that the rarer large enclosed sites may have functioned more as "aggregation centres" than subsistence settlements (Ford 1987b, 129). In addition, the emphasis on blades and narrow flakes in Earlier Neolithic assemblages has been seen as a reflection of a still essentially mobile way of life - that Earlier Neolithic communities "travelled light" (Bradley 1987, 184).

Where excavated, Earlier Neolithic flint scatters seldom produce features indicative of substantial structures and it is more common to find deliberately back-filled bowl-shaped pits (Edmonds 1995, 35). These often contain selections of carefully sorted and chosen "refuse" - potsherds, bone and flint - and have been interpreted as the final acts of ceremonial feasts and ritualised flint-working (*ibid.*, 43). These deposits may have been intended to ensure the fertility and continuity of the communities involved or to mark and ensure their rights of access to significant places (*ibid.*, 45). Such scatters may also support the notion that Earlier Neolithic communities retained a measure of routine mobility (*ibid.*, 35).

In general, industrial or quarrying sites are characterised by core reduction in discrete, high density scatters of preparation flakes, primary waste material, broken flakes and wasted nodules. Settlement areas are characterised by lower density tertiary material with higher percentages of cores and retouched artefacts. Extractive tools such as axes and arrowheads occur across a wider hunting and foraging domain, while settlement areas are characterised by the presence of maintenance artefacts such as scrapers. Although higher artefact densities do not necessarily equate to the size or longevity of the settlements involved, it is still possible that the dominance of scrapers in Early Bronze Age assemblages points to denser and more permanent settlement (Schofield 1994, 91).

4.2 Neolithic Land Use

Evidence for pre-elm decline agriculture in the Brecon Beacons and western Black Mountains is scanty, though the presence of ribwort plantain at Llyn Mire during an elm depression may indicate local agricultural clearance in the Wye Valley. Although cereal pollens are recorded at Black Mountains sites, Neolithic agricultural activity seems to have been small in scale and clearances short-lived (RCAHMW 1997, 6), but it still led to the inception of blanket peat in upland areas (Caseldine 1990, 49). Accelerated silting at Llangorse Lake in the period 5,000-2,000 B. P. may have been due to forest clearance (*loc. cit.*)

The landscape (Fig. 5) was slowly colonised by farmers. The siting of the Mynydd Troed long cairn (B-CT 2) on a high coll suggests Neolithic agricultural land-use at high altitudes. However, Neolithic fields, if they ever existed, have not survived (RCAHMW 1997, 206), but lithic distributions in Brecknock indicate Neolithic farming communities settled in diverse topographical locations right across the county (*ibid.*, 24). Most of the excavated Brecknock chambered tombs have produced evidence of domestic occupation close to, or even on the tomb sites themselves (*ibid.*, 28). The use of emmer wheat is attested at Gwernvale (B-CT 11) and the collection of hazelnuts at Pipton (B-CT 8). Cattle, sheep and pig bones were identified at Pen y Wyrlod-Talgarth (B-CT 4), Gwernvale and Tŷ Isaf (B-CT 3) and the latter two sites also produced deer bone (*ibid.*, 6).

The Black Mountains chambered tombs (see below) are mainly sited on the boundary between good, freely-drained soils and wetter soil; in the Neolithic between two kinds of oakwood, one damp, the other dry and open. In these woods, it has been suggested that the valleys may have supported cattle and pigs with sheep on the lower hill-slopes. In summer, both cattle and sheep would have moved to the better-drained soils adjacent to the tombs (Webley 1976, 28). In this light, the Black Mountains have been seen as the territory of people dependent on grazing animals. Finds of

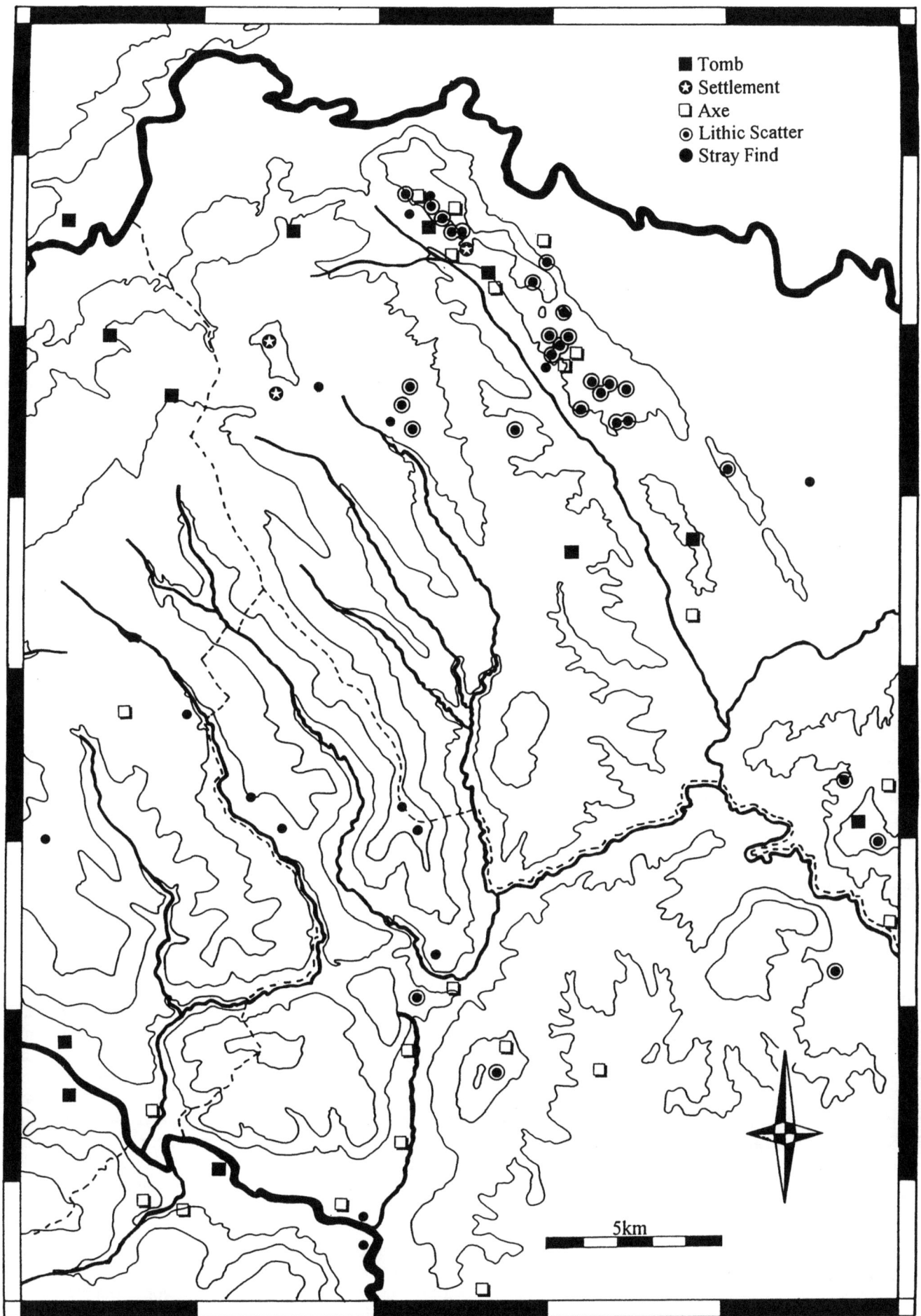

Fig. 5: The Earlier Neolithic Landscape

11

ox horn-cores in ritual positions in the forecourts of Tŷ Isaf and Pipton seem to support the view that pastoralism was the main economy of the region (*ibid.*, 29). The possibility has also been raised of long-distance herd movements between the Cotswolds and the Black Mountains with valley-bottom chambered tombs marking the major routes into the Black Mountains (*ibid.*, 30). This has in turn been put forward as a possible mechanism for long-distance contact and trading (*ibid.*, 33).

There appears to be a distinct divergence in land use between valley and upland sites in mid-Wales in the Earlier Neolithic period. The absence of cereal pollen or other indicators of arable farming at upland sites indicate that forest clearance here was solely for the creation of upland pasture (Britnell and Savory 1984, 138).

Lowland sites produce different evidence. Post-elm decline horizons from a peat mire at Newbridge in the Wye valley contain a wide variety of pollen types associated with cultivation as well as cereal pollens themselves. The evidence has been interpreted as a cyclical pattern of clearance and cultivation by a single family group over the course of about a century. Final abandonment was due to soil depletion.

The range of finds dating to the pre-cairn phase at Gwernvale clearly illustrated the establishment of local arable and pastoral systems by about 3100 b. c. (c. 3900 cal. B.C). Emmer wheat was moderately abundant in the buried soil and querns and rubbing stones found within and beneath the cairn indicate that cereals were cultivated locally and processed for consumption on site. Domesticated cattle, sheep and pigs also played a part in the local economy, though the total assemblage was too small to assess the relative importance or function of each species (Britnell and Savory 1984, 141).

The picture therefore emerges of an economy based on the arable cultivation in the valleys coupled with pastoral exploitation of the uplands.

4.3 Neolithic Settlement

Convincing evidence for Neolithic settlement in the Brecon Beacons and western Black Mountains is scanty in the extreme. However, excavations at Cefn Cilsanws (B-US 90) revealed a flimsy, stake-built rectangular house. Finds included flint and chert tools and arrowheads, hazelnut shells and sherds of three Neolithic pots. The house seems to have had internal divisions and part of the building could have been constructed of ash withies (RCAHMW 1997, 24; Webley 1958).

There is considerable evidence of Neolithic activity at Gwernvale before the construction of the cairn. Some of the evidence points to the existence of a small-scale settlement and some to the presence of ceremonial structures pre-dating the chambered tomb (Britnell and Savory 1984, 138). A single radiocarbon date of 3100 ± 75 b. c. (c. 3900 cal. B. C.) is associated with this activity.

It is uncertain whether the bedding trenches and six post-holes found beneath the northern horn of the tomb and the forecourt all constitute parts of a single structure (Fig. 6). However, in view of the abundance of other evidence for domestic activity on the site, the excavator regarded it as reasonable to suggest the presence of an Earlier Neolithic roofed building similar in ground-plan to other excavated examples at Ballynagilly, Co. Tyrone; Ballyglass, Co. Mayo and Llandegai, Gwynedd. Like Gwernvale, all of these sites occupied the highest point on the edge of a terrace and all appeared to stand in isolation, possibly representing individual farmsteads (*ibid.*, 139). At least a percentage of extant lithic scatters must represent the remains of such settlements (Darvill, 1987, 57).

It is also possible that the bedding trenches and post-holes found at Gwernvale represent stratigraphically separate structures with the six-poster still standing at the time of the tomb's completion, whereas the bedding trenches are overlain by the cairn (Britnell and Savory 1984, 140). Similar patterns of posts have been found at Fussell's Lodge, Wilts., and Wayland's Smithy, Berks. At the latter site, the structure was interpreted as an exposure platform for the excarnation of bodies prior to the deposition of bones within the tomb. The excavator at Gwernvale seemed satisfied that the six-poster's primary function was a ceremonial one (*ibid.*, 141).

Herefordshire has very little evidence of Neolithic settlement sites. Only three extensive Neolithic settlement sites have been recognised in the county as a whole (Fig. 7).

At Dorstone Hill (HN 8), we are fortunate in having an excavated example of a "settlement site" initially identified only by the surface collection of lithic artefacts. The site lies on the edge of an escarpment and commands views across the Wye Valley to the N and the Golden Valley to the S. Field-walking in 1958 produced eleven complete or fragmentary leaf-shaped arrowheads, four fragments of axe heads, twelve implements of shale and chert, three strike-a-lights, 291 blades and blade fragments, 456 utilized flakes and 384 unworked flakes. With eleven Mesolithic flints, this gave a total of 1,290 artefacts from the hill (Pye 1958, 82).

By the early 1960s, the same field had yielded 3,000 surface lithic finds. These included many Neolithic leaf-shaped arrowheads and 50 fragments of polished stone axes and seemed to indicate an extensive Neolithic settlement. A two day excavation in 1965 found an old ground surface with traces of burning covered by a collapsed rough sandstone wall, 0.75m wide and probably not more than 0.60m high originally. This had been built to consolidate a line of stakes 12.7cm in diameter. An undisturbed occupation soil behind this wall contained waste flint, a polished axe fragment and Western Neolithic pottery. A trench through the site of the densest flint scatter yielded more pottery (Houlder 1965, 10).

Further excavations in 1967 in the interior of the promontory fort produced definite evidence of Neolithic occupation. A layer which produced two leaf-shaped arrowheads and a Neolithic sherd sealed a storage pit. The pit contained a scraper and other unworked flints, charcoal and a few sherds of Western Neolithic pottery (Pye 1967, 8).

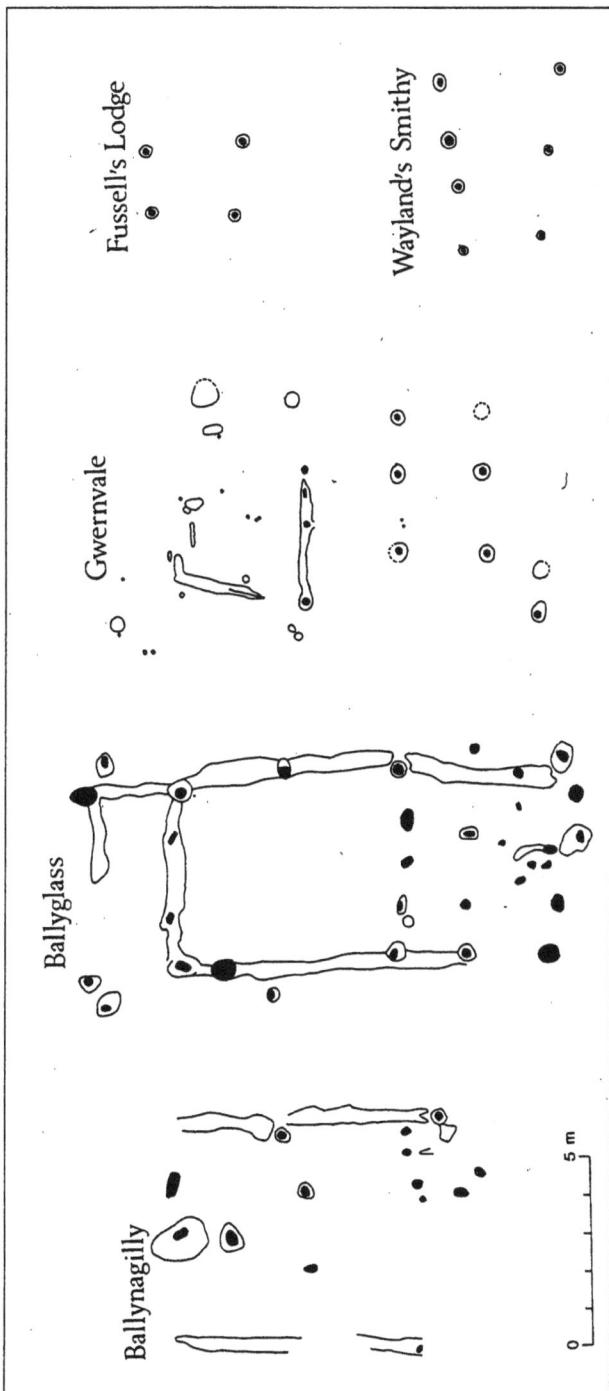

Fig. 6: Top – Neolithic timber structures (after Brittnell
and Savory 1984); bottom – Ballynagilly Neolithic house
(after Parker Pearson 1993).

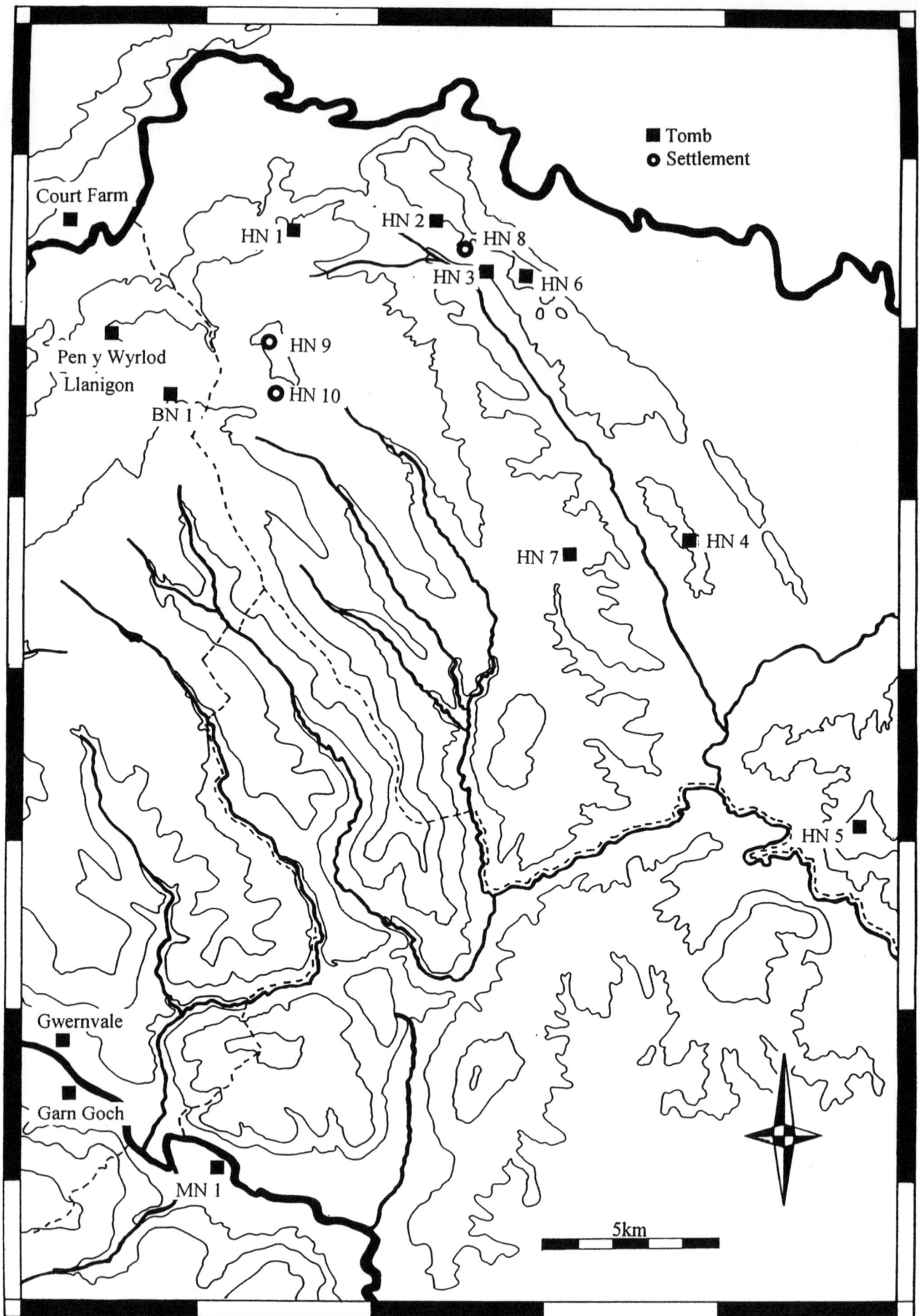

Fig. 7: Earlier Neolithic Tombs and Settlements.

More evidence of Neolithic occupation was discovered in 1968 in part of the adjoining Forestry Commission woodland. A ditch (0.75m wide) and slight bank were located and some very abraded pottery and a few flints were recovered from the primary silt. A hearth some 2.0m across (which produced a fragment of pottery and some flint flakes) had been constructed on top of the silted ditch. The hearth was overlain by a hut-floor and post-hole - this layer produced an arrowhead made from a flake of polished axe. Another hut-floor, of different plan, was located some distance away and a scatter of flints found in its floor (Pye 1968, 8-9).

In 1969, a total of five phases were noted on the site of the bank and ditch examined the previous year. Charcoal from a fireplace of Phase III (which immediately preceded a possible house site) was dated A. D. 40-90. The bank and ditch had been levelled and a sub-rectangular house built on the site. This area represents extra-mural settlement of the small promontory fort 200 yards to SE (HI 1). Some 70 flints were found in the derived soil, including a leaf-shaped arrowhead and a crescentic microlith indicating intense Neolithic occupation (Pye 1969, 11). The site also produced Mesolithic, Bronze Age, Iron Age and Roman material. It is nothing short of a scandal that one of the most significant Neolithic settlement sites ever excavated has never been published - all the finds remain in private hands.

Parallels can be drawn between Dorstone Hill and the causewayed enclosures of the Cotswolds. It is now becoming clear that these sites performed a variety of functions and that their roles changed through time. Periodic occupation for ritual festivals of some kind may have been their original function, but, over time, they became sites of more permanent settlements (Bradley and Edmonds 1993, 175-176). They were certainly closely involved in the circulation of axes and have been described as geographically marginal and socially liminal (ibid., 170). In its later phases, Crickley Hill, Glos., represents nothing less than a fortified village with areas set aside for flint-working, ritual and other activities. Carn Brea in Cornwall, may have been home to up to 200 people at any one time (Darvill 1987, 59-62).

At "Cefn Hill Site A" (HN 9) on the northern end of the plateau of Cefn Hill, the flint scatters which Robinson regarded as "living floors" covered an area of some 2 acres (0.8ha) with several discrete, dense clusters which he identified as hut sites. No evidence of actual dwellings was discovered but various patches of darkened soil were also thought to represent hut sites and the site was interpreted as a Neolithic settlement (Robinson 1946, 34-35).

On the western slopes of Cefn Hill, at "Abbey Farm Site A" (HN 10), a ploughzone flint scatter was discovered in 1950 on a site which had not previously been cultivated. The discrete scatter consisted of a large number of flint flakes, scrapers and chips covering an area of about a quarter of an acre (0.10ha) (Robinson 1950, 112). There were also stone "rubbers or hones" and, outside the immediate scatter, a "few flakes scattered here and there over the ploughed field". Several areas of blackened soil in the area were interpreted as the result of medieval charcoal burning by the monks of Craswall Priory as there were no flints found in association

with them (ibid., 113). A piece of grooved sandstone was tentatively identified as a Bronze Age loom-weight. In the same field, but not within the scatter, were found two complete Neolithic polished stone axes (ibid., 115).

Gavin Robinson also equated other Herefordshire flint scatters (Fig. 8) with settlement and identified three common factors in the location of the sites, namely water, observation and "safety for their crops and themselves from wild animals". The sites are all on hilltops, which Robinson interpreted as being for reasons of inter-communication by signals between the various "settlements" and with hunting parties in the valley bottoms (Robinson 1934, 54).

In the Golden Valley as a whole, Robinson noted occasional stray finds of flint in almost every field above the 150m contour line. Below that height, he only ever found two other flints and was of the opinion that had flint been present in any quantity, he would certainly not have missed it. He felt it impossible to say whether all the sites were "occupied" simultaneously but postulated the presence of a fairly dense population living on the hilltops in little "settlements" (ibid., 59).

At Stockley no. 1 (HN 45), practically all the flints came from a strip some 90m by 45m with a dense area some 27m square where Robinson estimated the density to be "several flints per square foot" (ibid., 55). On the basis of flints and scrapers which had been re-worked over patination, Robinson postulated protracted activity at this site. This led him to postulate that each "settlement" was allotted a separate hunting ground and were individually sited to command different areas for mutual protection and to cover their own hunting grounds (ibid., 58).

At "Greenway No. 2" (HN 39), Robinson postulated the presence of a Neolithic settlement covering about 2 acres (0.8ha) with a flint-working floor some forty yards (36.4m) square on a small ridge with a wide view down the Golden Valley. This site produced two leaf-shaped arrowheads (ibid., 61) and other implements made from "drift" stones. Robinson speculated that this material was resorted to due to shortage of suitable flint in the area (ibid., 48).

Seemingly foreseeing objections to his identification of these sites as settlements, Robinson later offered a cogent argument in favour of his theories:

> *Provided that flints of definitely Neolithic type are found in fair numbers, in conjunction with the debris of a chipping floor, with spindle whorls, pot boilers, rubbing stones or burnishers etc. . . . the reasonable inference is that the living site has been located. More especially as the soil in the case under consideration (HN 9) has never been moved since the Neolithic remains were deposited, and a concentration such as we are dealing with is in a very different category from the miscellaneous flint debris widely scattered over, say, the Cotswolds, which bear no relation to any given spot, persistent ploughing having transported them far from any centralised chipping floor.* (Robinson 1946, 36)

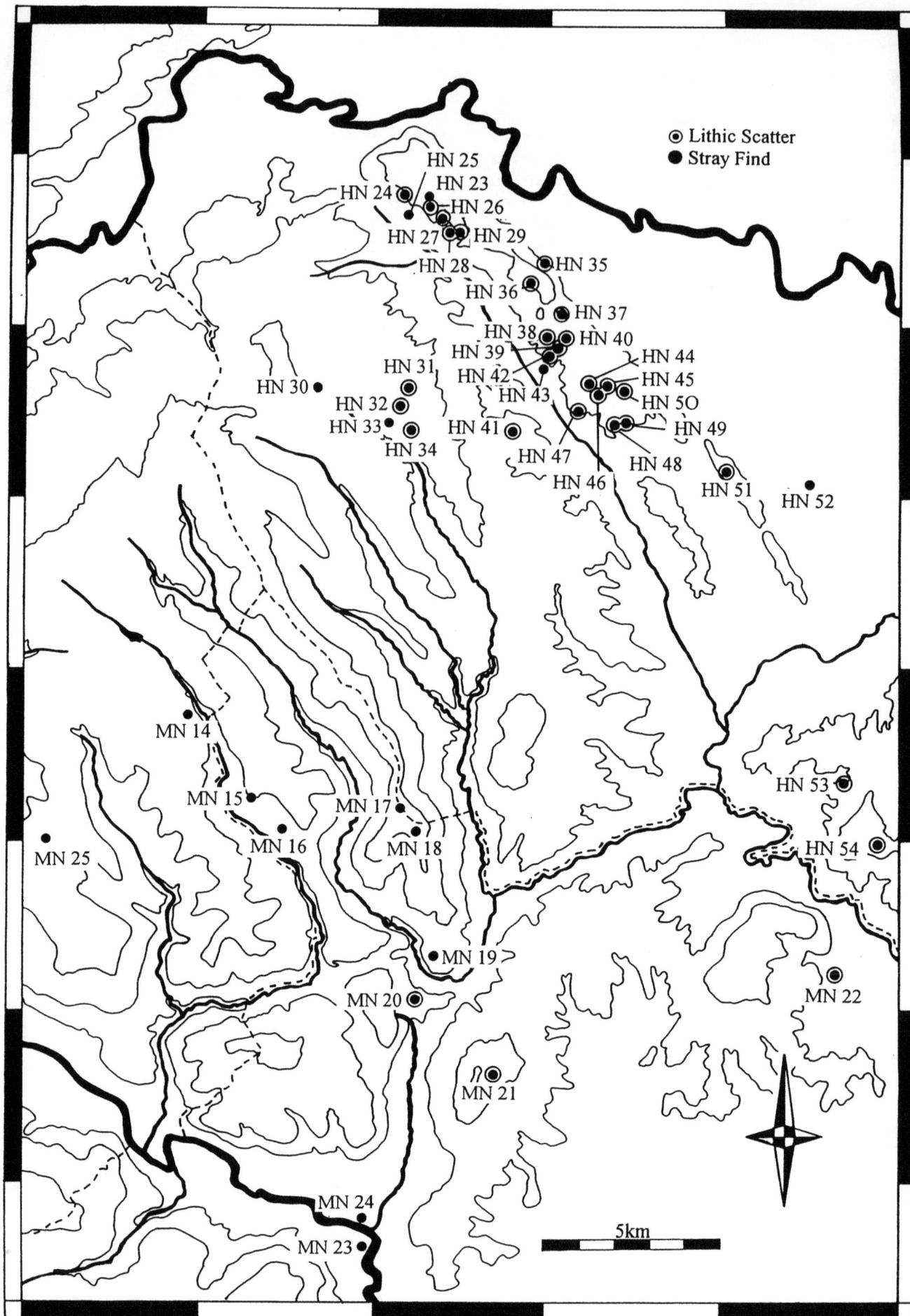

Fig. 8: Earlier Neolithic Lithic Finds.

Gavin Robinson was also far in advance of the modern "pioneers" of the new science of taphonomy!

Of the Monmouthshire sites in the Grwyne Fawr valley, only the scatter to the NW of Tŷ Isaf farm (MN 16) produced diagnostic evidence of on-site flint-working in the form of cores and rejuvenation flakes. The other finds in this area (MN 14-15) can probably be best interpreted as losses during hunting-foraging expeditions or as the remains of hunting stands comparable to that at Moel y Gaer, Flintshire (Darvill 1987, 57).

At Pen y Clawdd (MN 20) and Skirrid Fawr (MN 21), on the other hand, the presence of hammer stones and significant numbers of cores and rejuvenation flakes implies flint-working of some scale and longevity. Where excavated, such Earlier Neolithic flint scatters have been interpreted as the final acts of ceremonial feasts and ritualised flint-working (Edmonds 1995, 43). They may have been deposited to ensure the fertility and continuity of the communities involved or to mark and ensure rights of access to significant places in a way of life which retained a measure of routine mobility (ibid., 35).

It is possible that the Earlier Neolithic material at Pen y Clawdd and Skirrid Fawr may represent the residue of such periodic visits to significant places and that essentially mobile Earlier Neolithic groups were attracted to the particularly striking hills at these sites (namely Bryn Arw and Skirrid Fawr itself) as foci for periodic social/ritual gatherings analogous to the seasonal activities attested at the causewayed enclosures of other areas. This could also be compared with the importance of particular hills for the chambered tomb builders of Brecknock (see below).

Neolithic axes (Fig. 9) are associated with forest clearance to provide grazing for animals, the preparation of the ground for agriculture and wood-working - especially the construction of the sort of wooden buildings discussed above (Savory 1980b, 210). Smaller and medium-sized Group VIII axes (Fig. 10) are also seen as primarily utilitarian tools (Chappell 1987, 255) and their local distribution is likely to reflect areas of Earlier Neolithic clearance in the Golden Valley (HN 15), the Gavenny Valley (MN 5-6) and the lowlands of NE Monmouthshire (MN 8).

Axes have also been interpreted as prestige items owned and controlled by powerful individuals and symbolising power, prestige and a stratified society - evidence of a socially and politically complex society involved in large-scale alliances between social groups (Children and Nash 1994, 19). The exchange of Group XXIII and Group VIII axes in the Earlier Neolithic probably served to maintain contact between people in different areas of southern and central Wales (Chappell 1987, 250).

Apart from two finds on the highest ridges (MN 2 and HN 11), the distribution of Neolithic axe heads in the eastern Black Mountains is confined to the lowland areas and river valleys. Five of the Monmouthshire axes are from the Gavenny Valley (MN 3-6, 9), two are from the eastern lowland area (MN 7-8) and the remainder from the valley of the River Usk (MN 10-13). These include a hoard of four axes from Llangenny (MN 13).

The main concentration of Herefordshire axe finds is in the Golden Valley. The find-spots (HN 12-15, 17-18, 20) range from Dorstone in the N to Abbey Dore in the S. The Golden Valley evidently saw intensive Neolithic occupation and activity. It is possible that the Dorstone Hill "settlement" (HN 8), the chambered tomb at Arthur's Stone (HN 2) and the long barrow at Cross Lodge (HN 3), together with their associated clusters of lithic scatters (HN 24, 27-29), stray axes and flints (HN 12-14, 23, 25) formed a core area for an extensive territory occupying the whole of the valley E of the Dore. If Dorstone Hill fulfilled some of the functions of the causewayed enclosures of other areas (see above), this core area may have combined ritual at the tombs with seasonal gatherings on the hill. Its hinterland may be reflected in the concentrations of lithic scatters centred on Stockley Hill (HN 44-50) and of lithic scatters (HN 35-40, 42,43) and axe finds (HN 17-18) centred on the Greenway Farm area.

The axes from the Abbey Farm Site "A" settlement (HN 11) and Marresses Farm, St. Margaret's (HN 19), together with the flint scatters spread along the length of Vagar Hill and Urishay Common (HN 30-34) may also represent the extent of a territory centred on the Cefn Hill and Abbey Farm settlements and bounded by the three chambered tombs - Maes Coch-Twyn y Beddau (BN 1) to the W, Mynydd Bach (HN 1) to the N and Park Wood (HN 7) to the SE.

Despite the general paucity of evidence for the area, the extent of another territory centred on Grey Valley may be represented by the Dunseal long barrow (HN 4) to the W and the Brampton Hill lithic scatter (HN 51) to the E.

The exceptions to this pattern are two axe finds from near Garway Hill (HN 21-22) which, together with the Garway Hill long barrow (HN 5) and a series of flint scatters (HN 53-54; MN 22), may represent a separate territory centred on the Monnow Valley.

It is possible to postulate a core area centred on the Gavenny Valley with its lithic scatter at Pen y Clawdd, valley-bottom clearance attested by numerous axe finds (MN 3-10) and a possible summer pasture/hunting hinterland extending into the valleys of the Honddu (MN 8, 10, 17) and Grwyne Fawr (MN 14-16). It is possible that, as in Mesolithic times, the lithic scatter site at Skirrid Fawr stood at the boundary of two distinct zones - the Gavenny Valley to the W and a wider territory extending into the eastern lowlands and represented by axe finds on the Full Brook (MN 7) and at Llanddewi Rhydderch (MN 8).

A similar territory may have been based on the Usk Valley and associated with the possible long cairn at Battle Tump (MN 1) and the axe finds from Gilwern (MN 11-12). It seems not beyond the realms of possibility that the stray axe from the summit of Y Gadair (MN 2) and the Llangenny axe hoard (MN 13) reflect a northern hinterland associated with Gwernvale.

Overall, the pattern suggests that the axe finds and flint scatters reflect the areas of most intense Neolithic activity. The valley bottoms doubtless saw clearance for both cereal agriculture and pastoralism (Savory 1980b, 207). It is therefore possible to suggest the existence of eight Neolithic

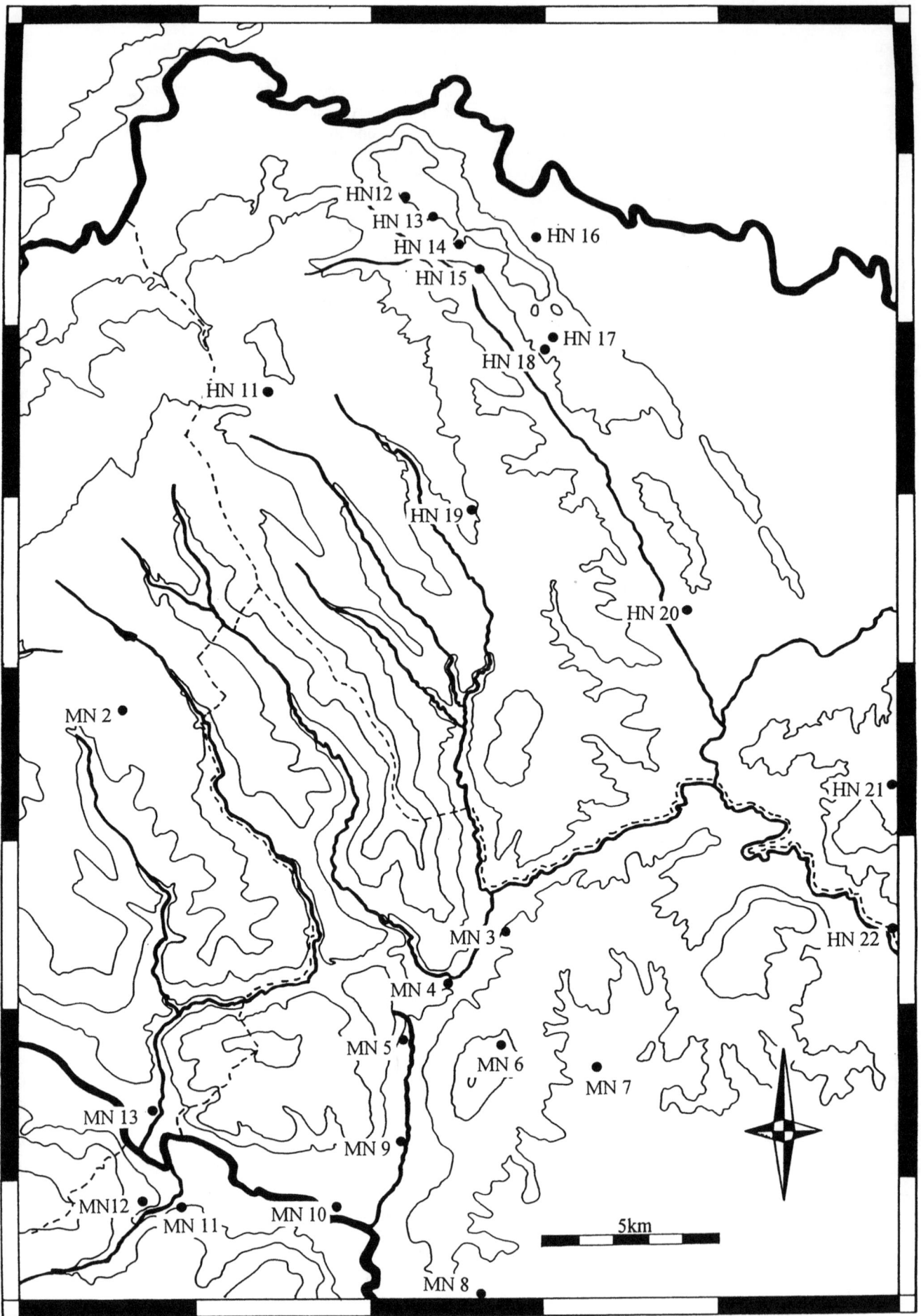

Fig. 9: Neolithic Axe Finds.

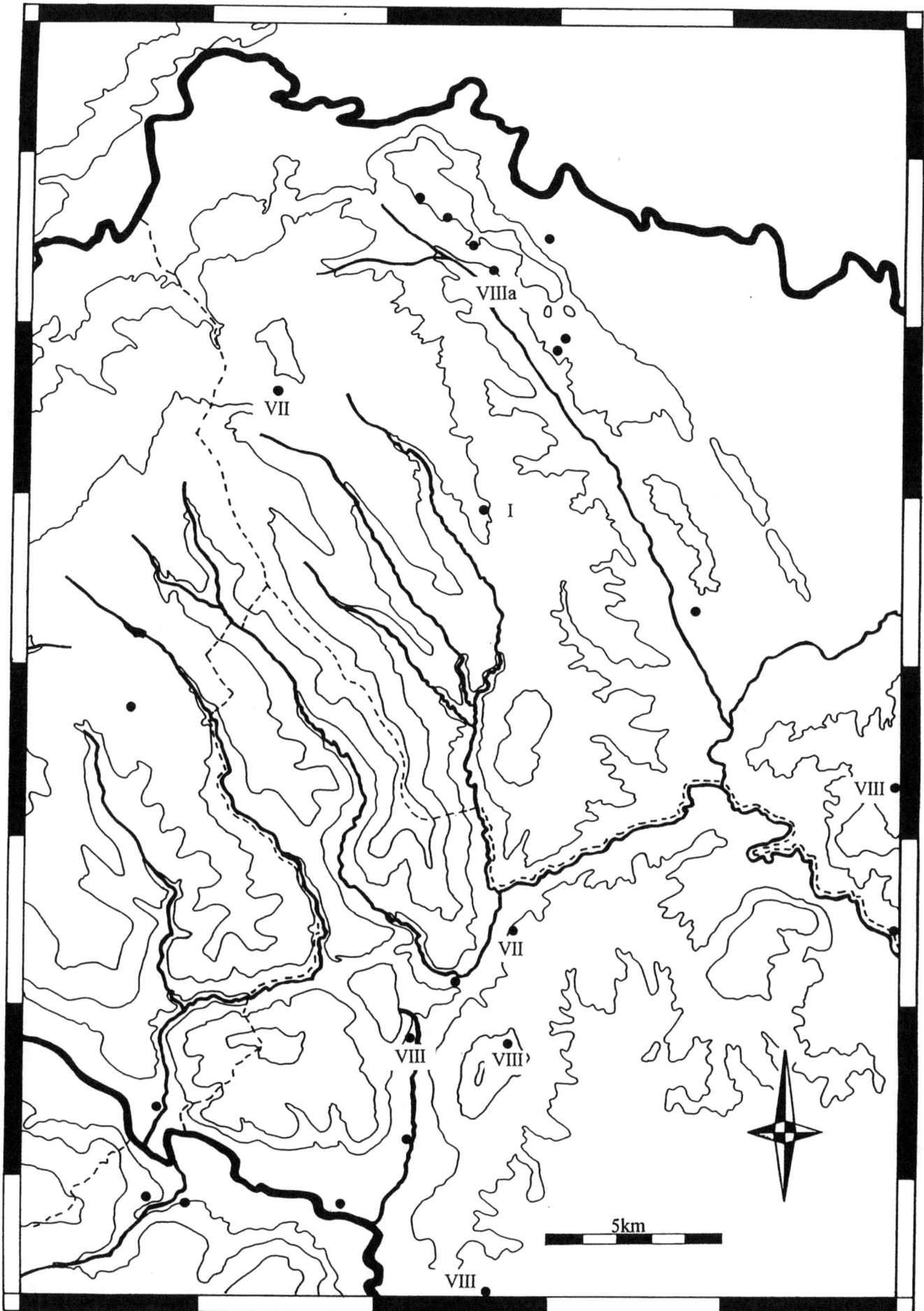

Fig. 10: Neolithic Axe Finds by Group (where known).

territories (Fig. 11) in the eastern Black Mountains based on the Golden Valley (A), Urishay Common-Cefn Hill (B), Grey Valley (C), Garway Hill-Monnow Valley (D), the Gavenny Valley (E), north-east Monmouthshire (F), the Usk Valley-Gilwern (G) and Gwernvale-Grwyne Fawr (H).

4.4 Neolithic Ritual

Chambered Tombs – Their Uses and Meanings

It has often been suggested that, in origin, long barrows or cairns represent some kind of transformation of the idea of the longhouse (Hodder 1990, Bradley 1993, Sherratt 1995). They certainly seem to copy the ground plans of older longhouses (Bradley 1998, 38). It is possible that in the settlements on the loess of eastern and central Europe, longhouses were abandoned and left to decay when one of the occupants died. Familiarity with the decay of these houses and their final ruined form may be the origin of the long mounds (ibid., 15).

The possibly primary round structures at Severn-Cotswold sites such as Pen y Wyrlod-Llanigon (B-CT 12), Tŷ Isaf (B-CT 3), Pipton (B-CT 8) and Notgrove (Corcoran 1969, Figs. 10, 12, 22, 23) have been seen as a reflection of Mesolithic domestic structures (Sherratt 1990, 338) - the hunter's tent made monumental (Sherratt 1995, 367).

The symbolic "messages" of the earliest monumental structures may in part have been directed at Mesolithic communities where farming and foraging lifestyles met and interacted (Sherratt 1990, 335; 1995, 361). Megalithic construction in Brittany, western Britain and Denmark has been interpreted as a product of the adoption by their indigenous Mesolithic populations of a largely pastoral farming lifestyle as part of a total package of economic, social and ideological practices. Sherratt sees this process as part of the development of social stratification and "conical clan structures" (1995, 365). Indeed, he has also argued that it was the construction of the tombs which forged the sense of community necessary for the successful adoption of a farming lifestyle (1990, 336-7). In the Black Mountains (see below), the continued importance of Mesolithic ancestral places in the Neolithic and the siting of chambered tombs near clusters of Mesolithic scatters seems likely to reflect this process of "conversion".

But, Bradley argues, the monuments are found in areas where little is known of the subsistence economy of the period and there is even less evidence for intensive farming (Bradley 1998, 40), where agriculture was adopted late by indigenous hunter-gatherers and where people may have adhered to a mobile way of life longer than elsewhere (ibid., 53). He even questions the conventional description of these monuments as tombs and emphasises their use for ancestor rituals rather than as purely funereal monuments (ibid., 54).

It has often been assumed that chambered tombs represent differences in power and social control within and between Neolithic communities. The elaborated treatment of the dead being connected with the concept of ancestry, known individuals were transformed into anonymous ancestors

through whom claims to social position and resources could be legitimated (Thorpe 1984).

Whittle rejects arguments that these processes reflect the emergence of socially dominant groups such as lineages or clans (Sherratt 1995, 365) and argues that the monuments had more to do with a Neolithic belief in mythical ancestors. The human dead were placed in the tombs as offerings to unite the living with their beginnings. A sense of sacred beginnings, he postulates, made time seem endless. The monuments involved a collective memory, the living and the dead were linked in a "a collectivity of shared experience" which lay at the heart of the Neolithic way of life (Whittle 1996, 261).

Megalithic tombs also embody the symbolism of the communal effort involved in their construction - they are emblematic of the unity of the group. Sherratt maintains that the sedentary Neolithic communities of eastern and central Europe invested effort in the construction of domestic structures - villages and longhouses - as statements of social organisation and control. However, in areas where livestock rearing and hunting played a larger part in the economy, villages and domestic buildings were not appropriate to a more mobile lifestyle. Alternative social and ritual focal points were needed and this, Sherratt argues, is the central social role of megalithic tombs (1995, 359).

The proper treatment of the ancestors at these sites demanded careful observance of procedures and appropriate behaviour - visits and ceremonies were marked by the deposition of artefacts as well as of human remains. Nor are they simply funerary monuments - both death and megalithic structures are identified with the realm of the "other", where the ancestors have a powerful existence. Access to the "other" may be gained by appropriate rituals carried out at appropriate times. It may be that the astronomical alignments sometimes claimed for chambered tombs were intended to ensure that ceremonies took place at the correct times (ibid., 355).

Whittle argues that the construction of chambered tombs cannot be reduced to variables of resources, cultural history or social difference. He sees them as the central point of a cult focused on fusion of the past with the present and a powerful ordering principal which fostered cohesion, integration and collectivity of action. The emergence of beliefs of this kind could have accelerated the process of convergence between Mesolithic foragers and Neolithic cultivators. Their spiritual and religious dimension needs to be revived (1996, 248).

The Black Mountains Tombs in their Landscape

The laterally chambered Severn-Cotswold tombs often contain large deposits of human remains formed by successive acts of deposition. These may be the result of successive secondary burials (i.e. old articulated burials being scattered to make room for new ones) or depositions of already disarticulated and incomplete remains. In some, such as Hazleton North (Savile 1990), whole bodies were brought into the tombs. This may represent transformation within the

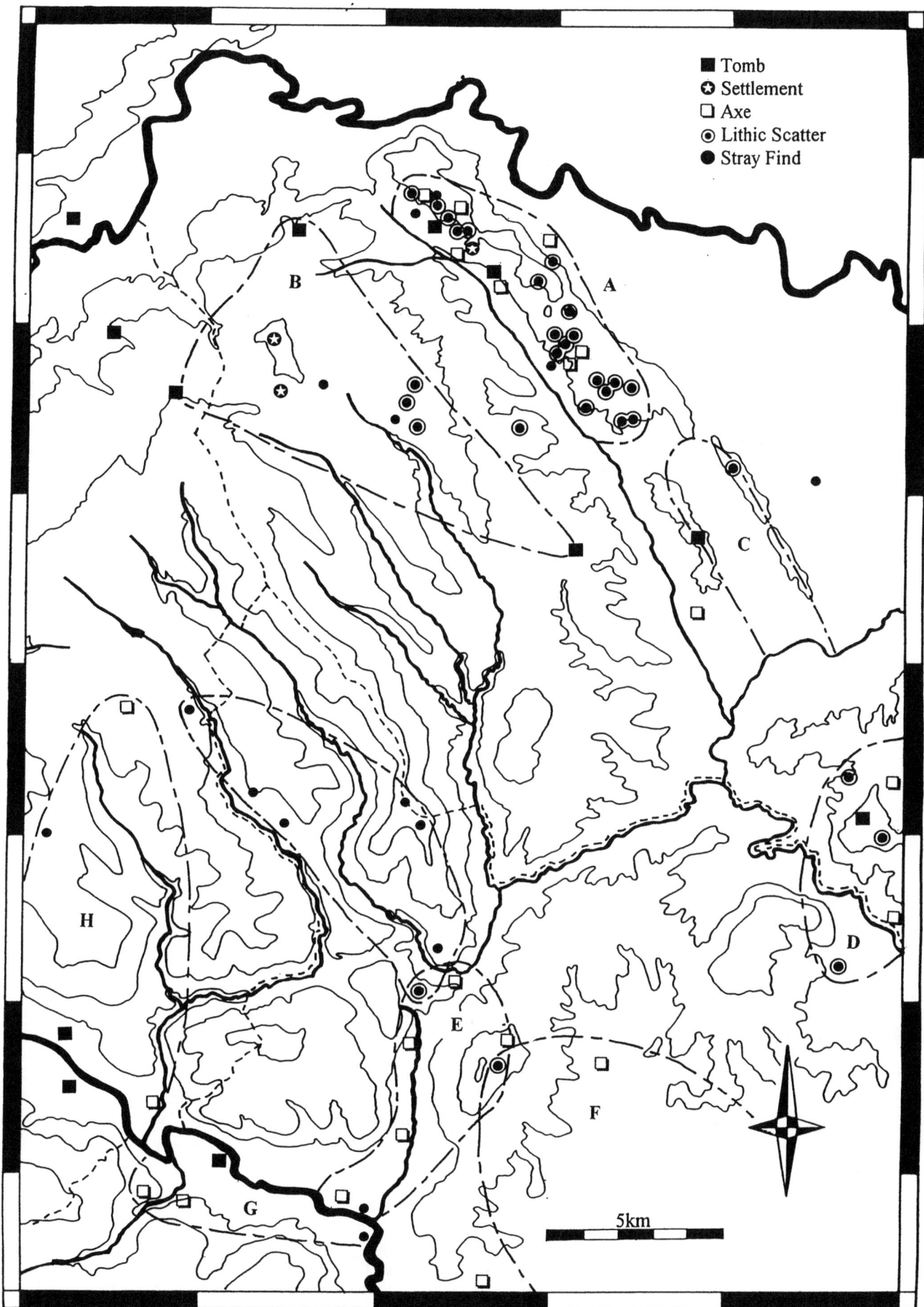

Fig. 11: Earlier Neolithic Territories.

21

monument (Graslund 1994) and suggests that many bones were never left in the chamber deposits (Whittle 1996, 259).

Several modes of deposition may have been used at each monument and at some there is also evidence for the sorting of bones by age, sex and body part. At West Kennet, the innermost chamber held male remains, adult and young; the inner pair of facing chambers held mainly adult males and females while the outer pair contained mainly old and young people (Piggott 1962). Bones from the tomb may also have been removed and circulated elsewhere (Whittle 1996, 260).

Thomas (1988) characterises laterally chambered tombs like Hazleton North as early in the sequence and transepted tombs such as Notgrove as later. The separate transepted chambers and the associated sorting of the bones on the basis of age and sex at sites such as West Kennet suggests more complex attitudes toward and treatment of the dead (Bradley 1998, 55) and, in this sequence, Bradley sees a gradual shift from burial rites where the bodies are disposed of and left undisturbed to ancestor rites where human remains are used by the living. Ancestor rites imply an idea of continuity between the past and the present which was a later development not associated with the earliest experiments in farming (*ibid.*, 63). It is therefore at this, later, stage, he argues, that chambered tombs may have acted as territorial markers (*ibid.*, 64).

Darvill sees tomb-building groups as forming part of a social system made up of "segmentary" or small scale societies - politically and economically autonomous communities of not more than a few hundred people. Within these groups, the primary social entity is a "residence unit" - a village or set of dispersed households - and relationships within the group are defined by kinship links. Under population pressure, such units undergo "fission", so that groups separated by considerable distances are still related by kinship and may keep up ongoing social relationships.

In the Severn-Cotswold area, strong evidence for the exchange of material goods in the form of stone and flint axes, flint, pottery, shale beads and marine shells shows the existence of an "interaction network" operating over considerable distances between such kinship groups. At Gwernvale, the pre-cairn pottery showed affinities with both Grimstone-Lyles Hill material from the western coasts of Wales and the Irish Sea area and with Abingdon Ware. While definitely locally produced, the pottery suggested a fusion of these two ceramic traditions with affinities to both the west and the east (Britnell and Savory 1984, 141). In addition, three ogival arrowheads and axe fragments from pre-cairn contexts may have arrived at the site as finished products (*ibid.*, 132). The material used is similar to that available at Beer Down, Devon and it is possible that ogival arrowheads were prestige products characteristic of the Severn-Cotswold "province" and transmitted over large distances from sources in SW England (Green 1980, 98-99). The knowledge of tomb building could have passed along the same networks (Darvill 1982, 80). It is in this way that a superficially coherent group of monuments like the Severn-Cotswold chambered tombs can display such great variation in detail between individual monuments (*ibid.*, 78).

Within the Severn-Cotswold tradition as a whole, the Black Mountains chambered tombs form a compact and isolated inland group (Fig. 12), though it is difficult to determine how far the current distribution reflects their true original density or is a result of differential preservation. None of the Herefordshire sites has been excavated and, due to the fragmentary nature of many of the Brecknock sites and the damage caused by poor early excavations, the group throws very little light on the question of the evolution of tomb morphology; though lateral chambers are more characteristic of the Brecknock sites as a whole (RCAHMW 1997, 27-28).

It is equally difficult to discuss phasing and dating, though the rotundae incorporated in the long cairns at Tŷ Isaf (B-CT 3), Pipton (B-CT 8) and Pen y Wyrlod-Llanigon (B-CT 12) may well represent earlier, independent structures comparable to that at Notgrove, Glos. (Darvill 1987, 64-66). Pen y Wyrlod-Llanigon (B-CT 12), Mynydd Troed (B-CT 2) and Ffostyll South (B-CT 5) may also be multi-period, but without excavation it is impossible to be certain (RCAHMW 1997, 28).

The cairn at Gwernvale (B-CT 11) was probably built after c. 3100 b. c. (3900 cal. B. C.) and formally closed at about 2500 b. c. (3000 cal. B. C.). In its original form, the outer walls of the cairn may have risen to from an impressive facade at the forecourt (Britnell and Savory 1984, 144). On completion the tomb probably appeared as a long trapezoidal cairn with sides carefully faced with vertical dry-stone walling, gradually diminishing in height away from the forecourt (*ibid.*, 148).

Chamber 1 at Gwernvale is polygonal and entered by a crooked passage. The shape of the chamber is similar to those at Belas Knap, Glos., but the closest parallel is with that at Arthur's Stone (HN 2, Fig. 13) which also has a long polygonal chamber entered by a crooked passage. Another crooked passage is found at Pipton (B-CT 8) and they seem to be features restricted to the Black Mountains group (*ibid.*, 144).

The lack of large bone deposits at Tŷ Isaf, Pipton and Gwernvale has been taken as evidence that the removal of bone from the chambers was part of the normal use of laterally chambered tombs. The effects of acid soil might equally be to blame (RCAHMW 1997, 29). Despite this, there is evidence that at Pen y Wyrlod-Talgarth (B-CT 4), bones were piled against the side walls of chamber 2 with skulls placed against the N wall (Britnell and Savory 1984, 19). Skulls were placed in the same position at Tŷ Isaf (Grimes 1939, 141-42). The use of the Black Mountains tombs in feasting cycles is attested by the bones of sheep, cattle and pigs in the chamber and forecourt areas, especially the presence of hearths and pits in the forecourt of Pen y Wyrlod-Talgarth (RCAHMW 1997, 29).

All but two of the Black Mountains chambered tombs are built on Old Red Sandstone glacial drift deposits. Only Gwernvale and Garn Goch (B-CT 10) are on alluvial gravels and sands (Webley 1959, 291). Excavations at Mynydd Troed showed that in Neolithic times the monuments were set in clearings in open, dry, climax oak forests with local heathlands on the uplands (Crampton and Webley 1966). Webley envisaged a significant element of transhumant

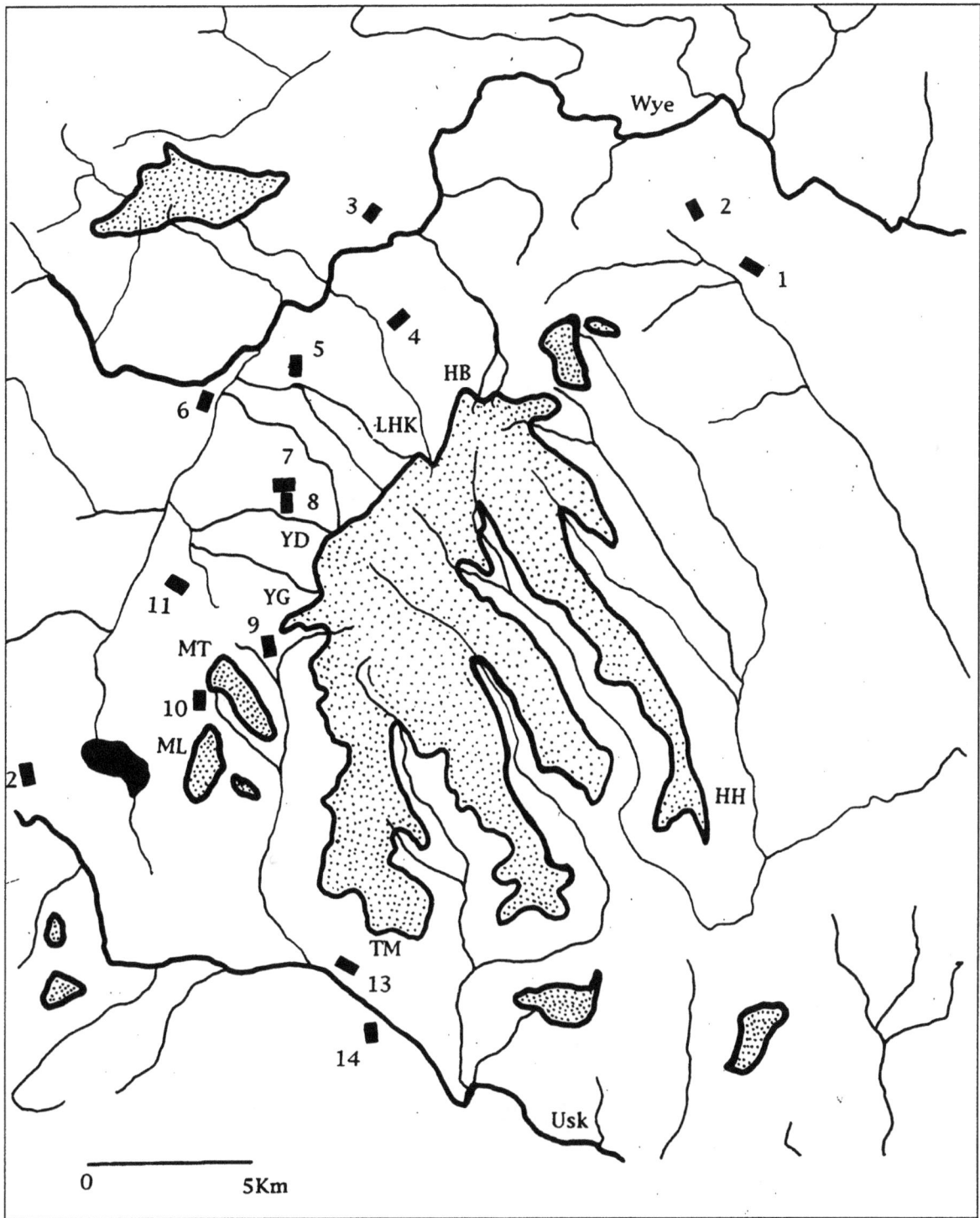

Fig. 12: The Black Mountains Chambered Tombs – Distribution and Alignment (after Tilley 1994).
1 - Cross Lodge, 2 - Arthur's Stone, 3 - Court Farm, 4 - Pen y Wyrlod-Llanigon, 5 - Little Lodge, 6 – Pipton, 7 – Ffostyll North, 8 – Ffostyll South, 9 – Tŷ Isaf, 10 – Mynydd Troed, 11- Pen y Wyrlod-Talgarth, 12 - Tŷ Illtyd, 13 – Gwernvale, 14 – Garn Goch. MT – Mynydd Troed, YD – Y Dâs, LHK – Lord Hereford's Knob, HB – Hay Bluff, TM – Table Mountain, HH – Hatterall Hill, ML – Mynydd Llangors, YG – Y Grîb.

Mynydd Bach Long Cairn
Llannerch y Coed, Clifford, Herefordshire.
NGR: SO 2765 4287
c. 260m above OD

Surveyed 23/11/99
Graham Makepeace, Frank Olding, Neil Phillips

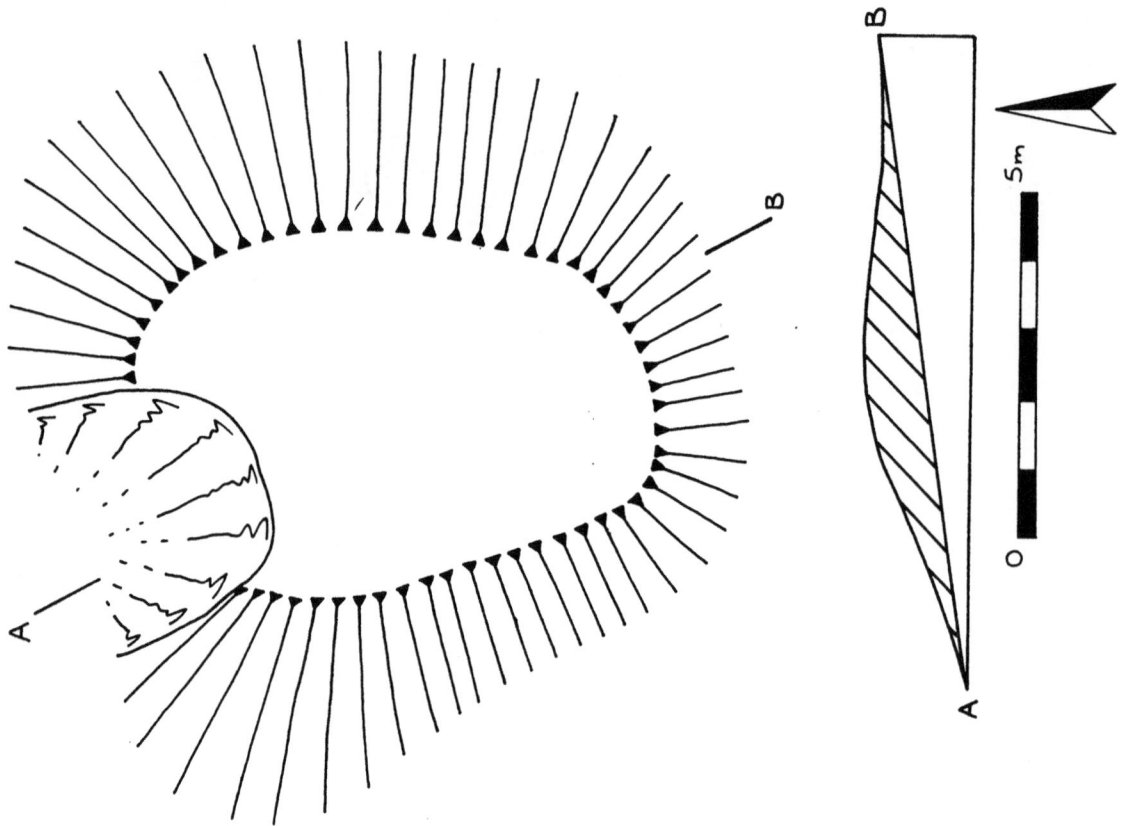

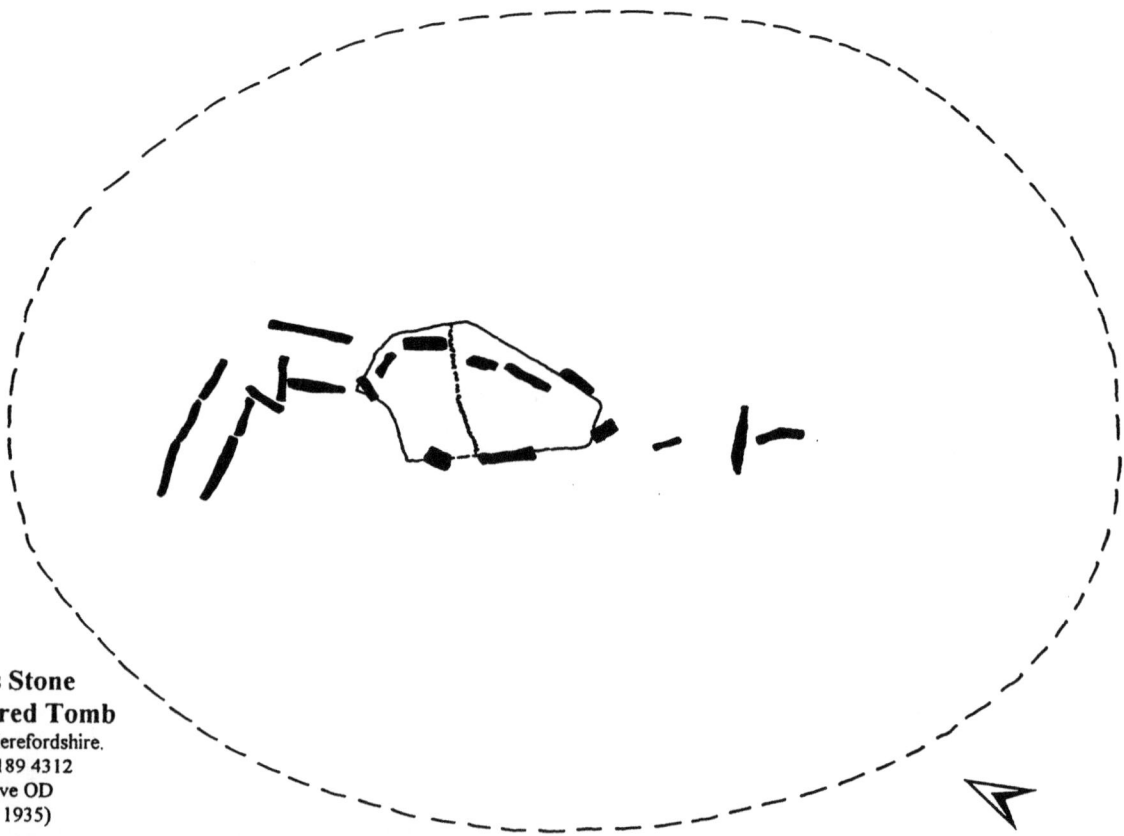

5m

**Arthur's Stone
Chambered Tomb**
Dorstone, Herefordshire.
NGR: SO 3189 4312
c. 280m above OD
(after Hemp 1935)

O   10m

Fig. 13: Top - Mynydd Bach (HN 1); bottom – Arthur's
Stone (HN 2).

24

pastoralism in the local Neolithic economy and argued that the tombs were built in areas which would have served as summer pastures (1976, 30). Repeated visits to a tomb fixed a routine in the use of the surrounding landscape - ancestral worship at these sacred monuments and sacred areas served to attach people very closely to particular places in their landscapes, they fixed a sense of place (Whittle 1996, 257).

Sherratt hypothesises that Neolithic communities felt the need to make permanent statements about the nature of their society which were intended to be "read" very widely within their region (1995, 357). The tombs are monumental and visible. They were designed to make an indelible impact on the landscape. Their distribution and positioning serves to draw attention to and emphasise important features in the landscape (Tilley 1994, 142).

Within the Black Mountains group, two different principles regarding the alignment of the tombs' long axes have been identified (Fig. 12) - those which run parallel with the major rivers or their tributaries and those which are orientated towards particularly prominent points on the escarpment edges of the Black Mountains (Tilley 1994, 124). It has been suggested that these were sacred landmarks associated with ancestral powers (*ibid.*, 136). In short, river valleys, prominent hills and spurs, paths and landmarks whose ancestral significance had already been established during the Mesolithic were monumentalised during the Earlier Neolithic by the construction of megalithic tombs (*ibid.*, 142).

The site of the Gwernvale chambered tomb, for example, saw repeated Mesolithic use in the cycle of seasonal movement from lowland-coastal winter settlements to upland summer hunting camps (see above). It has been argued that it occupies a site which had become "embedded in social memory", a location which ritually linked the past and the present (Barrett 1994, 53; Tilley 1994, 117). In short, Gwernvale was already an ancestral place before the tomb was built. The complementary distributions of Mesolithic material and megalithic tombs in Wales has may be interpreted either as evidence of severe competition between hunter-gatherer populations and incoming agriculturalists or as indigenous development from one economic system to another (RCAHMW 1997, 29). The presence of rotundae beneath some of the Black Mountains tombs (see above) may indicate that the latter is the more likely scenario.

The same argument can be applied to Arthur's Stone (HN 2, Fig. 13). No less than five Mesolithic find-spots (HM 2-6) cluster in the immediate vicinity of the monument. The three lithic scatters among them (HM 3, 5 and 6) may represent summer camps. This goes some way to supporting Webley's hypothesis that the Black Mountains cairns are built within areas which would have been utilized as summer pastures by Neolithic pastoralists engaged in a seasonal pattern of movement similar to that of the Mesolithic, albeit under a different subsistence regime (1976, 30).

Mixed assemblages of Mesolithic and Neolithic material indicate that Neolithic patterns of movement included places that had been important for centuries. Spreads of already ancient debris probably reminded Neolithic people that these places had a "history" and may have contributed to the

process by which the landscape became cultural and by which Neolithic people developed a sense of place and belonging (Edmonds 1995, 35).

Tilley accepts Bradley's view of the essentially mobile nature of Earlier Neolithic populations (Bradley 1987, 184) and goes on to suggest that the chambered tombs aligned along the river valleys, such has Cross Lodge (HN 3,) served as markers along pathways from the lowlands to the uplands (1994, 120). The newly discovered long cairn at Maes Coch-Twyn y Beddau (BN 1, Fig. 14), with its long axis aligned on the shelf leading up to the Gospel Pass (NGR SO 2360 3505), may therefore be interpreted as marking a route from the Wye Valley up onto the northern escarpment of the Black Mountains - the very same migration path that the Earlier Mesolithic sites on Cefn Hill (HM 7) were best placed to exploit. It is interesting to note that both the Twyn y Beddau round barrow (B-RC 311) and the Pen y Beacon stone circle (B-SC 10) also appear to respect the same landmarks.

All the Herefordshire sites, with the exception of Park Wood (HN 7) are located along the eastern fringe of the Golden Valley. Both occupation sites and ritual monuments appear to be positioned in order to secure clear views of the Black Mountains and the mountains have been seen as acting as a "religious nucleus". The apparent paucity of Neolithic material on the mountains themselves has been seen as evidence of an ambivalence in the attitude of the Neolithic population towards them - they may have been both sacred and ritually dangerous (Children and Nash 1994, 20).

A more recent discussion has suggested that the layout of the tombs replicates their surrounding landscapes, creating a cultural and symbolic "map" where certain topographic features are symbolically incorporated into the tomb plan. The axis of a tomb may replicate the flow of rivers and its chambers and passages align on prominent landscape features. In this way, Tŷ Isaf, is seen as acting as a compass or central point within the landscape, its axis orientated to the flow of the river Rhiangoll, its chambers aligned east-west so as to "catch" the rising and setting sun, the life and death cycle (Nash 1997, 22). The bend in the passage at Arthur's Stone is seen as an attempt to encompass the whole sweep of the eastern Black Mountains within the tomb's structure. In this way, it is argued, the Black Mountains themselves are incorporated into the social and symbolic identity of the Neolithic population and ritual knowledge becomes instrumental in the formulation of a sense of belonging (*ibid.*, 23).

Part of Nash's argument is based on the notion that, when covered by their original mound or cairn, the tombs became hidden, invisible, part of the landscape itself (*ibid.*, 20). However, this seems to fly in the face of strong evidence for the striking monumentality of the tombs in their original condition (Britnell and Savory 1984, 143-146).

Current evidence points to the association of individual tombs with small social groups but little is known about the settlements of the tomb-building communities. Darvill postulates a pattern of small farmsteads somewhere near the tombs and also argues that each of the groups associated with a tomb would also have controlled a territory of some kind.

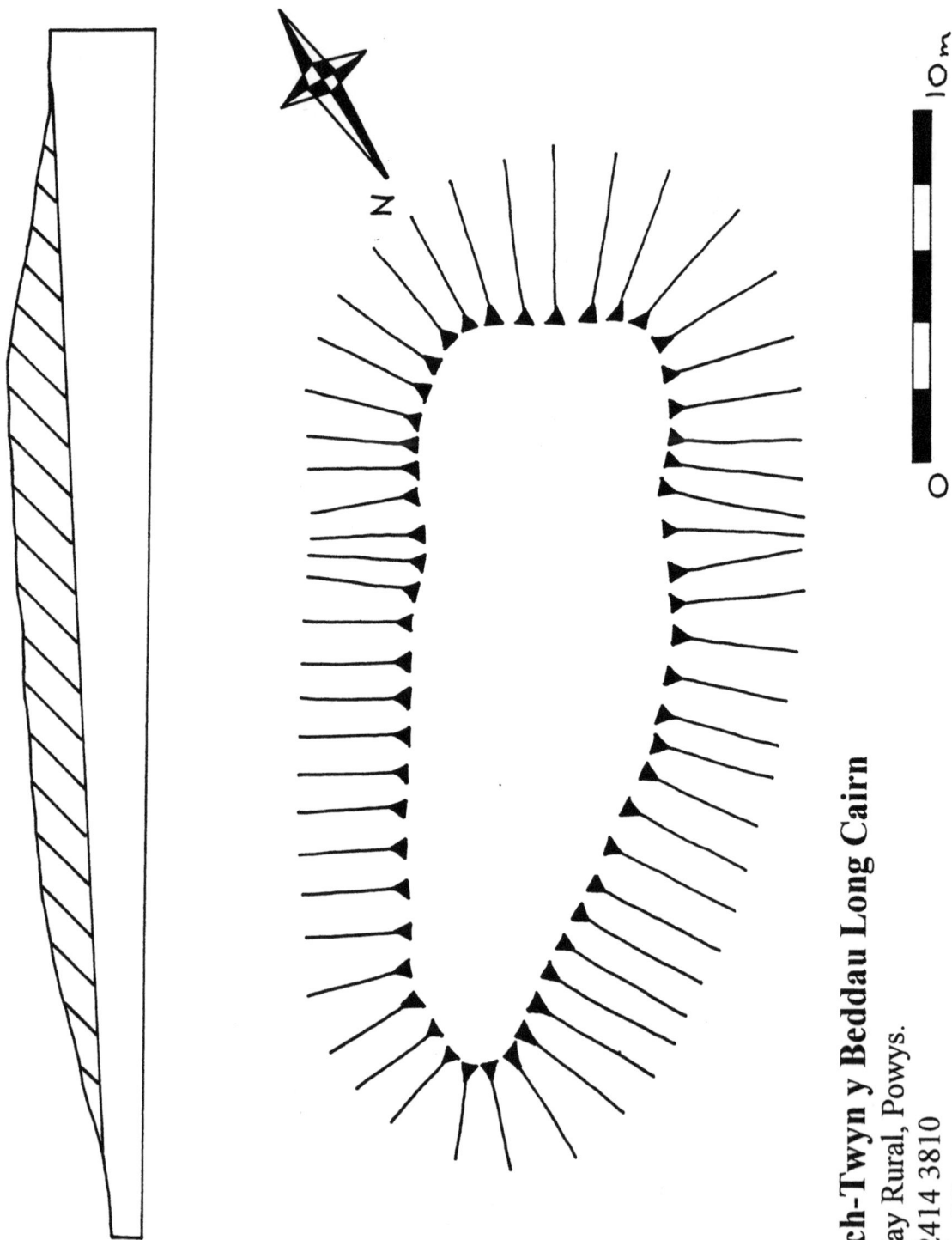

Maes Coch-Twyn y Beddau Long Cairn
Llanigon/Hay Rural, Powys.
NGR: SO 2414 3810
420m above OD

Surveyed 28/4/99
Graham Makepeace, Frank Olding,
Neil Phillips.

Fig. 14: Maes Coch-Twyn y Beddau Long Cairn (BN 1).

These may or may not have had formal boundaries, but would have had to have been capable of supporting the group. The tombs, built by the people for the people, take on the role of territorial marker, a seal of ownership putting the land under the guardianship of eternal spirits and/or gods. They were thus also intimately connected with the disposal of the dead and with ritual and symbolic acts such as ceremonial feasting and gift exchange (Darvill 1982, 82). Some see the tombs as lying at the centre or focus of territories (Renfrew 1973a, 1973b; Darvill 1979) others prefer to envisage them as marking their boundaries (Burl 1979, 95; Drewett 1975,139; Whittle 1977, 24). Fences have been found beneath a number of long barrows in Wiltshire and it has been suggested that they were sited on boundaries to avoid causing disruption to farmland (Darvill 1987, 53). It is also interesting to note that Neolithic activity around the completed chambered tomb at Gwernvale was markedly less intense than in the pre-cairn phase, suggesting that the tomb may have lain remote from contemporary settlement (Britnell and Savory 1984, 149).

In the Severn-Cotswold areas where causewayed enclosures occur (whether they be periodic meeting-places or settlements), the enclosures may have sat at the centre of a distribution with tombs around them, or, if tombs formed the foci of territories, the enclosures may have occupied the peripheries. The causewayed enclosure at Crickley Hill may have formed the centre of a territory some 2.3km in diameter with the periphery marked by four chambered tombs (Darvill 1982, 82-4, Fig. 16).

In the Black Mountains, Neolithic settlement never seems to have been far removed from the tombs. Most of the excavated Brecknock tombs produced evidence of domestic occupation close to, or even on the tomb sites themselves (RCAHMW 1997, 28). A comparable situation to that at Crickley Hill seems explicit in the spatial relationship between the Neolithic "settlement" on Dorstone Hill (HN 8) and the chambered tombs at Arthur's Stone (HN 2) and Cross Lodge (HN 3, Fig. 16). A similar relationship seems possible between the settlements on Cefn Hill (HN 9-10) and the tombs at Maes Coch-Twyn y Beddau (BN 1) and Mynydd Bach (HN 1, Fig. 13).

Carrying the hypothesis further, the Dunseal tomb (HN 4) may form the southern boundary of a territory centred on Stockley Hill and bounded to the north by Cross Lodge. It is also possible that Dunseal and the now destroyed Park Wood (HN 7) once formed a complementary river axis/hill alignment "pair" of the kind identified by Tilley (1994, 136). The tomb on Garway Hill (HN 5, Fig. 15) could also be interpreted as marking the northerly extent of a territory centred on the lower Monnow valley and marked by lithic scatters (HN 53-4; MN 22) and axe finds (HN 21-2).

4.5 The Later Neolithic

To date, no attempt has been made to identify a Later Neolithic element in the Herefordshire lithic assemblages and the evidence for Later Neolithic activity in Monmouthshire is also scanty, being largely confined to two small scrapers among the Pen y Clawdd scatter assemblage (MN 20), one tranverse and one oblique arrowhead among the Skirrid Fawr assemblage (MN 21) and stray finds of scrapers (MN 14, 15) and arrowheads (MN 23, 25). The discovery of Later Neolithic scrapers and Peterborough Ware during the Flannel Street excavations at Abergavenny (MN 24), combined with Mesolithic (MM 9) and Early Bronze Age material (MB 57) from the same site demonstrates the remarkable longevity of prehistoric activity at certain locations (Fig. 17).

The widespread expansion in the use of Group VII Graig Lwyd axes took place primarily in the Later Neolithic (Chappell 1987, 206; Bradley and Edmonds 1993, 186), exclusively for the production of utilitarian tools (Chappell 1987, 256) and the two local examples from Penbidwal (MN 3) and Cefn Hill (HN 11) should probably be assigned to this period. Cornish Group I axes also saw an expansion during the Later Neolithic (Bradley and Edmonds 1993, 192) and there is a single local example from Maresses Farm, St. Margaret's (HN 19).

The abundance and widespread distribution of Graig Lwyd axes at this period has been seen as a sign that intensified competition for land and resources may have increased the need for wide-spread alliances coupled with greater regional integration (Chappell 1987, 258). The period certainly saw greater competition for exchange goods and links with distant areas (Bradley and Edmonds 1993, 192).

The final closure of the tomb at Gwernvale is dated by two radiocarbon dates of c. 2440 b. c. and c. 2640 b. c. The tomb was closed partly by pulling down unstable stretches of cairn wall and partly by piling new stone against the cairn. This was probably designed to mask the external features of the monument and all took place more or less simultaneously. The intention seems to have been the production of a featureless cairn and the production of an "instant" archaic form may have been the prime objective. Deliberately deposited sherds of two Peterborough vessels are associated with the closing.

A great deal of effort was put into the closing of the tomb implying that it retained ritual or symbolic meanings apart from burial, possibly still connected with the ownership of territory (Britnell and Savory 1984, 150). There is also a strong possibility that some at least of the Herefordshire ring-banks discussed under the Bronze Age (see below) date to the Later Neolithic period.

The distributions of Neolithic and Early Bronze Age flint sites show a considerable amount of overlap and apparent continuity between the two periods. Two of the Herefordshire Neolithic scatters have also produced Bronze Age material: Wern Derries (HN 33-HB 65) and Greenway Farm (HN 39- HB 72). In addition, seven of the Herefordshire Mesolithic sites which had Earlier Neolithic material also produced Early Bronze Age flint: Arthur's Stone Ridge (HM5-HN 29-HB 59), the settlements on Dorstone Hill (HM 6-HN 8-HB 43), Cefn Hill (HM 7-HN 9-HB 44) and Abbey Farm (HM 8-HN 10-HB 45) and the scatters at Woodbury (HM 11-HN 35-HB 71), Stockley no. 1 (HM 12-HN 45-HB 73) and Pucha no. 1 (HM 14-HN 32-HB 64).

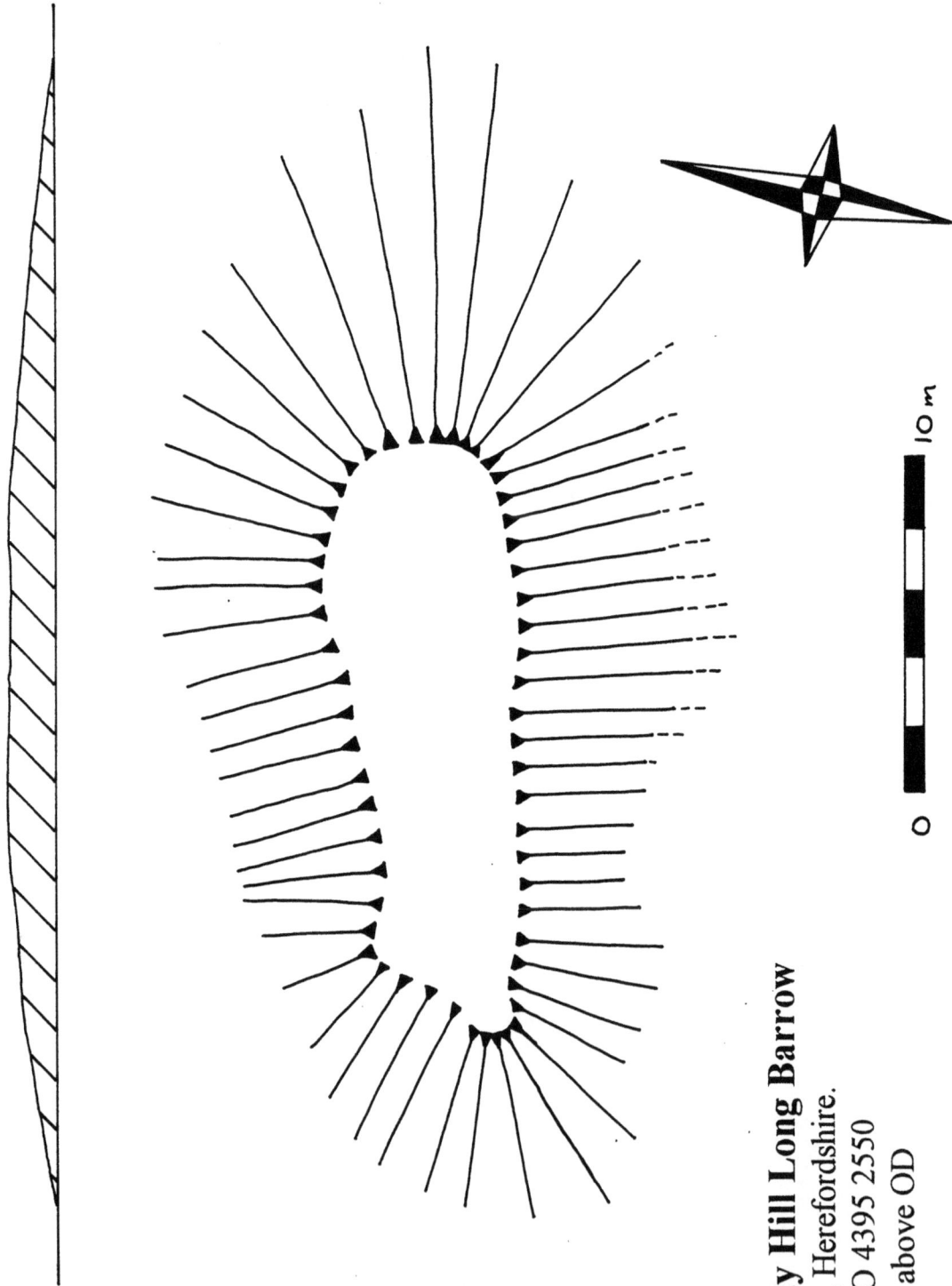

Garway Hill Long Barrow
Garway, Herefordshire.
NGR: SO 4395 2550
c. 335m above OD

Surveyed 14/7/99
Frank Olding, Neil Phillips,
Kieran Phillips.

10 m

0

Fig. 15: Garway Hill Long Barrow (HN 5)

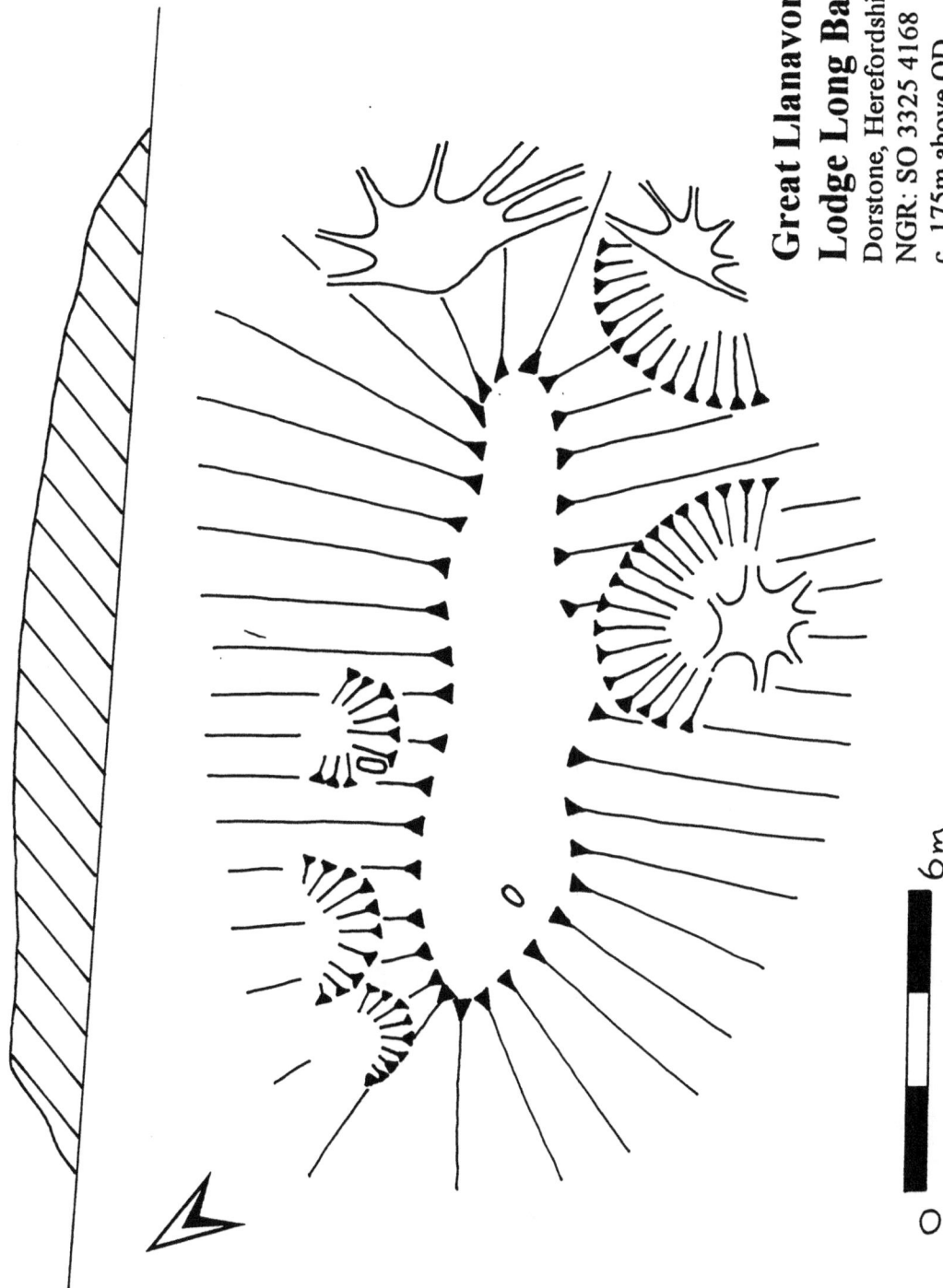

**Great Llanavon-Cross
Lodge Long Barrow**
Dorstone, Herefordshire.
NGR: SO 3325 4168
c. 175m above OD

Surveyed 9/8/99
Graham Makepeace, Frank Olding.

6m

**Fig. 16: Great Llanavon-Cross Lodge Long Barrow
(HN 3).**

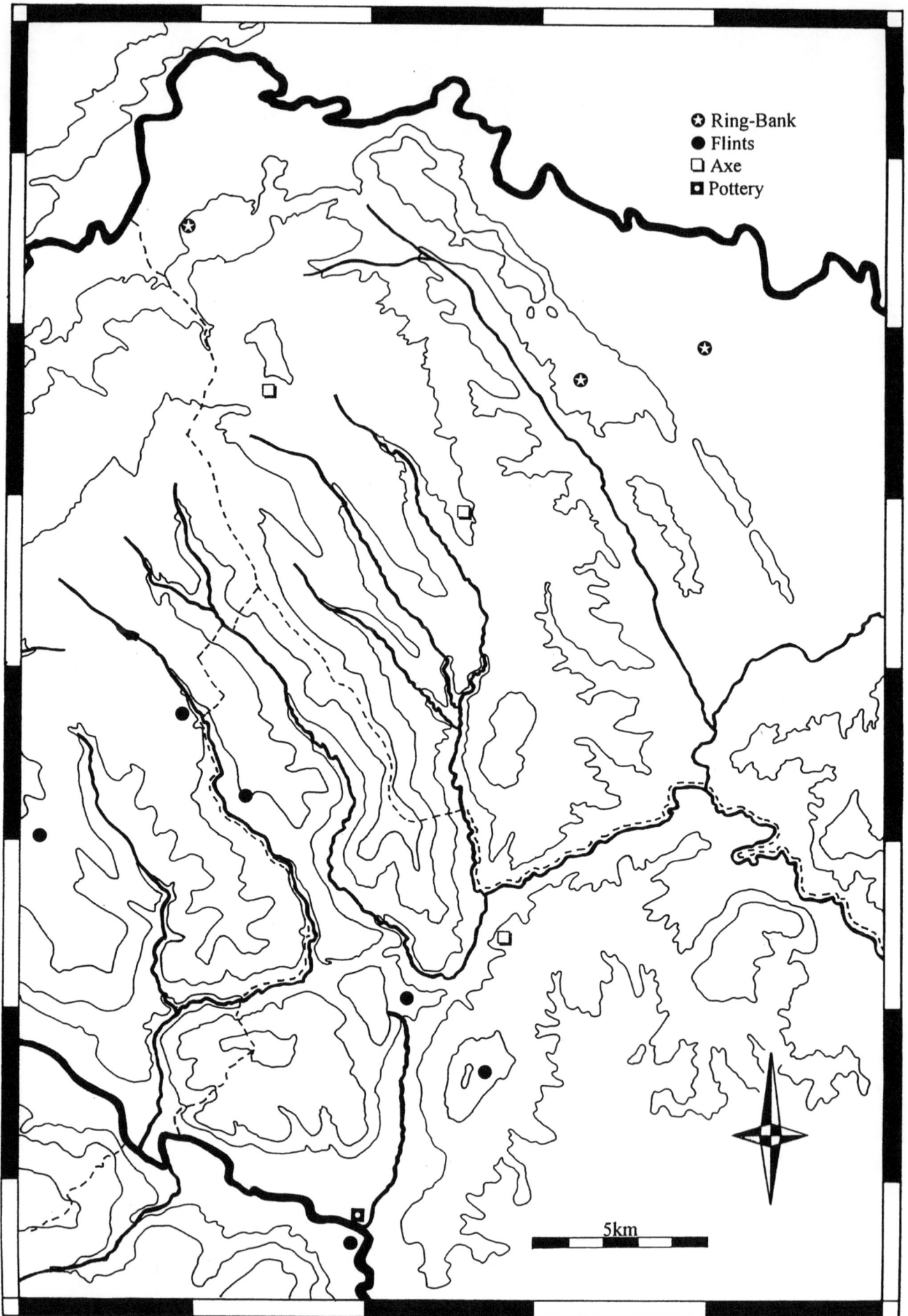

Fig. 17: The Later Neolithic Landscape.

30

In Monmouthshire, the same chronological depth of prehistoric activity from the Mesolithic through to the Bronze Age is only evident at Abergavenny (see above) and at Skirrid Fawr (MM 7-MN 21-MB 53). There was both Neolithic and Bronze Age material among the lithic scatter at Pen y Clawdd (MN 20-MB 52), at the flint find-spots in the Grwyne Fawr valley (MN 14-MB 47), on Hatterall Hill (MN 18-MB 50) and at Llanfoist (MN 23-MB 58).

5 - THE BRONZE AGE

5.1 Early Bronze Age Lithic Scatters

The adoption of metalwork did not, of course, mean the immediate end of flint-working. Metal is not the best material for all tasks and the number of flint artefact types decreases by stages as the range of metal tools grows (Ford *et al.* 1984, 165). For example, flint axes, adzes, burins and sickles went out of general use by or during the Early Bronze Age with bronze axes taking the place of flint axes and adzes. By the Later Bronze Age, the same had happened to flint arrowheads, though scrapers, awls, rods and knives continued in use for longer (*ibid.*, 166/7).

In summary, the Bronze Age saw a progressive deterioration in flint-working skills and a drastic reduction in the range of implement types as bronze tools were devised to replace them. There is also a relationship between the order in which different flint types went out of use and the production of metal artefacts which fulfilled the same functions (*ibid.*, 167).

5.2 Early Bronze Age Land Use

The Early Bronze Age in the Brecon Beacons and western Black Mountains saw a "devastating onslaught" of upland forest clearances in search of cultivable. Widespread deforestation seems to have been established by c. 3000 B.P with open ground at over 400m above OD on the Brecon Beacons around Coed Tâf soil (RCAHMW 1997, 6). Territories which had kept mainly to the lower ground during the Neolithic expanded onto the adjoining uplands (Fig. 18), becoming geographically more diverse in the process (Burgess 1980, 249).

In the Black Mountains, intermittent clearances were initiated at Pen y Gadair Fawr (SO 230 285) c. 3,500 B. P. and at Waun Fach (SO 217 300) c. 4.800-2,800 B. P. By the time of the construction of the two Bronze Age cairns at 280m above OD at Nant Helen in the western Beacons (B-RC 16-17), the upland landscape was dominated by heather or scrub (RCAHMW 1997, 7).

Such clearances may have been with a view to pastoral rather than arable activities (Webley 1976, 26). Some 75% of growth on modern mountain pastures in the Black Mountains is concentrated between June and September (*ibid.*, 32). However, it has been estimated that average overall temperatures during the Early Bronze Age were some 2 degrees higher than at present. Variations in seasonal growth would have been accentuated as a result and mountain soils would also have dried out quicker, causing a shorter summer grazing season (*ibid.*, 22).

On the basis of cairn distributions, the lack of known domestic sites and the presence of sheep bone in cists, it has been suggested that the Bronze Age people of the Black Mountains and Brecon Beacons were primarily pastoralists practising transhumance between valley-bottom bases and summer pastures on the high ridges. The presence of some valley-bottom cairns and barrows has been interpreted as reflecting winter habitats (*ibid.*, 32). However, arable

activity in the area is attested by an impression of emmer wheat on the base of a cordoned urn from Fan y Big in the Beacons (B-LBS 6) and the presence of rye at other Brecknock sites (RCAHMW 1997, 7).

Major deforestation c. 2,200-1,500 B. C. followed by widespread tillage had devastating effects on the landscape. By c. 1,200 B. C., blanket peat had begun to grow throughout the upland areas and poor soil management led to leaching and acidic soils. The upland areas were abandoned, possibly creating greater pressure on the available land (*loc. cit.*). The period has been characterised as an agricultural crisis (Burgess 1980, 258).

Although there is no direct dating for Bronze Age land clearance, field systems or territorial markers anywhere in the Black Mountains or Brecon Beacons, pollen evidence and the widespread distributions of cairns at high altitudes suggests that Bronze Age agricultural activity (probably mixed hill-farming) was ubiquitous (RCAHMW 1997, 206). In addition, the distribution of dated Early Bronze Age burials (see below) gives some indication of the chronology of the colonisation of upland areas. This points to the exploitation of the lower slopes in the early Beaker period c. 2500-2300 cal. B. C., some movement onto the higher ground in the later Beaker phase c. 2300-2050 cal. B. C. and intensive exploitation of the highest land during the full Early Bronze Age c. 2050-1500 cal. B. C.

5.3 Early Bronze Age Settlement

Although virtually nothing is known about Early Bronze Age settlement in the southern Marches as a whole (Stanford 1991, 29), four Herefordshire sites (HB 43-46) have been interpreted as settlements on the basis of the presence of lithic scatters (Fig. 19) and other evidence. However, the only excavated site with evidence of actual Bronze Age structures is Dorstone Hill (HB 43). A shallow depression "on the silting of which had been a large fire" was dated by C-14 to the Bronze Age. Above this was a floor level with a post hole which the excavators interpreted as a Bronze Age building.

Of the other Herefordshire "settlements", the ground at "Abbey Farm Site A" (HB 45) had never previously been ploughed and was shown on the 1883 and 1903 Ordnance Survey maps as forming part of the original Park Wood. When visited in 1950, the site had recently been ploughed and there was a large number of flint flakes, scrapers and chips on the surface covering an area of about a quarter of an acre (0.1ha) (Robinson 1950, 112).

On the basis of a lack of diagnostic Neolithic material and by comparing the assemblage with that of "Cefn Hill Site B" (HB 44, see below), Robinson assigned a Bronze Age date to the Abbey Farm scatter (*ibid.*, 115). In support, he cited the presence of a possible round barrow on the ridge above Abbey Farm (HB 2) which appeared to have been dug into in antiquity (*loc. cit.*). Some authors have written this off as a ruined building (Brown 1972, 315).

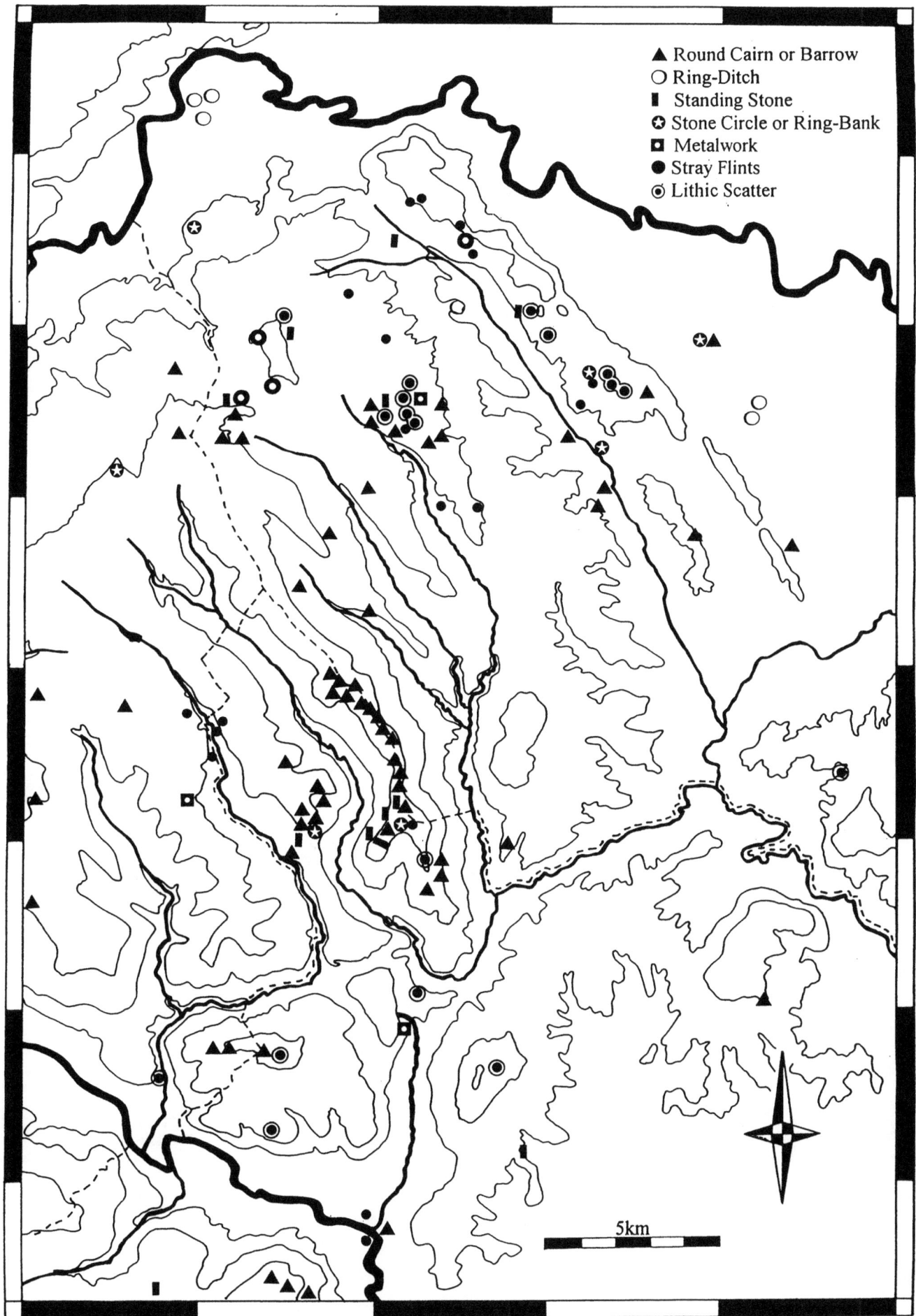

Fig. 18: The Early Bronze Age Landscape.

Legend:
- ▲ Round Cairn or Barrow
- ○ Ring-Ditch
- ▮ Standing Stone
- ✪ Stone Circle or Ring-Bank
- ▣ Metalwork
- ● Stray Flints
- ⊙ Lithic Scatter

5km

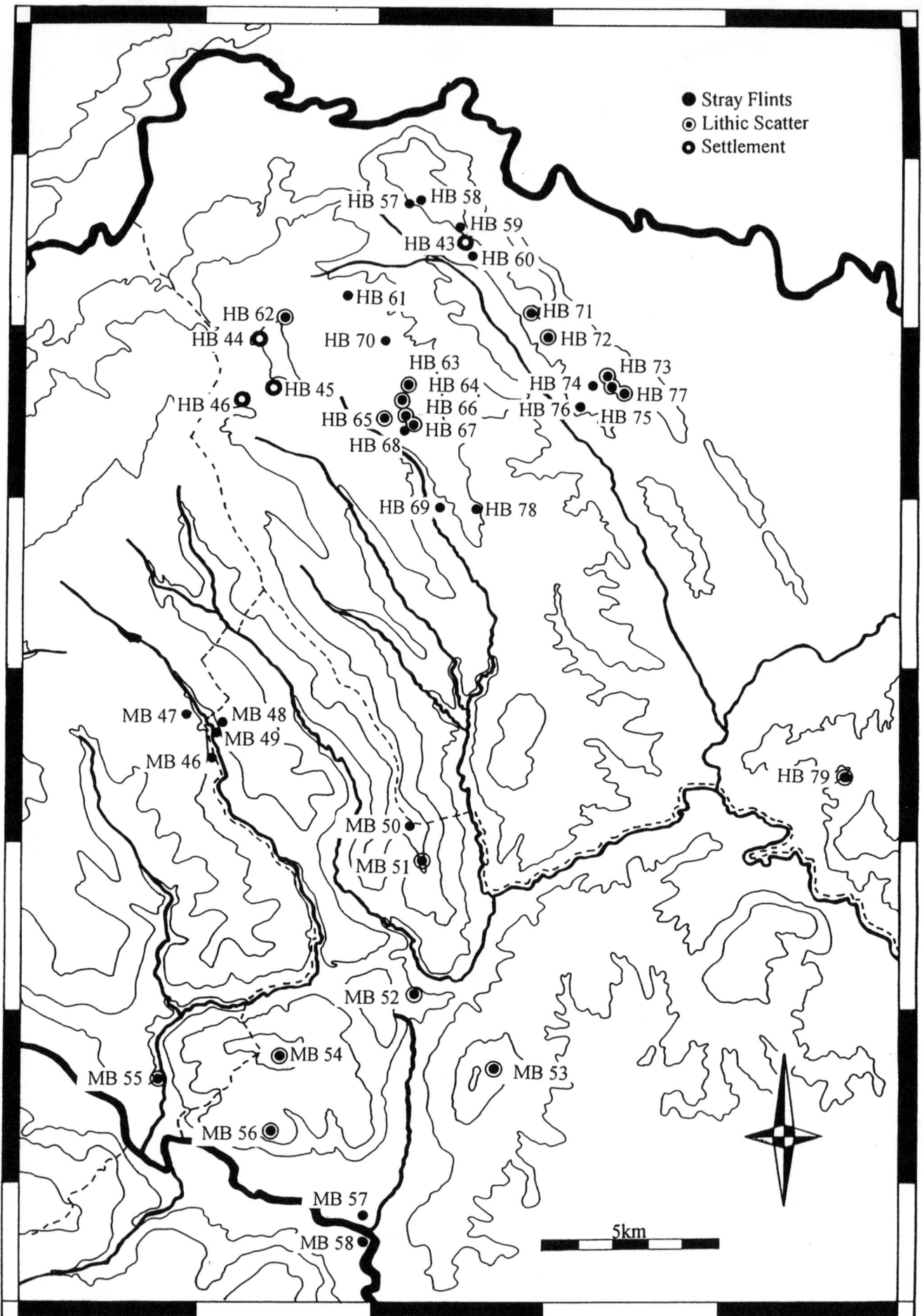

Fig. 19: Early Bronze Age Lithic Finds.

The flint scatter at "Birches Farm Site B" (HB 46) was situated towards the bottom of a slope on fairly flat ground adjoining an area which showed evidence of having been wet or swampy for a considerable period. The site was also marked by a large patch of whitish soil. The ground had not been cultivated previously and was immediately laid down to pasture again. Among the scatter was a very fine Early Bronze Age plano-convex flint knife which Robinson speculated may originally have come from a destroyed cist or round barrow (Robinson 1950, 116) and which he used to date the assemblage. Again, in support he cited the presence of a very small round barrow on Parc y Meirch (HB 3) not far from the Parc y Meirch standing stone (HB 42). Several large slabs lying against the adjacent hedge-bank were interpreted as possibly belonging to a destroyed cist. Another small barrow stood nearby and Robinson drew attention to the fact that the Olchon valley beaker burials (HB 8) did not appear to have covering barrows of any size. In short, Robinson interpreted the Abbey Farm and Birches Farm sites as a Bronze Age settlement complete with occupation sites and their associated barrows (ibid., 117).

On the N end of Cefn Hill at "Cefn Hill Site B" (HB 44), an indeterminate length of prehistoric dry stone wall was associated with coarse Bronze Age flints. Nearby, on a flat stretch of ground just W of the Hay-Michaelchurch road, "Cefn Hill Site C" (HB 44) produced chips, scrapers and borers as well as two barbed and tanged arrowheads. Robinson interpreted both sites as Early Bronze Age settlements.

These sites have all been classed as settlements on the basis of the presence of other evidence in addition to lithic scatters. Whether any meaningful distinction can be drawn between these and other Early Bronze Age lithic scatters in Herefordshire is still unclear. Whether seen as "settlements", "working floors" or "activity areas", their distribution gives some indication of the Early Bronze Age exploitation of the Golden Valley and adjacent areas.

There are marked clusters of scatters on Urishay Common (HB 63-68) and Stockley Hill (HB 73-77). It is interesting to note the relationship between distributions of round barrows or cairns and lithic scatters. On Urishay Common, the Wern Derries standing stone (HB 40) stands at the centre of a cluster of both lithic scatters (HB 63-68) and barrows (HB 13-18). The extant cairns are sited at the periphery of the lithic scatter concentration and it does not seem unreasonable in this case to suggest that the Urishay barrows may have fulfilled a similar role to that postulated for the local Neolithic chambered tombs and acted as boundary markers for a small but clearly defined territory on Urishay Common (Fig. 20).

A similar relationship seems possible between the settlement sites, lithic scatters, barrows and standing stones on Cefn Hill (HB 1, 2, 41, 44, 45, 62) and Parc y Meirch (HB 3-5, 42, 46). Seen in this light, the Gannols Farm and Willmastone standing stones (HB 38, 39) may once have been associated with territories centred respectively on Dorstone Hill settlement (HB 43) and Stockley Hill (HB 73-77). The Stockley Hill territory may also have possessed a ritual focus in the possible Later Neolithic-Early Bronze Age ring-bank at Poston (HB 34) and an eastern boundary marker in the

damaged barrow in Rushen Wood (HB 20) which still marks the Vowchurch-Tyberton parish boundary.

In this light, there seems to be a clear territorial role for both burial cairns/barrows and standing stones. Burgess has argued for the existence of Early Bronze Age territories incorporating centres of varying importance as foci for populations inhabiting scattered farmsteads and hamlets (1980, 245). It seems possible, therefore, that these areas formed ritual and social foci or "core areas" for five Early Bronze Age territories (Fig. 21) centred respectively on Parc y Meirch (I), Cefn Hill (II), Dorstone Hill (III), Urishay Common (IV) and Stockley Hill (V). It should also be borne in mind that these larger territories included access to the grazing lands on the high ridges. It is also possible that Bronze Age settlement was attracted to the area by the sandy soils which contrast with the heavy clays of northern Herefordshire (Stanford 1991, 33).

In Monmouthshire, there is less evidence, but the dominance of scrapers in the Early Bronze Age assemblages from the lithic scatters at Pen y Clawdd (MB 52) and Skirrid Fawr (MB 53) may indicate denser and more permanent use of these sites at this period. The exploitation of the high uplands implied by the distribution of ritual monuments is also attested by the high altitude Early Bronze Age lithic scatter on Hatterall Hill (MB 51) and two distinct territories centred on the ritual complexes at Garn Wen (VI) and Garreg Las (VII) can also be postulated (Fig. 21).

Across the eastern Black Mountains as a whole, single finds of Early Bronze Age flint knives (MB 47-49; HB 59), barbed and tanged arrow-heads (MB 50, 51, 57, 58; HB 61, 62, 70) and scrapers (MB 46, 51; HB 60) and the distribution of small assemblages of points, blades and scrapers (MB 55, 56; HB 58, 59) reflect the ubiquitous exploitation of the landscape at this period and should probably be regarded as losses by herdsmen or hunters. Although the bow and arrow may have functioned as an object of war and display (Pitts and Jacobi 1979, 174), it has been suggested that stray finds of barbed and tanged arrowheads may still represent hunting expeditions (Ford 1987b, 121). It is also possible that the stray finds of spindle whorls (HB 57), adzes (HB 69) and whetstones (HB 74) represent activity of a more domestic nature. The spindle whorl also implies sheep-rearing and the manufacture and use of woollen cloth as elements in the local Bronze Age economy. The sole battle-axe find (HB 70 - a re-used Neolithic axe) could have originated in either a ritual or domestic context (Clarke et al. 1985, 173).

5.4 Early Bronze Age Ritual

Dated Early Bronze Age Burials

In the eastern Black Mountains, we are fortunate in having a spread of Early Bronze Age cairns which have produced datable finds (Fig. 22). Their distribution presents an intriguing picture. The early beakers of Needham's Period 1 c. 2500-2300 cal. B. C. (Needham 1995) from the Pen y Wyrlod-Llanigon chambered tomb (B-BB 28) and the Olchon Valley cists (HB 8) both occur on the lower slopes at 265m and 325m above OD respectively and a later handled beaker of c. 2300-2050 cal. B. C. comes from Pen Gloch y

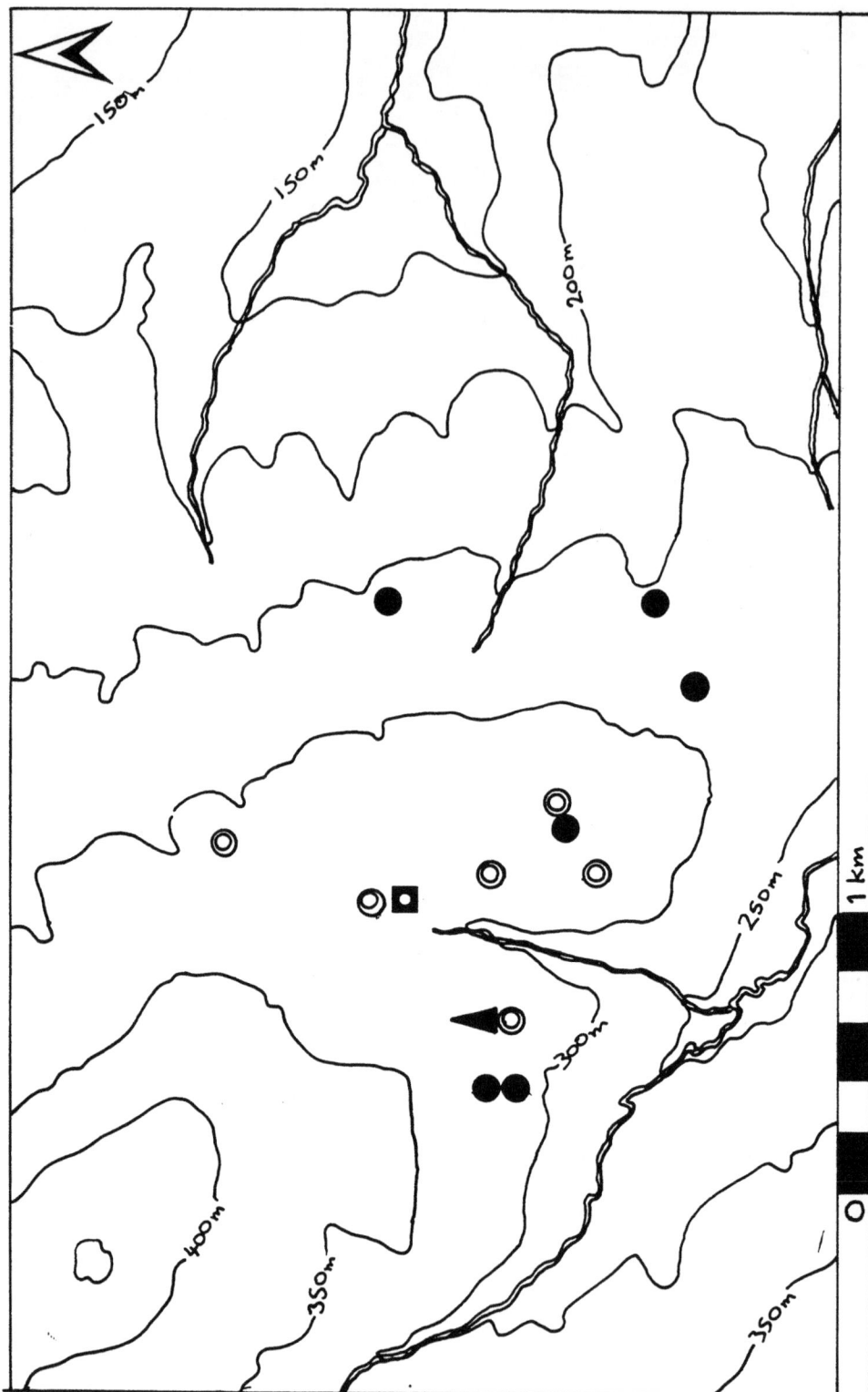

Fig. 20: The Urishay Common Core Area.

Round Barrows
Lithic Scatter
Metalwork
Standing Stone

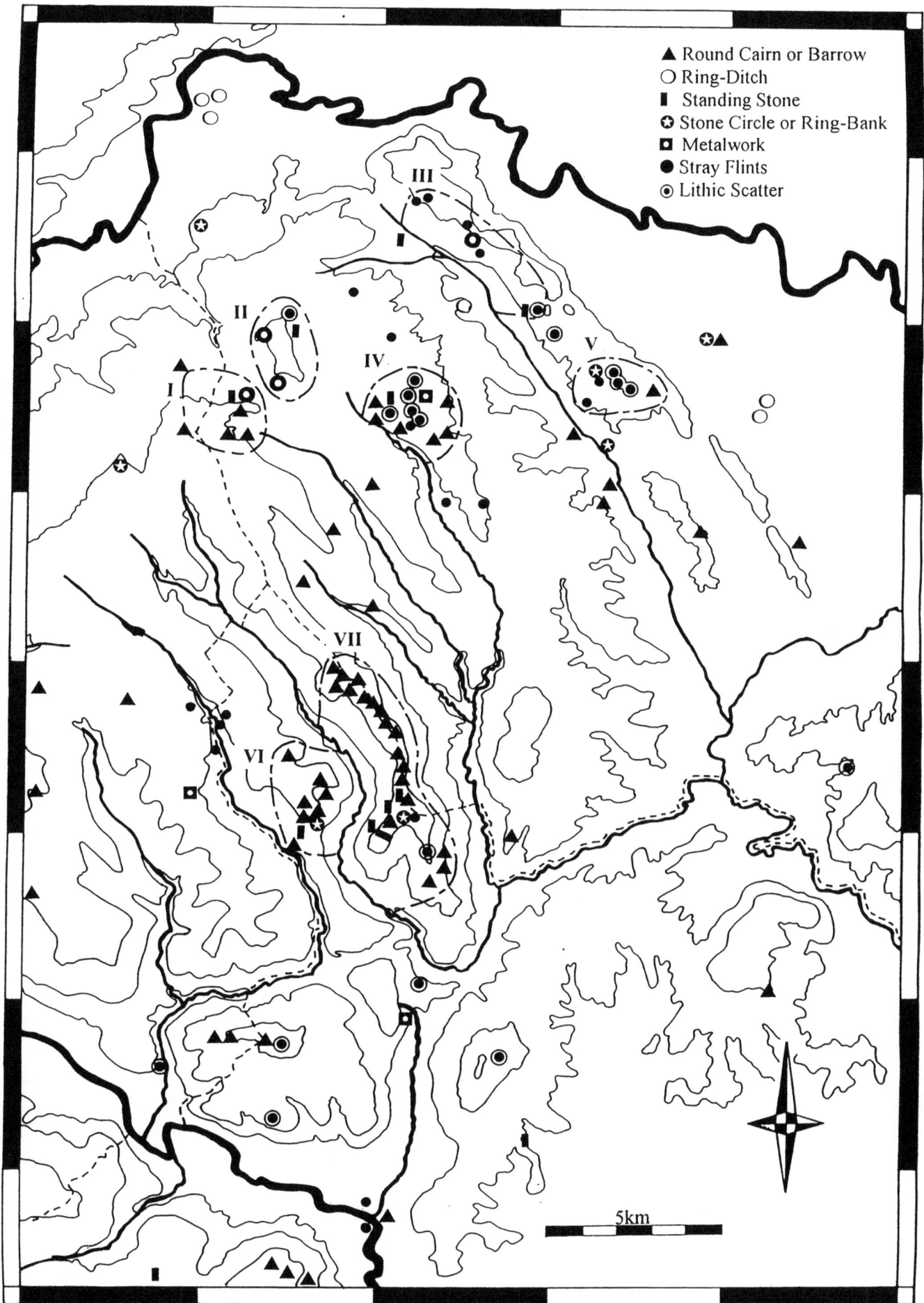

Fig. 21: Early Bronze Age Territories.

Pibwr (B-RC 302) at c. 655m above OD. The collared urn from the Craig Ddu cairn at 480m above OD (MB 3) cannot be dated more closely than to the Early Bronze Age (Needham's periods 3 and 4) c. 2050-1500 cal. B. C., while the pygmy cup from Pen Allt Mawr at 455m above OD (B-RC 300) is assigned to Needham's period 4 c. 1700-1500 cal. B. C. which sees the total domination of cremation in the burial record (Burgess 1980, 257).

This distribution gives some indication of the chronology of the colonisation of upland areas. This points to the exploitation of the lower slopes in the early Beaker period c. 2500-2300 cal. B. C., some movement onto the highest ground in the later Beaker phase c. 2300-2050 cal. B. C. and intensive exploitation of the highest land during the full Early Bronze Age c. 2050-1500 cal. B. C.

Round Cairns and Barrows

Even with careful excavation, it is sometimes difficult to distinguish between cairns whose primary function is burial and those used for other ritual purposes. Some may have entirely agricultural origins (RCAHMW 1997, 67).

The diameters of sites in the Brecon Beacons and western Black Mountains range from 2.5m to 30m or even up to 50m, though few are above 1m in height. Twyn y Beddau on Hay Bluff (B-RC 311) once stood to a height of 2.8m and is still a substantial monument (*ibid.,* 69). About 10% of Brecknock cairns have kerbs. While kerbs obviously perform a practical function in revetting the cairn mass, they have also been interpreted as architectural features designed to give a mystical and aesthetic quality to the cairns which served to relate their builders to the surrounding landscape (Lynch 1975).

Only a small proportion of Brecknock sites are earthen barrows, though excavation has shown that some cairns, such as Twyn Bryn Glas (B-RC 127), Ynys Hir (B-RC 138) and Nant Maden (B-RC 111), incorporated layers of earth within their stone structures. Conversely, the excavated barrow at Twyn y Beddau in the Black Mountains (B-RC 311) included layers of stone in its earthen structure. It has been speculated that many or most of the Brecknock cairns may have had cappings of earth in their original form (RCAHMW 1997, 71).

Extant distribution patterns (Fig. 23) owe much to factors of differential survival and the apparent absence of burial cairns and barrows from valley floors is probably due in large measure to human activity and natural processes of erosion and alluviation (*loc. cit.*). In the Brecon Beacons and western Black Mountains, aerial photographs have proved singularly unsuccessful at locating barrows on valley ploughland and it is difficult to relate the number and distribution of cairns and barrows to population estimates (*ibid.,* 69). An exactly similar situation exists in the eastern Black Mountains (see Appendix) and the albeit fragmentary evidence for valley-bottom cist burials such as Ysbyty Farm, Abergavenny (MB 24) gives some indication of the number and distribution of sites which may have been lost. Elsewhere in Wales, aerial photographs show burial monuments to be more common in valley locations than on hills and valley bottom settlement

was probably much denser than is suggested by surveys of upstanding monuments (*ibid.,* 73).

While it is undoubtedly true that surviving cairns and barrows only partially reflect their original densities and distributions (Roese 1981b, 575-87), it is surely altogether too mechanistic an approach to reduce cairn siting to the need to avoid invasion of prime agricultural soils. To maintain that the siting of burial monuments "held limited importance for cairn builders" (RCAHMW 1997, 73) is an exercise in *reductio ad absurdum*. The evidence for excavated cairns and barrows acting as foci for long-term cemeteries would seem to contradict this minimalist stance (Warrilow *et al.* 1986).

In his survey of Herefordshire barrows, Grinsell (1993) identified 63 round barrows and 73 ring-ditches. Of the latter, he estimated that about 40% represented the sites of round barrows. Even the great barrow wight himself found identifying barrows in the county unusually difficult. Elsewhere, he lamented, they are normally on hills and seldom in valleys, here they are also found in valleys and may often be confused with Norman mottes - of which there are a great many (Grinsell 1993, 301).

The distribution and siting of the Herefordshire barrows differs considerably both from the Gloucestershire sites - which are mainly on the Cotswolds - and from those of Wessex - which are largely situated on the chalk downlands. In Herefordshire, they may be found on hill tops (e.g. Ganarew 1-7, Llanveynoe 1-2a) or on valley floors beside rivers and streams (e.g. Walford 1 and 2) (*ibid.,* 302). It has been argued that even in the Early Bronze Age rivers held a special place in people's minds. Bronze Age farmers may have worked the light soils of the river terraces and buried their dead near their settlements, or the deceased may have been brought "to Jordan from afar" (Stanford 1991, 34).

The results of excavations (of varying quality) have led to a broad typology of Herefordshire burials. The Beaker phase is represented by the crouched interment of a child with a bell-beaker at Aymestrey 2 and beaker sherds at Eastnor 1, though it is uncertain whether either of these sites was actually covered by a round barrow (Grinsell 1993, 302). An Early Bronze Age knife came from a ring-ditch at Adforton 1, though again the presence of a barrow is far from certain. Early-Middle Bronze Age dates are assigned to Grinsell's Craswall 2 (HB 6), Leominster 1, St. Weonards 1a-b and Walford 1 or 2 and part of a Middle-Late Bronze Age barrel- or bucket-urn was discovered at Eastnor 1. Here again, the presence of a covering barrow is uncertain (*ibid.,* 303).

More locally, Grinsell considered the "Wessex-type" barrows claimed for Chilstone (HB 19, 35) as highly unlikely and dismissed the seventeen barrows identified within the parish of Peterchurch altogether on the grounds that they did not appear in the records of the Archaeology Division of the Ordnance Survey and were not reflected in field names based on the tithe maps of the parish (*ibid.,* 306).

The contents of the double cist burial at Olchon Court, Llanveynoe (HB 8) have been interpreted as a local versions of the earliest fine imported beakers and the inhumation as

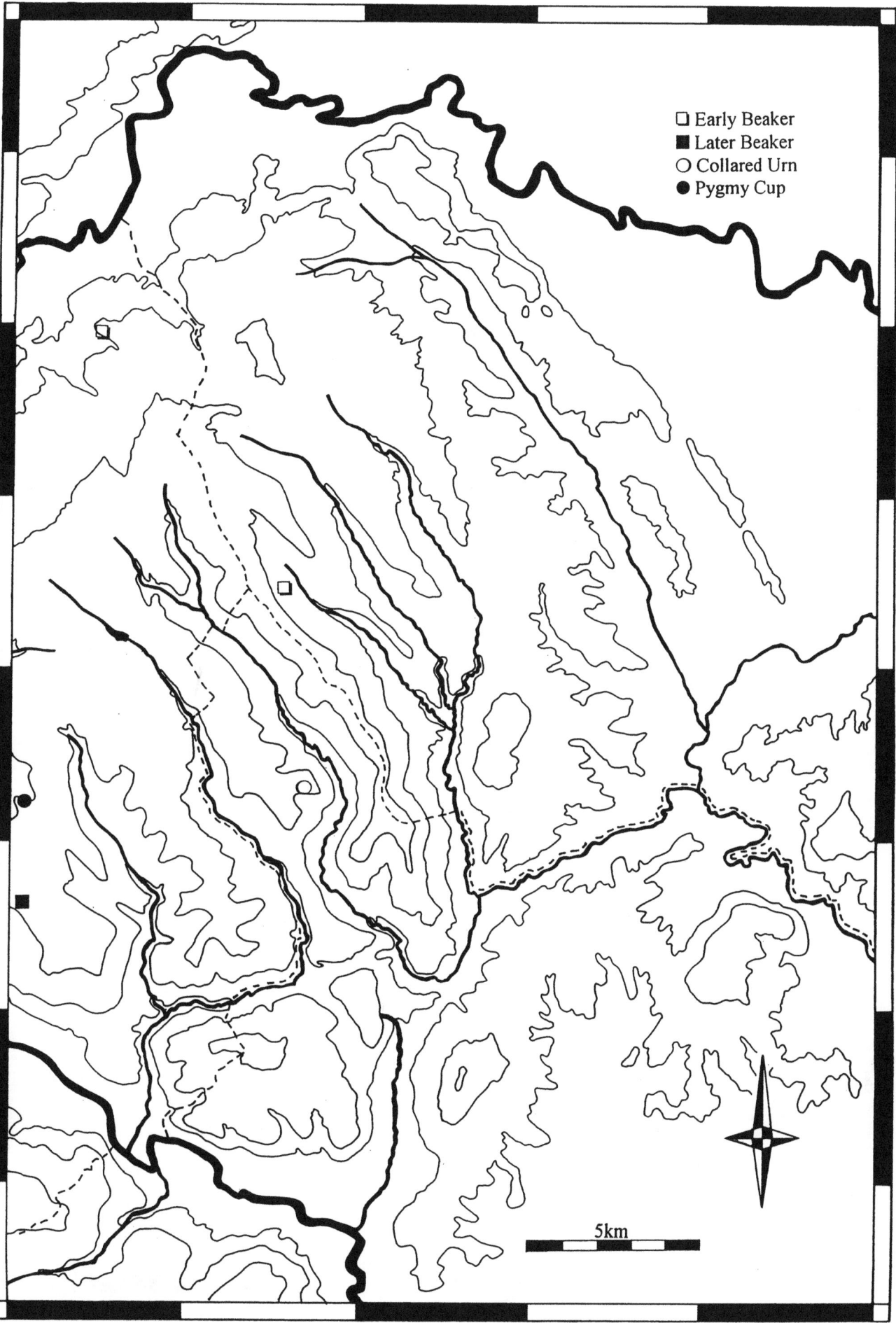

Fig. 22: Dated Early Bronze Age Burials.

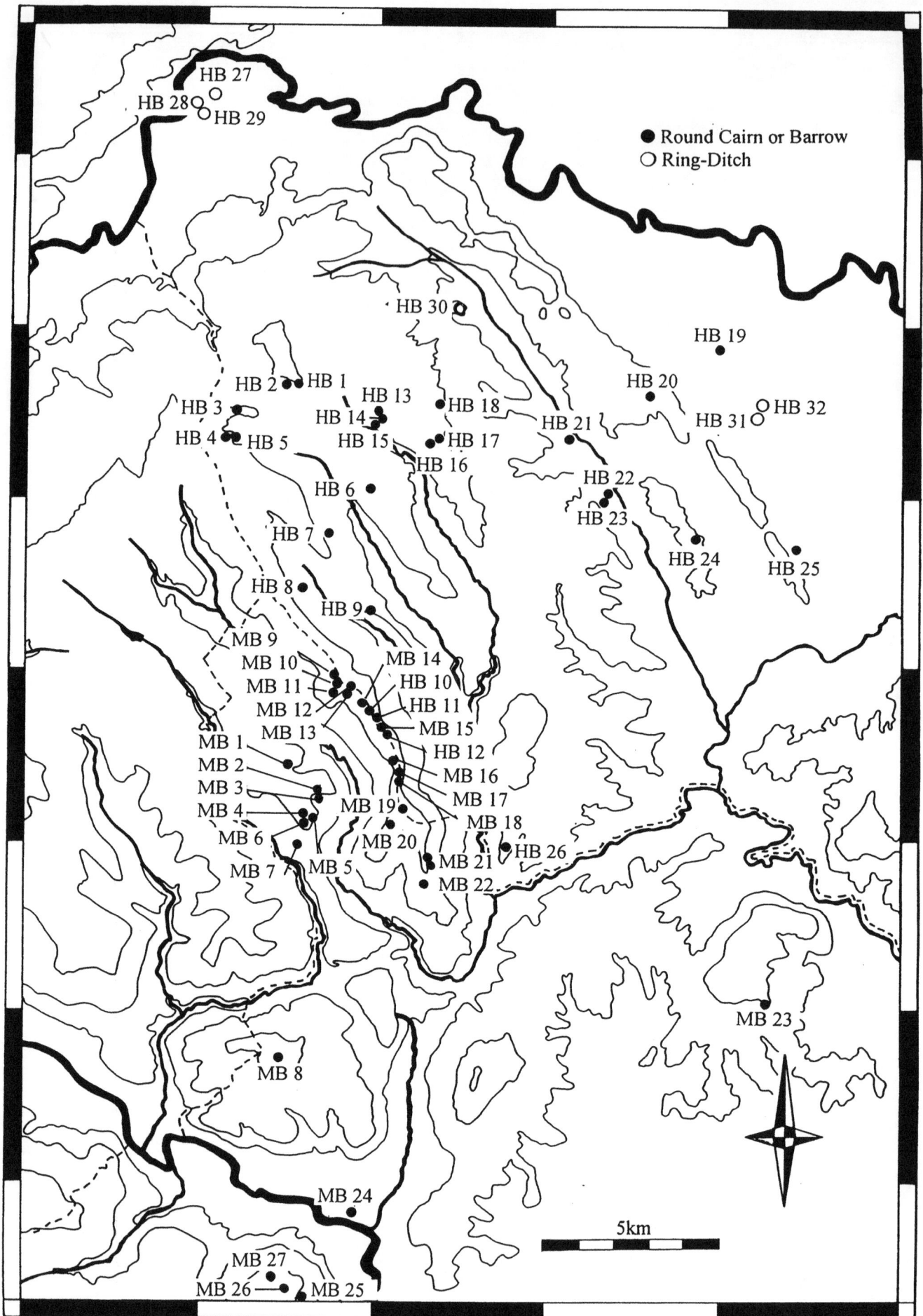

Fig. 23: Early Bronze Age Cairns and Barrows.

that of a young noble (Children and Nash 1994, 42). Inhumation was probably always a minority rite in Wales and the Marches and reserved for the privileged few (Burgess 1980, 255). The possibility has also been broached of the use of beakers for ritualised drinking - either as part of a general "ecstatic" cult or, more particularly, as part of the inhumation process itself. As the only excavated beaker burial in the eastern Black Mountains, the site merits detailed discussion.

Cist 1 was small, oriented exactly to magnetic N and S and contained a crouched male inhumation facing E with the head to the N. An intact bell beaker lay behind the thigh bones and a barbed and tanged arrowhead was found at the bottom of the cist (Marshall 1932, 147).

Cist 2 was also small and lay 1m E of the first, nearly parallel with it but oriented slightly to the W. The capstone was missing and the cist partly filled with earth. The contents were poorly preserved, probably due to the loss of the capstone. Small amounts of charcoal and the outlines of the larger bones of another inhumation were still visible and, at the centre of the cist, was another bell beaker which contained a flint knife with slight secondary working (*ibid.*, 148). There was no sign of any covering mound (*ibid.*, 150).

Both beakers had a curved collar at the rim and have were originally assigned to a "degenerate" B1 beaker group (Savory 1963, 37). Clarke assigned them to his North/Middle Rhine group (1970 Vol. 2, 533). Case (1993) assigned them first to his Group D/Style 2 group, but has since refined his definition and now includes them in his Group Ba dated to c. 2500-2000 B. C. (1999; pers. comm). Other authorities favour an earlier date c. 2500 B. C. (R. J. Harrison pers. comm.).

The well-preserved skeleton in the first cist was that of a young man aged about 25 to 30 years of age and short in stature (approx. 1.69m) but "his mentality was considerably above the average of his race" (Marshall 1932, 150). The pathology report appended to the excavation report comments especially on the outstanding strength of the bones of his shoulders and arms, especially of the right humerus (*ibid.*, 151). This is probably consistent with long practice of archery. The condition of his jaws and teeth suggested that his food was well prepared and cooked (*ibid.* 153). It was impossible to assign gender to the second skeleton, but Marshall speculated that the presence of a knife, rather than an arrow head, indicated a female (*ibid.* 151). However, statistical analysis of the contents of Beaker burials has shown that some 82% of flint knives are deposited with male inhumations. The likelihood, therefore, is that the second Olchon cist also contained a male (Clarke 1970, Appendix 3.3).

Many of the Herefordshire hilltop barrows or cairns are not actually visible from the surrounding countryside and it may be that their significance was essentially localised to their immediate surroundings as local, specific markers (Children and Nash 1994, 43).

The cairn on the Hereford side of Loxidge Tump (HB 10) stands on the eastern slope of the ridge which obscures sight-lines to N or W. To the S, the tops of the ridges of the Black Mountains can be seen, but to the E the site enjoys panoramic views over the valleys of Olchon, Escley and the Golden Valley and all of Herefordshire and NE Monmouthshire as far as the Malvern Hills to the E and southern Shropshire to the NE. Again, this cairn seems to have been sited with reference to what may be seen from it rather than to its own visibility. It is not visible from the valley floors to W or E and can only be seen from the S from the ridge on which it stands.

The neighbouring cairn and contentious "stone circle"(HB 11, 37), at a height of some 530m above OD, enjoy outstanding views in all directions. Immediately below, in the Olchon Valley, is the site of the discovery of the Olchon Valley Beaker cists (HB 8). It has been suggested that a direct ritual relationship exists between the Loxidge Tump cairn-circle complex and the cist burials (*ibid.*, 59).

Other mounds recorded in the county can be regarded as the results of various natural processes or miscellaneous human activity. A mound at St. Margarets (SO 359 338) was probably created by pond cleaning or quarrying (RCHM 1931, 227; TWNFC 1933-5, lxxxiv), one of the cairns at Craswall (HB 2) has been regarded as a ruined building. Another mound at Orcop (SO 464 282) is a rabbit warren (Brown 1972, 315).

Other sites are more enigmatic and, by the time of Brown's survey in the 1970s, widespread destruction had made field evaluation almost impossible in many cases. A possible round barrow at Pentwyn Farm, Urishay (HB 15) shown on photographs of the 1930s (TWNFC 1933-5, lxiii, lxxxiv, 57, 62) had been completely destroyed by 1972 (Brown 1972, *loc. cit.*). In the 1950s, the series of mounds associated with the Chilstone ring-bank (HB 35, Fig. 25) were still preserved in pasture - they too had been badly damaged by 1972 (*loc. cit.*) and have since been completely obliterated. Barrows recorded at Parc y Meirch in 1950 (HB 3) could not even be traced in 1967 (*ibid.*, 317).

The two major Monmouthshire concentrations of round cairns occur on Hatterall Ridge-Loxidge Tump (MB 9-22) and the ridge of the Ffawyddog (MB 1-7). From the evidence of the distribution of dated Early Bronze Age burials in the eastern Black Mountains, it seems likely that these sites situated on the highest ridges date to the full Early Bronze Age (c. 2050-1500 cal. B. C.) and reflect the intensive exploitation of the uplands postulated for this period. On both ridges, the cairns are associated with standing stones and ring-cairns/stone circles and form an element in extended ritual complexes (see below).

About 50m SW of the Garreg Las ring-cairn (MB 29) stands a small cairn (MB 21) and some 200m to the NE another small, and irregular mound (MB 19) is the most southerly of the fourteen cairns which are strung out in linear formation along the highest part of Hatterall Ridge (MB 9-19, HB 10-12). It seems reasonable to consider the group as representing a linear cairn cemetery associated with the ring-cairn.

The tight group of three cairns at Garn Wen (MB 4-6) stand in association with a possible, very fragmentary stone circle

(MB 28), a standing stone (MB 31) and a smaller, outlying cairn (MB 7) and form a distinct ritual complex (see below).

About 1km to the NE of Garn Wen and intervisible with it across a steep-sided valley, is the Craig Ddu cairn (MB 3). The published account of the episode of reckless fossicking at this site is very inadequate but it seems likely that the cist contained the remains of a collared urn and should be assigned to the Early Bronze Age c. 2050-1500 cal. B. C. (Needham's Periods 3 and 4). The cairn stands on a S facing shelf of Craig Ddu with extensive views to the S and SE over the Dyffryn Ewias. It is intervisible with the large cairn at Garn Wen, but is not visible from the valley floor. On Bâl Mawr, some 1.7m N of Garn Wen, is the Cwm Bwchel cairn (MB 1) whose position on a SE facing shelf overlooking a steep valley mirrors that of Craig Ddu.

As in Herefordshire, although many of the cairns are situated to command extensive views over the surrounding landscape from both the Ffawyddog (MB 1, 3, 7) and Hatterall Ridges (MB 13, 16, 17, 21; HB 10-12), none are visible from the valley floors immediately below them and they do not form prominent landmarks from a greater distance. The position of the most westerly of the Loxidge Tump cairns (MB 11) on a high shelf on the SE side of the hill means that views are obscured to the N, E or W. However, the site offers commanding views of Dyffryn Ewias to the S. The cairn is not visible from the valley floor and only comes into view on a false crest from a position some 460m above OD on the hillside to the SE. This strongly implies that their topographical significance lay in what could be seen from them rather than in their own visibility.

Stone Circles

Brecknock boasts the largest number of stone circles in south Wales. Of the ten sites across the county as a whole, five are in the Brecon Beacons and one in the western Black Mountains at Pen y Beacon (B-SC 10, the site is also known as Blaen Digedi and Blaenau). Some occur in pairs or groups, others are associated with cairns, standing stones or stone rows. All have been assigned to Later Neolithic or Early Bronze Age contexts (RCAHMW 1997, 143).

In the past considerable emphasis has been placed on the ritual functions of stone circles (Burl 1976), though currently more attention is paid to their communal or public role in prehistoric society (Barnatt 1989, 211-226). The two spheres need not have been mutually exclusive or even separate in the minds of their builders, of course. Astronomical activities have also been postulated (Thom 1967), but burial and/or associated ritual are by far the most likely activities to have taken place at these sites (RCAHMW 1997, 145). It is possible that a few important centres served wide areas (Stanford 1991, 27).

Most of the Brecknock sites survive in remote upland locations, but it is clear that these areas were reasonably densely settled in the Early Bronze Age. The stone circles originally occupied populated landscapes. Pollen analysis at an Early Bronze Age complex at Cefn Gwernffrwd in Carmarthenshire suggested that the site stood in a wooded setting which had been affected by agriculture since Neolithic times (RCAHMW 1997, 145).

The remarkable survival rate among the Brecknock sites may partly be a result of their later use as highly visible route markers through the sometimes treacherous terrain of the Brecon Beacons and Black Mountains. Some e.g. Nant Tarw (B-SC 2) and Trecastle (B-SC 4) were associated with major drovers' routes. The circle and standing stone of Cerrig Duon (B-SC 3) and Maen Mawr (B-SS 3) have long acted as markers of a route from the head of the Tawe valley over the moors to source of the Usk at Trecastle. The circle at Pen y Beacon marks the route from the Wye valley via the Gospel Pass over the northern escarpment of the Black Mountains (RCAHMW 1997, 144). These historic uses may also give some indication of the circles' original use as focal points for scattered populations.

There are only two open stone circles recorded in Herefordshire (Fig. 26). Near the flint scatter at Stockley no. 1 (HN 45), stood an oval enclosure (HB 36) marked by stones of various sizes with two large outliers of limestone. The stones were removed with the intention of re-erecting them in Gavin Robinson's garden at Poston (Robinson 1934, 55-56)! The contentious example on Loxidge Tump close to the Welsh border (HB 37) was interpreted by Grinsell (1993, 309) as the site of a small cairn but others argue for its being a small stone circle (Children and Nash 1994, 59). The sole Monmouthshire example is the very fragmentary open circle (MB 28) at 472m above OD which forms part of the Garn Wen ritual complex (see below) and which may originally have measured some 50m in diameter (Fig. 28).

Ring-Banks and Ring-Cairns

The Wye Valley and Golden Valley have an unusually high number of ring-banks (Fig. 26). Photographs taken in 1924 show that the "disc barrow" at Upper Chilstone (HB 35) was, in fact, a superbly preserved ring-bank (Fig. 25). The monument measured some 23m in diameter with a 3.5m wide bank and a nearby bell barrow (HB 19) measured some 10m in diameter. Four other, smaller, round barrows surrounded the ring-bank to the S and E. The very well-preserved earthen ring-bank with extensive views over the Wye Valley between Hawks Wood and Mouse Castle Wood in Clifford (HB 33, Fig. 25) is approx. 11m in diameter internally with a small gap or entrance on the S side. In Bradley's Wood, Poston (HB 34), the base of the Iron Age mound (HI 14) consisted of a ring-bank of fine soil some 16.5m in diameter and about 1.2m in height (Fig. 24). Although the excavator assumed that the structure represented a single phase of construction (Marshall 1933b, 32), the site is comparable in size and lay-out with the other Herefordshire ring-banks and it is likely that a pre-existing ring-bank was incorporated in the Iron Age mound.

These sites may be compared with the "earthen embanked enclosures" of Ireland - a type of ceremonial site which consists of a large earthen bank, without an obvious ditch, forming an enclosure around an area from which the soil has been scraped, creating a lower surface inside the monument than outside. They are generally a lowland, river valley phenomenon and are closely associated with passage tombs

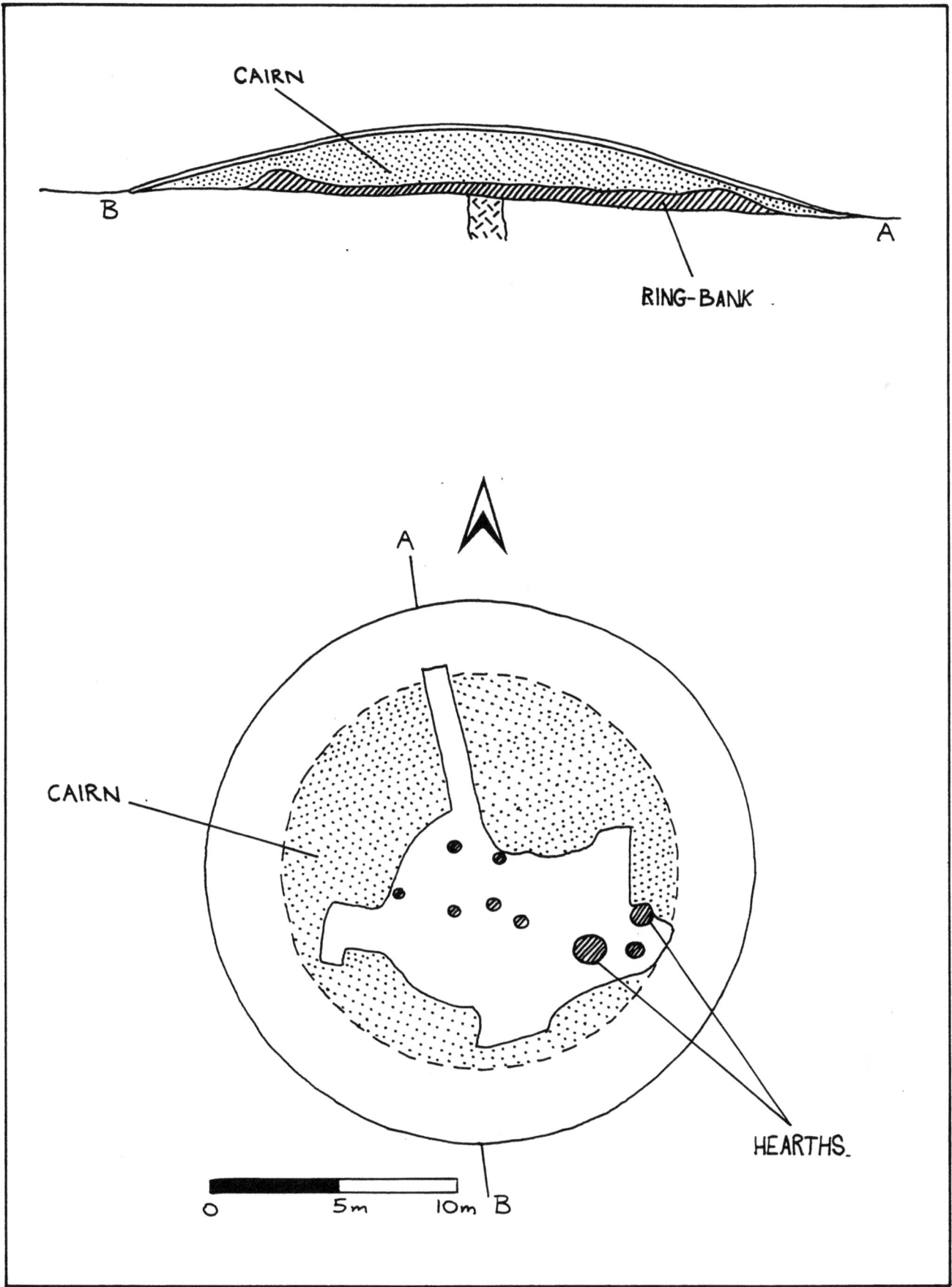

CAIRN

RING-BANK.

A

CAIRN

HEARTHS.

0   5m   10m B

Fig. 24: The Poston Mound (HI 14) and Ring-Bank (HB 34) (after Marshall 1933b).

43

Clifford Ring-Bank
Clifford, Herefordshire.
NGR: SO 2484 4275
c. 215m above OD

Surveyed 23/11/99
Graham Makepeace, Frank Olding, Neil Phillips

10m

30m

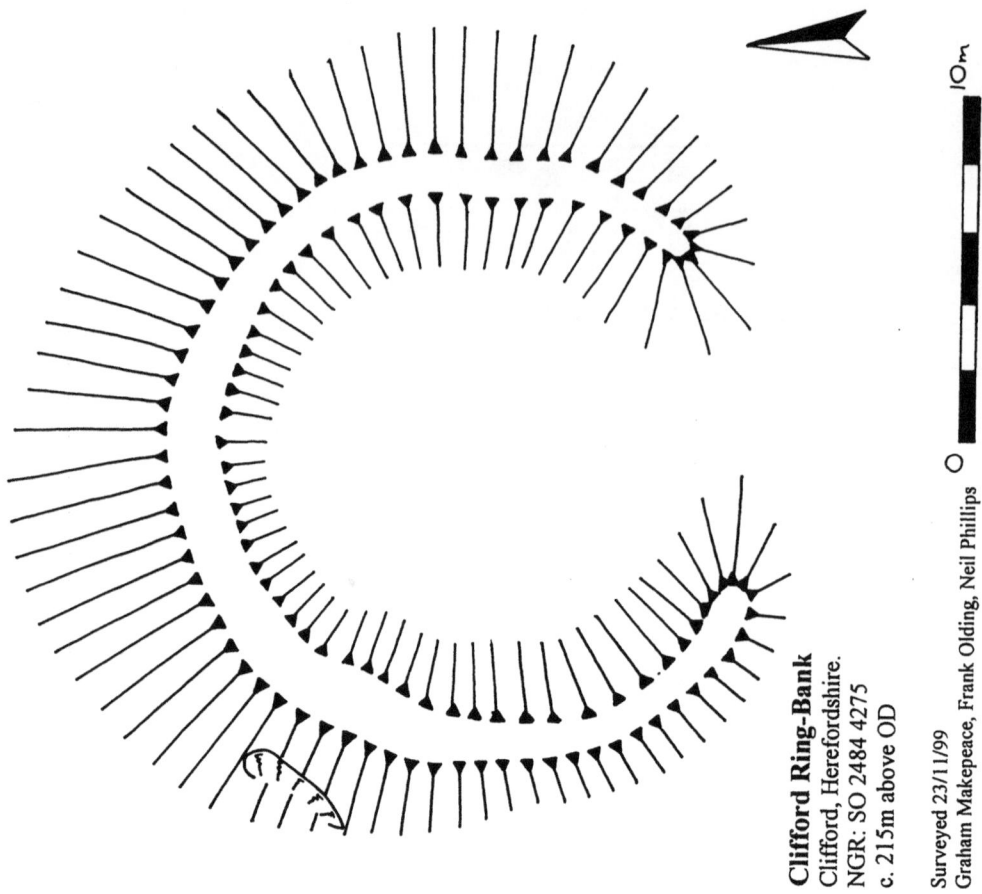

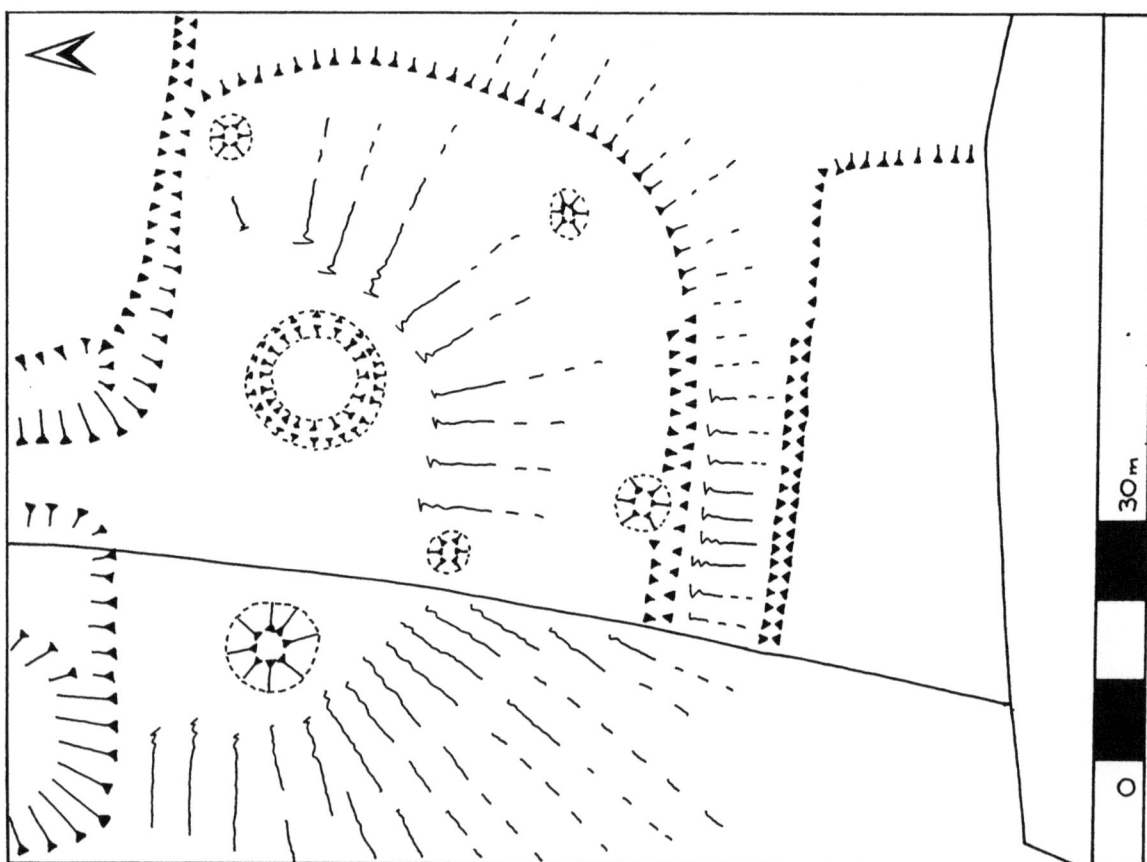

Fig. 25: Top – The Clifford Ring-Bank (HB 33); bottom –
The Upper Chilstone Ring-Bank and Barrow Cemetery
(HB 35).

44

(Condit and Simpson 1998, 45/7). However, two of the Irish examples (at Boyle, Co. Roscommon) are situated on hilltops, one of them on a terrace of the hill (*ibid.*, 47).

Although the Irish embanked earthen enclosures are generally large monuments ranging from 50m to 70m in diameter (*ibid.*, Figs. 4.2-3), smaller examples ranging from 12m to 24m in diameter do occur (*ibid.*, 47-50). The Irish sites have Later Neolithic/Beaker associations (O' Kelly 1989, 132-136) and this raises the possibility of a similar date bracket for the Herefordshire examples. The disposition of the five round barrows which once surrounded the Chilstone ring-bank (HB 35, Fig. 25) strongly suggests that they were attracted to a pre-existing ring-bank and strengthens the case for an earlier date.

In Wales, similar monuments have been termed "embanked earth circles" and assigned to the Bronze Age. They are defined as a bank of earth and/or stone, with no visible ditch, approximately oval or circular in plan, generally with a simple single entrance (Grimes 1963, 95). Only four certain examples could be cited in 1963 (*ibid.*, 105) and, of these, only two have survived critical re-evaluation - namely Ffridd Newydd N and Penmaenmawr Circle 278. Ffynnon y Brodyr (*ibid.*, 141; SN 122 191) has been redefined as a defensive or domestic structure (Harding and Lee 1987, 323), while excavation proved Dan y Coed (Grimes 1963, 143; SN 077 187) to be an Iron Age fortified settlement (Harding and Lee 1987, 429-30).

Ffridd Newydd N and Meini Gŵyr have recently been re-classified as western circle-henges (Barnatt 1989, 59/60). The rusticated beaker sherds from Ffridd Newydd N form the only dating evidence for Barnatt's entire Class L ("Western Irregular Circles and Circle-Henges"), though he postulates a possible Later Neolithic origin for the class as a whole. At Meini Gŵyr, Carms. (Grimes 1963, 143; SN 142 267), the stone circle post-dates the bank and a hearth containing food vessel sherds of the period c. 2050-1700 cal. B. C. (i.e. Needham's Early Bronze Age Period 3) overlay one of the empty stone holes. The construction of the bank therefore dates to before that period (Rees 1992, 38). It has been suggested that the builders of these sites were copper prospectors influenced by the Kerry/Cork recumbent stone circles (Burl 1976, 256).

The excavator of circle 278 at Penmaenmawr - "a broad low overgrown ring about 40ft. in diameter" (Griffiths 1960, 318) - regarded the presence of a collared urn in a pit containing burnt earth as an indication of a Middle Bronze Age date for the construction of the embanked earth circle (*ibid.*, 329). However, C-14 assays from wood beneath the bank gave dates of 1520 b. c. ± 145 (c. 1750 cal. B. C.) and 1405 b. c. ± 155 (c. 1630 cal. B. C.) (Burl 1976, 269) and Savory assigned the site to his Early Bronze Age II c. 2000-1750 B. C. (1980b, 28). The main currency of collared urns is now reckoned as c. 2050-1500 cal. B. C. - Needham's Early Bronze Age.

Barnatt classes the Penmaenmawr site with his Earlier Bronze Age "embanked stone circles". He has also argued that lowland embanked stone circles may have Later Neolithic origins while the upland sites date to the Earlier

Bronze Age which saw the first extensive exploitation of upland areas (1989, 128).

Recent surveys have found other examples of Welsh earthwork circles. Two lie in the Brecon Beacons - Rhyd Uchaf is a complex double ring-bank approx. 23m in diameter with an eastern entrance (RCAHMW 1997, 88-89; SN 9233 1896). Tir yr Onnen is a hengiform bank 12.5m in diameter, 2.0m wide and 0.3m high with an entrance to the E (*ibid.*, 93; SN 9633 1296). This site differs from the others in having slight traces of an internal ditch. Both sites have been assigned to the Earlier Bronze Age (*ibid.*, 67). There is yet another example in Glamorgan at Tor Clawdd, some 305m above OD, with an internal diameter of approx. 16m, 3m wide and 0.3m high with a SE entrance (RCAHMW 1976, 55; SN 6703 0630).

Ring-cairns have been described as lying "midway between the stone circles and the burial cairns" (Lynch 1975, 124). In the Brecon Beacons and Black Mountains, they are sometimes difficult to identify. A ring of stones may be all that remains of a robbed-out burial cairn and it is sometimes no easy matter to distinguish ring-cairns from hut-circles (RCAHMW 1997, 71). There are 19 possible or recorded ring-cairns in Brecknock. Most are of stone, but two at Ystradfellte (B-RC 78-9) in the western Beacons are complex earthworks associated with early, though undated, settlement features (B-US 45-6).

The Garreg Las ring-cairn (MB 29, Fig. 27) can be compared with similar sites in Glamorgan. That at 250m above OD on the summit of Graig Fawr in Glamorgan is formed of a rubble bank approx. 52m in diameter, 1.5m wide and 0.3 high with entrances to S and NE (RCAHMW 1976, no. 57; SN 6286 0633) while Pebyll, at 500m above OD, is some 30m in diameter and formed of a stony bank varying from 1.5m to 4m in width and up to 0.6m high, with entrances to NW and SSE (*ibid.*, no. 348; SS 9105 9724). There is a rather smaller ring of grass-grown limestone rubble on Morlais Hill at Merthyr Tydfil, Glam., at 380m above OD which is 25.9m in diameter, approx. 4m wide and 0.8m high with a southern entrance (*ibid.*, 67; SO 0526 0964).

Of excavated examples, the construction of ring-cairn Brenig 44 has been assigned to the period c. 1700-1600 b. c. (c. 2000-1890 cal. B. C.) and compared with dates of c. 1590 b. c. (c. 2140 cal. B. C.) from Moel Goedog I (Lynch 1993, 135). Brenig 44 continued in use to c. 1200 b. c. and all these dates fit into Needham's Early Bronze Age I (Period 3 c 2050-1700 cal. B. C.). The stone circle and ring-cairn at Ynys Hir, Brecs., were assigned by Savory to his Early Bronze Age III c. 1750-1450 B. C. and characterised by him as marking the end of the circle tradition in Wales (Savory 1980a, 29). This was on the basis of the presence of a pygmy cup in a burial outside the ring-cairn but under the later covering mound. The main currency of Aldbourne Cups is now seen as late in the Early Bronze Age c. 1700-1500 cal. B. C. (Needham 1996, 132). The main phase of these monuments therefore seems to span the Beaker period and Early Bronze Age.

Barnatt has argued that embanked stone circles and complex ring cairns should all be classed as one monument type and the Welsh ring-cairns are seen as the functional equivalent of rings of orthostats (1989, 11-12). In Wales, ring-cairns seldom occur in isolation and are often associated with barrow cemeteries or groups of more elaborate monuments (Lynch 1993, 143). The Garreg Las complex is therefore typical of the class as a whole. Larger stone circles and/or ring-cairns are clearly designed for communal gatherings (Barnatt 1989, *loc. cit.*) and competition between communities may have stimulated the construction of neighbouring monuments of similar type (*ibid.*, 213). This may account for the siting of the Garreg Las and Garn Wen complexes and implies that each site belonged to a discrete territory - territories VI and VII (see above).

While the lowland equivalents of ring-cairns remain elusive, Lynch draws strong parallels between the regionally concentrated distribution patterns and ritual uses of ring-cairns and pond-barrows which she regards as the chalkland equivalent of the ring-cairn (1993, 138-140). This throws an interesting new light on the Herefordshire ring-banks (see above).

Standing Stones

Standing stones (Fig. 26) remain enigmatic and difficult to classify - some were certainly erected with a ritual intention and many have acted as waymarkers or boundary stones in recent times. Elsewhere in Wales, excavations have served to shed some light on the role of prehistoric standing stones. The Devil's Quoit at Stackpole Warren, Pembs., was found to be central to a series of Bronze Age ritual and habitation features (Williams 1988, 96-100; RCAHMW 1997, 163).

Excavations at other west Wales sites suggest two basic types of standing stone - large stones which appear to be central to ritual or burial activities (e.g. Kilpaison at Rhoscrowther, Rhos y Clegyrn at St. Nicholas, the Longstone at St. Ishmael's and the Devil's Quoit itself (Williams 1988, 73-75, 89-91, 92-94 respectively)) and smaller stones which are found, often in multiples, in association with other burial/ritual monuments and some of which were erected to mark the site of burial pits (RCAHMW 1997, 163). At Aber Camddwr, Ceredigion, two small standing stones were set in the kerb of a cairn covering pits which contained charcoal and cremated bone and were explained as defining a temporary entrance through the cairn's kerb. The cairn was adjoined by an annexe and the excavator interpreted the whole complex as a skuomorphic Bronze Age timber round-house - a stone house for the dead (Marshall and Murphy 1991, 62).

Stones of this sort seem to have existed at the Twyn y Beddau round barrow (B-RC 311) and small stones close to a number of Brecknock cairns and circles may have served the same purpose (RCAHMW 1997, 163).

In historic times, other Brecknock standing stones like Maen Mawr (B-SS 3) have acted as waymarkers to assist safe movement over moorland and it is possible that such was also part of their prehistoric purpose. Roese (1978, 129-35; 1980, 645-55) also noted the regular proximity of Brecknock standing stones to water courses whether on flood-plains, valley slopes or in passes and also that their longer sides are always aligned at right-angles to the water courses (*ibid.*,

133-4). Despite this, some authors have doubted whether any of the Brecknock stones can be assigned with any certainty to later prehistory (RCAHMW 1997, 163), though this almost certainly represents too bleak a view.

As with ring-cairns, the principal function of standing stones seems to have been ritual rather than burial *per se* though cremations do occur. Charcoal-filled pits are the most common feature at ring-cairns and related monuments and the Aber Camddwr II stones seem to represent a merging of ceremonial traditions with standing stones, charcoal-filled pits and round cairns all playing a part (Marshall and Murphy 1991, 72).

Although some writers assign standing stones in the Marches to the Beaker period (Stanford 1991, 27), examples of dated Welsh standing stones include Stackpole Warren c. 1870-1490 cal. B. C., Mynydd Llangyndeyrn c. 1600-1050 cal. B. C. and Gors, Llangynog c. 1740-1430 cal. B. C. Round cairns and standing stones were erected and used contemporaneously (Marshall and Murphy 1991, 72).

Bearing in mind that, of all the Herefordshire standing stones, only Wern Derries (HB 40) is known to be in its original position, it is very difficult to offer any valid explanation for their past use and current distribution. Considering the eastern Black Mountains as a whole, two main types of use seem possible - as territorial or way-markers and a ritual function.

In Herefordshire, some of the sites have been interpreted as territorial markers (Children and Nash 1994, 44) and a strong case can be made that at least some of them (MB 38-40) marked the core areas or boundaries of Early Bronze Age territories (see above). Other stones are ideally placed to act as way-markers along paths from the valley bottoms to the ridge tops (MB 32-34) or via valleys and passes over or through the high moorland (HB 41-42). Such way-markers may also have possessed a ritual significance as a safeguard to travellers. Whether stones of this type are all of prehistoric date is difficult to ascertain without excavation. However, analogy with some of the Brecknock sites would suggest a prehistoric origin for a least a proportion of them.

Other Black Mountains standing stones are found in obvious association with Early Bronze Age ritual monuments and form an element in ritual complexes (see below).

Ritual Complexes

The Garreg Las ring-cairn (MB 29) sits at some 525m above OD on Hatterall Hill and is 57m in diameter and formed of a rubble bank some 7m wide and standing to an average height of approx. 0.75m. Some 600m to the SW of the ring-cairn, a massive drystone cross-dyke (MB 30) cuts across the promontory of the northern arm of Hatterall Hill. The cross-dyke is of similar construction to the ring-cairn and may be contemporary with it. About 50m SW of the enclosure stands a small cairn (MB 21) and some 200m to the NE is the most southerly (MB 19) of the fourteen cairns which form the Hatterall Ridge cairn cemetery (MB 9-19, HB 10-12). The three standing stones which mark the way from the

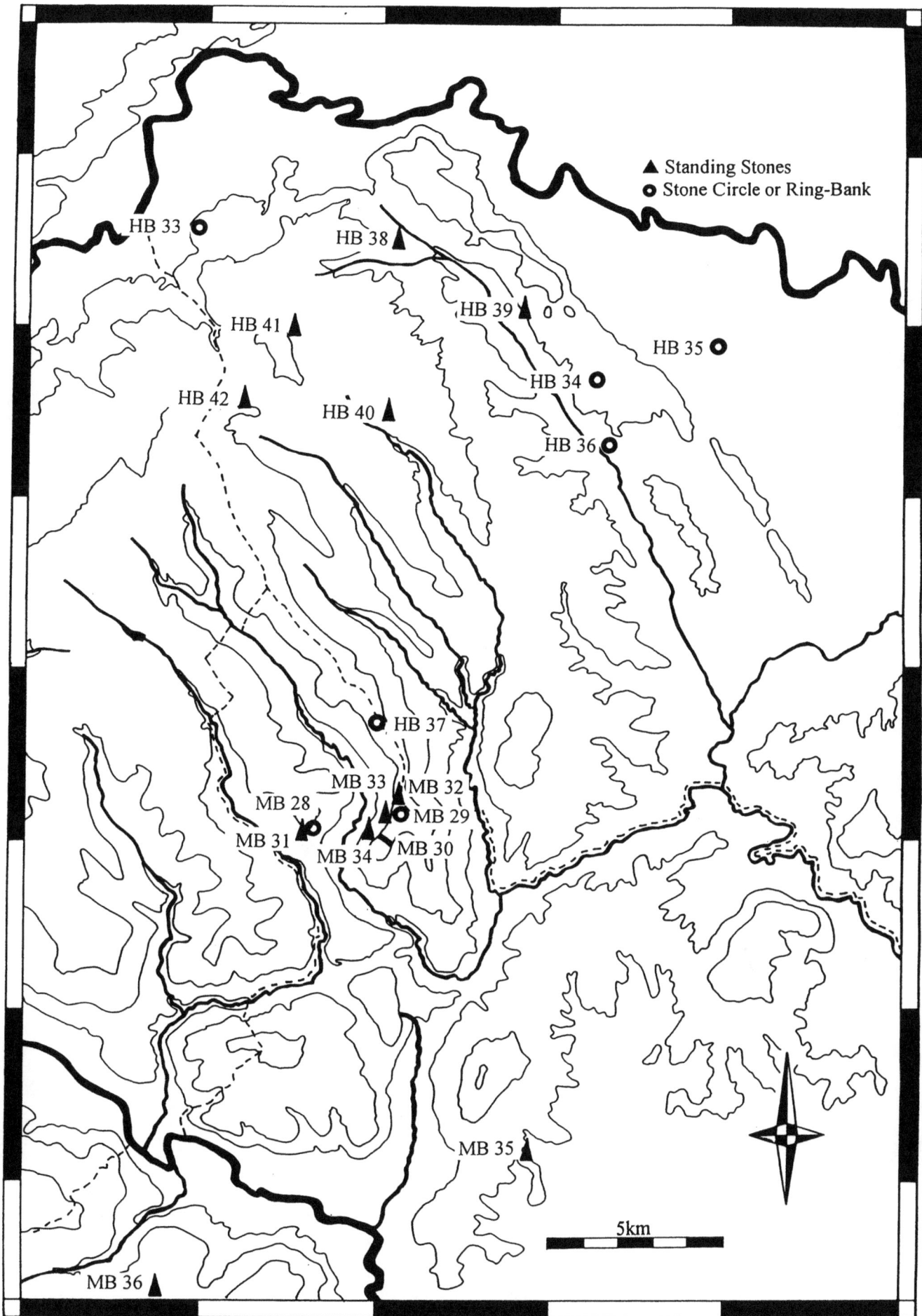

Fig. 26: Standing Stones, Stone Circles, Ring-Cairns and Ring-Banks.

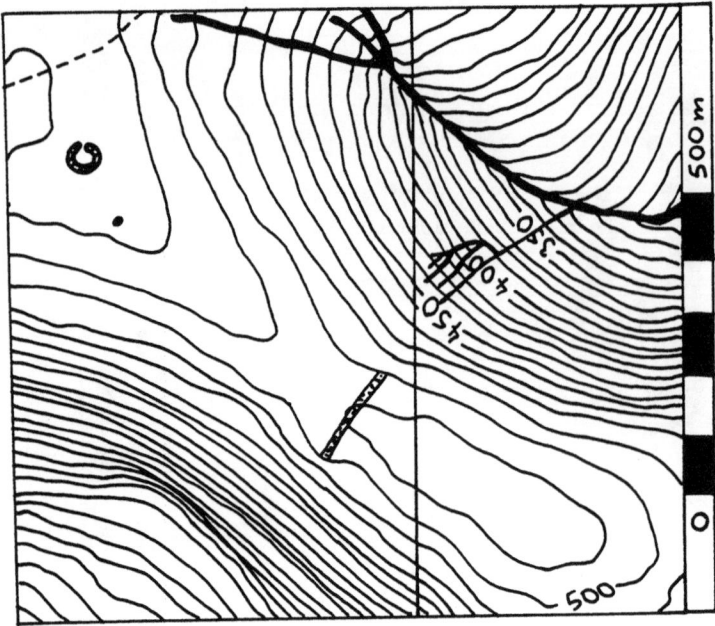

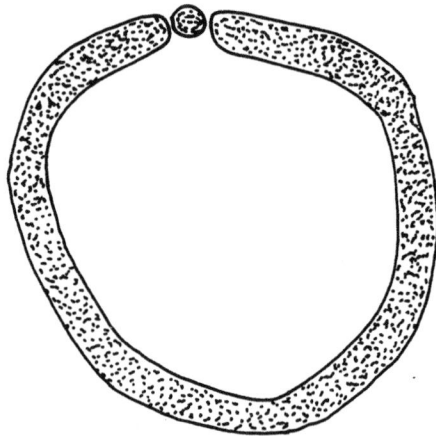

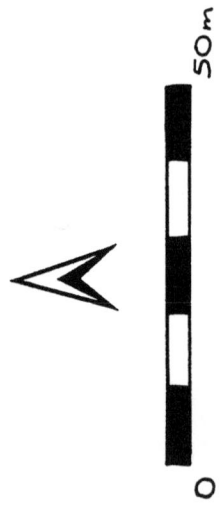

Fig. 27: The Garreg Las Ritual Complex
Round Cairn (MB 20) and Ring-Cairn (MB 29). Inset (W to E): Dyke (MB 30), Round Cairn (MB 20), Ring-Cairn (MB 29).

48

Round Cairn (MB 4) ⊛

Round Cairn (MB 5) ⊛

Round Cairn (MB 6) ⊛

Garn Wen Ritual Complex

⊛ Round Cairn

•—·—·—• Stone Circle

● Standing Stone

Stone Circle (MB 28)

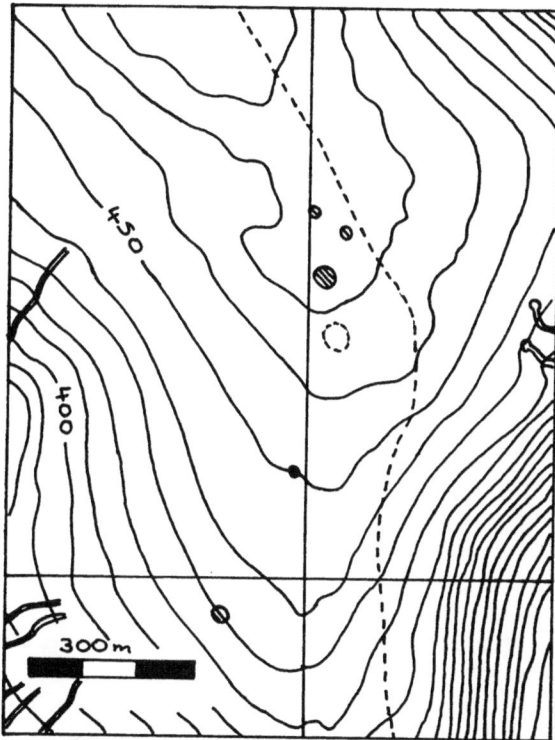

450

400

300m

● Standing Stone (MB 31)

Round Cairn (MB 7)
⊛

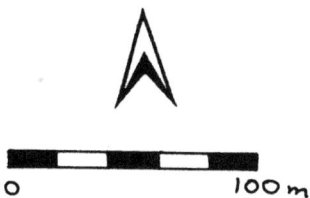

0   100 m

Fig. 28: The Garn Wen Ritual Complex.

49

Bronze Age Ritual Complexes

● Round Cairn

○ Stone Circle/Ring-Cairn

▲ Standing Stone

3 km

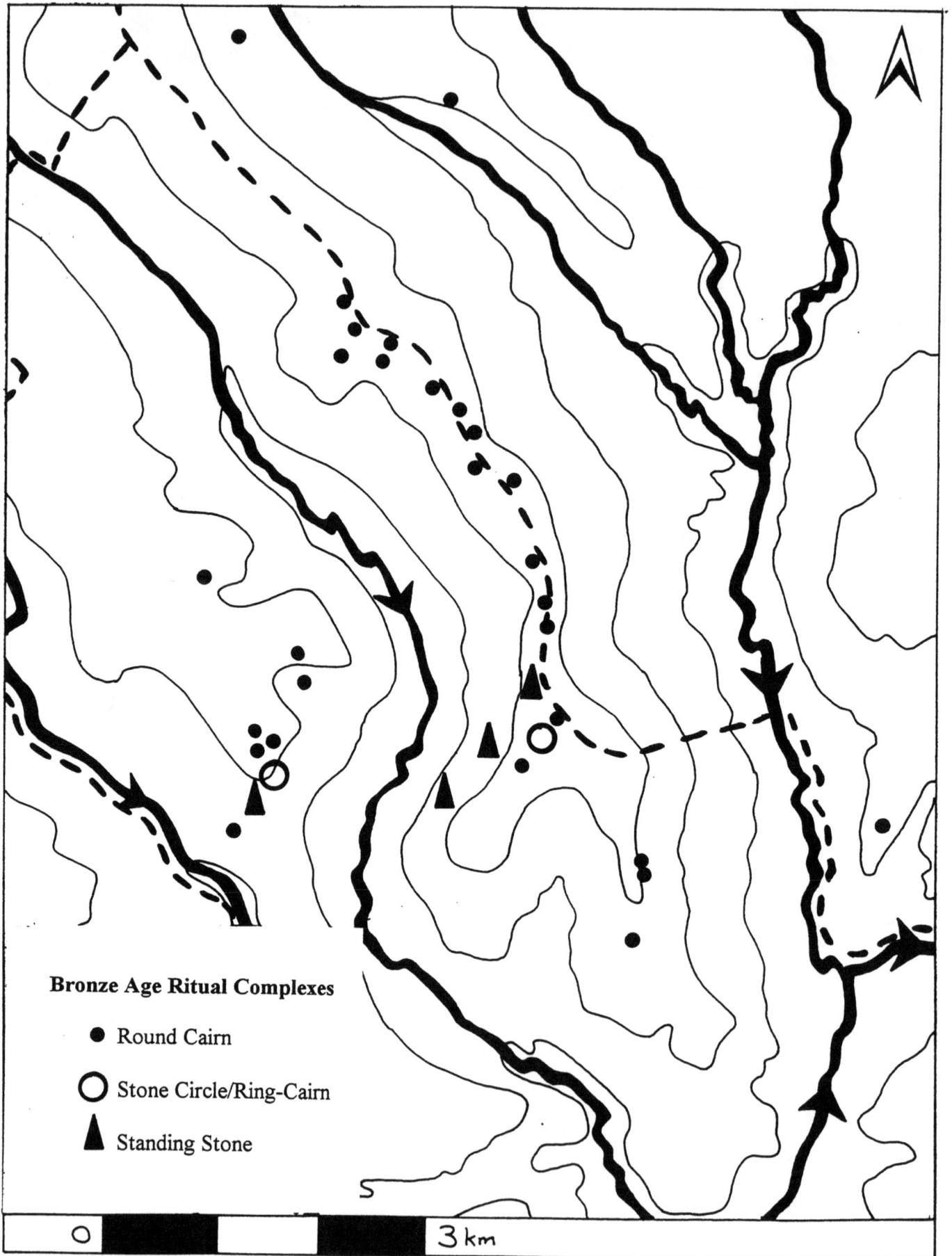

Fig. 29: The Garn Wen and Garreg Las Ritual
Complexes and Hatterall Hill Cairn Cemetery.

valley bottom to the ridge (MB 32-34) may also form part of the complex (Figs. 27, 29).

The eponymous and particularly large cairn at Garn Wen (MB 6) and its two smaller satellites (MB 4-5) stand some 90m NW of an extremely fragmentary stone circle (MB 28) which may originally have been some 50m in diameter. About 350m SSW of the circle stands an isolated standing stone (MB 31) and approx. 265m SW of the standing stone is a previously unrecorded small round cairn (MB 7) with extensive views to S and SW (Fig. 28).

Nash has offered the tempting suggestion that in these contexts standing stones mark ritual pathways from the ring-cairn or circle to barrow cemeteries (Children and Nash 1996, 53). He postulates that one of the many social and ritual uses of ring cairns and circles was as a venue for ceremonies linked with death. Having passed through the necessary funerary rituals, the deceased was then carried on his or her ritual journey to the final resting place along a ritual pathway marked by standing stones. The circle-stone-barrow complex represents a physical expression of the liminal space and time between the death of the body and the departure of the spirit. Such a scenario could certainly explain the lay-out of the ritual complexes at Garreg Las and Garn Wen (Fig. 29). The recurring ring-cairn-barrow combination was also to be seen at Chilstone (HB 35), though here its seems likely that the barrows were attracted to a pre-existing ring-bank (Fig. 25).

5.5 Early Bronze Age Metalwork

Metalwork has been assigned a central role in the milieu of conspicuous display and prestige associated with emerging chiefdoms in the Early Bronze Age. Possession of high quality metal objects, together with beakers and the burial practises associated with them, may have symbolised legitimate power over both people and economic resources. Children and Nash have postulated the existence in Bronze Age Herefordshire of hereditary aristocracies supported by tribute paid by farmers for the use of their land. The wealth thus generated may have been redistributed in the form of feasts and gift-exchange which served to further consolidate the status of the hierarchies (Children and Nash 1994, 46).

However, Early Bronze Age metalwork is extremely scarce in the eastern Black Mountains (Fig. 30). In Monmouthshire, only the haft-flanged axe from Cwm Ddeunant (MB 37) and the Acton Park 1 palstave from Blaengavenny (MB 39) can be assigned to the period. The sole Herefordshire find is the winged palstave from Tanner's Place (HB 48) and even this may belong to the Early-Middle Bronze Age transition.

5.6 The Middle and Late Bronze Age

As in Wales and the Marches as a whole (Burgess 1980, 263), evidence for Middle and Late Bronze Age activity in the eastern Black Mountains is entirely confined to finds of metalwork (Figs. 30, 31). So far, there is no evidence for the large scale land divisions seen in other upland areas such as Dartmoor, though some of the early rectangular enclosures

discussed under the Iron Age may have their origins in this period (see below).

All of the Late Bronze Age metalwork from Monmouthshire (Fig. 30) is assigned to the Llantwit-Stogursey tradition and dated to Needham's Period 7 c.950-750 cal. B. C. The material includes four hoards (HB 40, 41, 44 and 45) and three stray finds (MB 38, 42 and 43). The vast majority of the finds are the ribbed and socketed "South Wales" axes so typical of south-east Wales, though one of the Llantilio Pertholey hoards (MB 41) included fragments of a rapier and two of the plain, pegged spear-heads also typical of the Llantwit tradition (ibid., 272). Another spear-head came from Llantilio Crossenny (MB 42). The Llanddewi Skirrid axe hoard (MB 44) has been interpreted as a founder's hoard containing outmoded implements and scrap for re-working (Stanford 1991, 31).

However, traditional classifications of such material into founders', merchants' and personal hoards (Bradley 1984, 100) seem no longer satisfactory and hoards similar to those from Llantilio Pertholey (MB 40-41) containing fragments of swords, spears and axes have been re-interpreted as votive offerings of personal equipment and possessions (Parker Pearson 1993, 117).

The distribution is entirely lowland. There are no finds from the high ridges and the only find from the Black Mountains themselves is from the floor of the Honddu valley at Llanthony (MB 38). Three of the findspots - Llantilio Crossenny spear-head (MB 42), the anomalous axe from Llanarth (MB 43) and the Llanddewi Skirrid hoard (MB 44) - occur in the area which later produces evidence of small, defended Iron Age farmsteads (MI 8-10).

In Herefordshire (Fig. 30), none of the Middle and Late Bronze Age metalwork has so far been assigned to specific metalwork traditions and a comprehensive re-appraisal of the material is badly needed. However, there is one stray palstave of very late Early Bronze Age date (HB 48), one Middle Bronze Age hoard (HB 51) and a single Middle Bronze Age looped and socketed spearhead (HB 52). The Late Bronze Age material includes a hoard of twelve socketed axes from Madley (HB 54), two socketed axes from Dorstone (H 47), two stray axes from Turnastone (HB 49) and Vowchurch (HB 50) and the hoard of spear ferrules from Park Wood, St. Margaret's (HB 53).

As in Monmouthshire, the distributions of both Middle and Late Bronze Age metalwork displays a marked bias to low ground and valley bottoms. Three out of the four Middle Bronze Age finds form a distinct cluster around Vowchurch (MB 50-52) on the floodplain of the river Dore. The Late Bronze Age finds again seem to prefigure Iron Age settlement patterns. The enigmatic Eaton Bishop finds (MB 55-56) cluster near the hill-fort there (HI 6) and the Turnastone axe (HB 49) was found within a kilometre of Poston Camp (HI 2) and the possible Iron Age settlement at Vowchurch (HI 9). Across the Marches, such finds have been seen as evidence of intensified exploitation of the lowlands during the Middle to Late Bronze Age (Stanford 1991, 33).

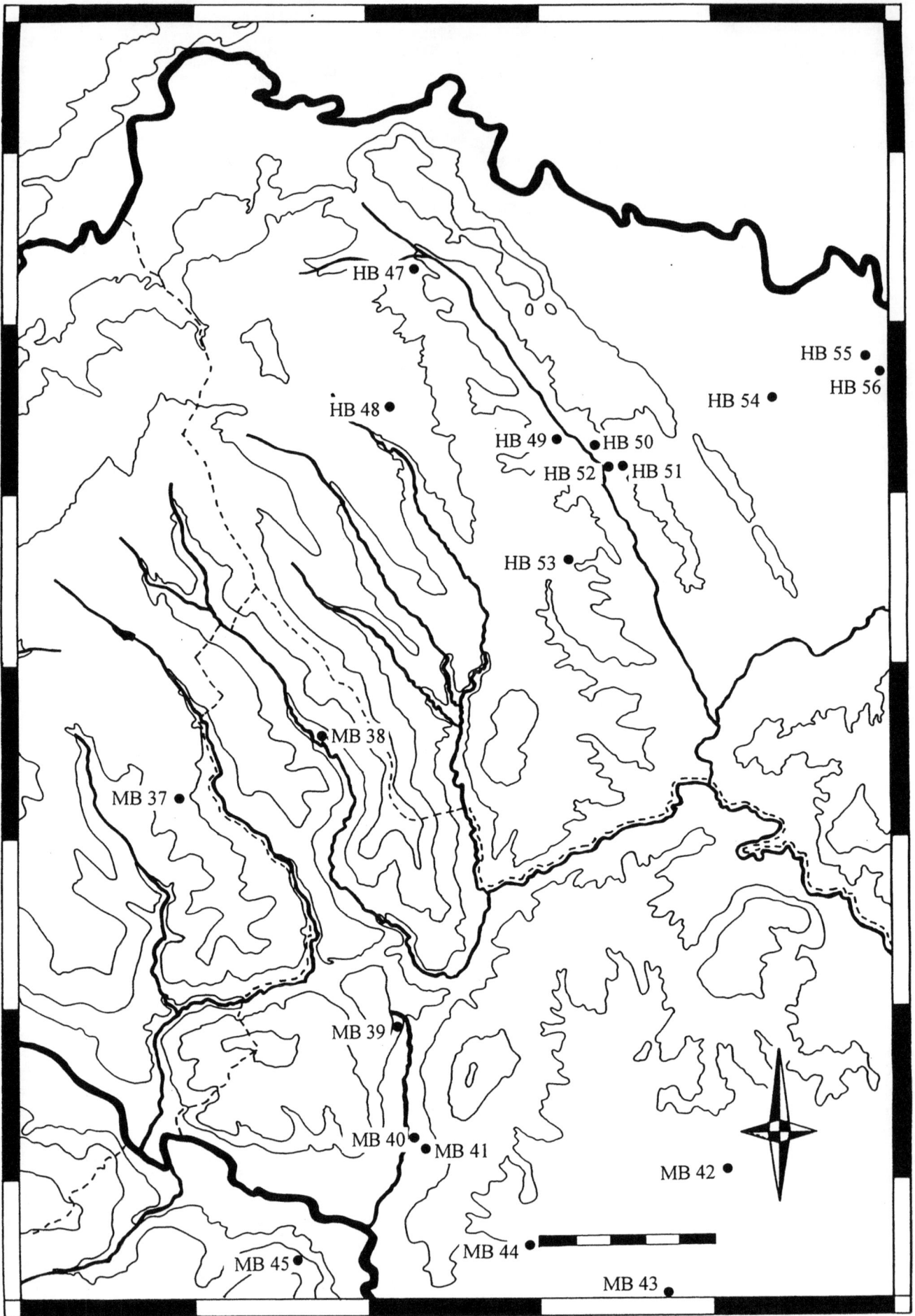

Fig. 30: Bronze Age Metalwork Finds.

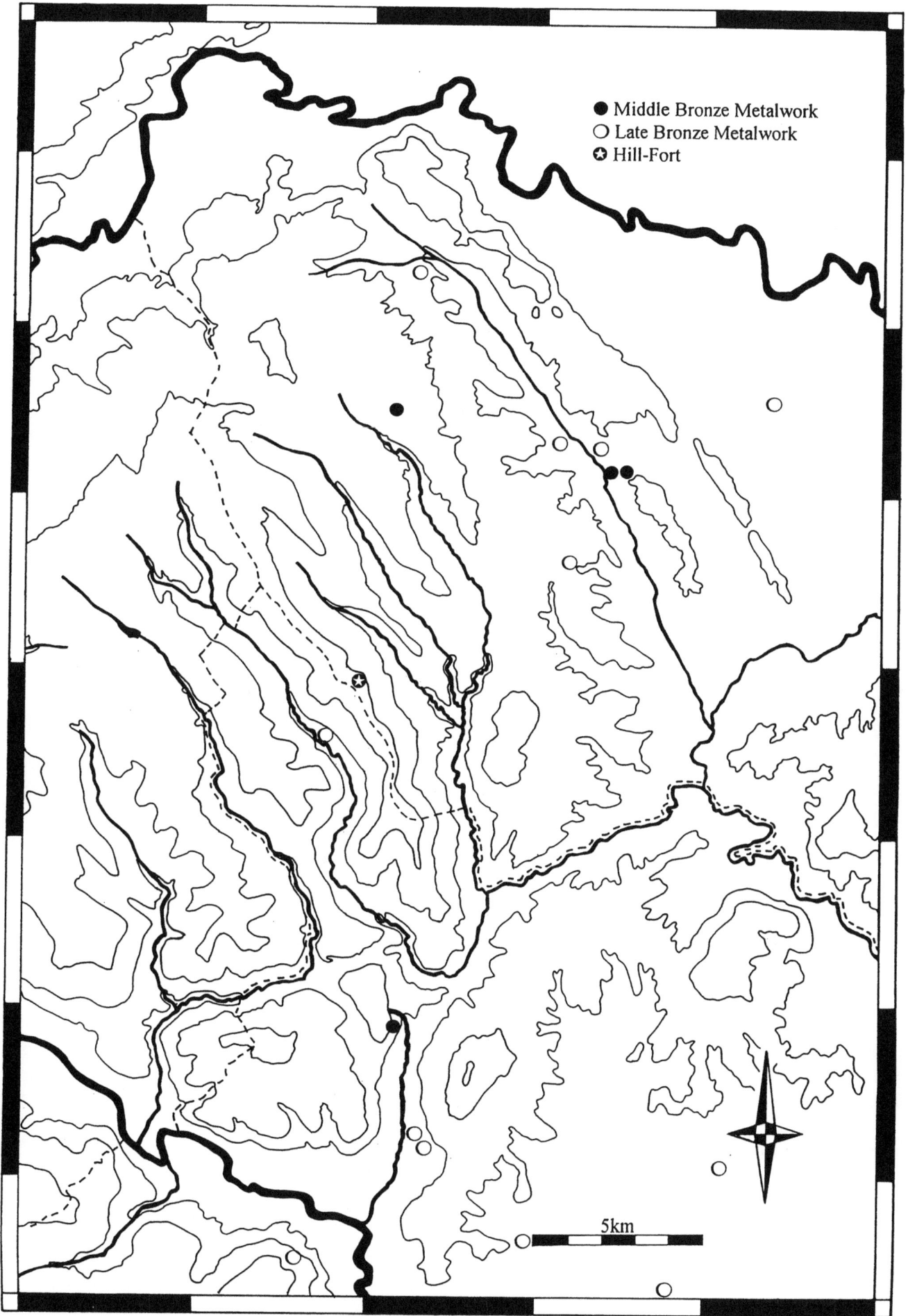

Fig. 31: The Middle and Late Bronze Age Landscape.

Middle Bronze Metalwork
Late Bronze Metalwork
Hill-Fort

5km

53

Black Darren (Daren Ddu) Hill-fort
Llanveynoe, Herefordshire.
NGR: SO 2968 3470
500m above OD

Surveyed 28/4/99
Frank Olding
Graham Makepeace

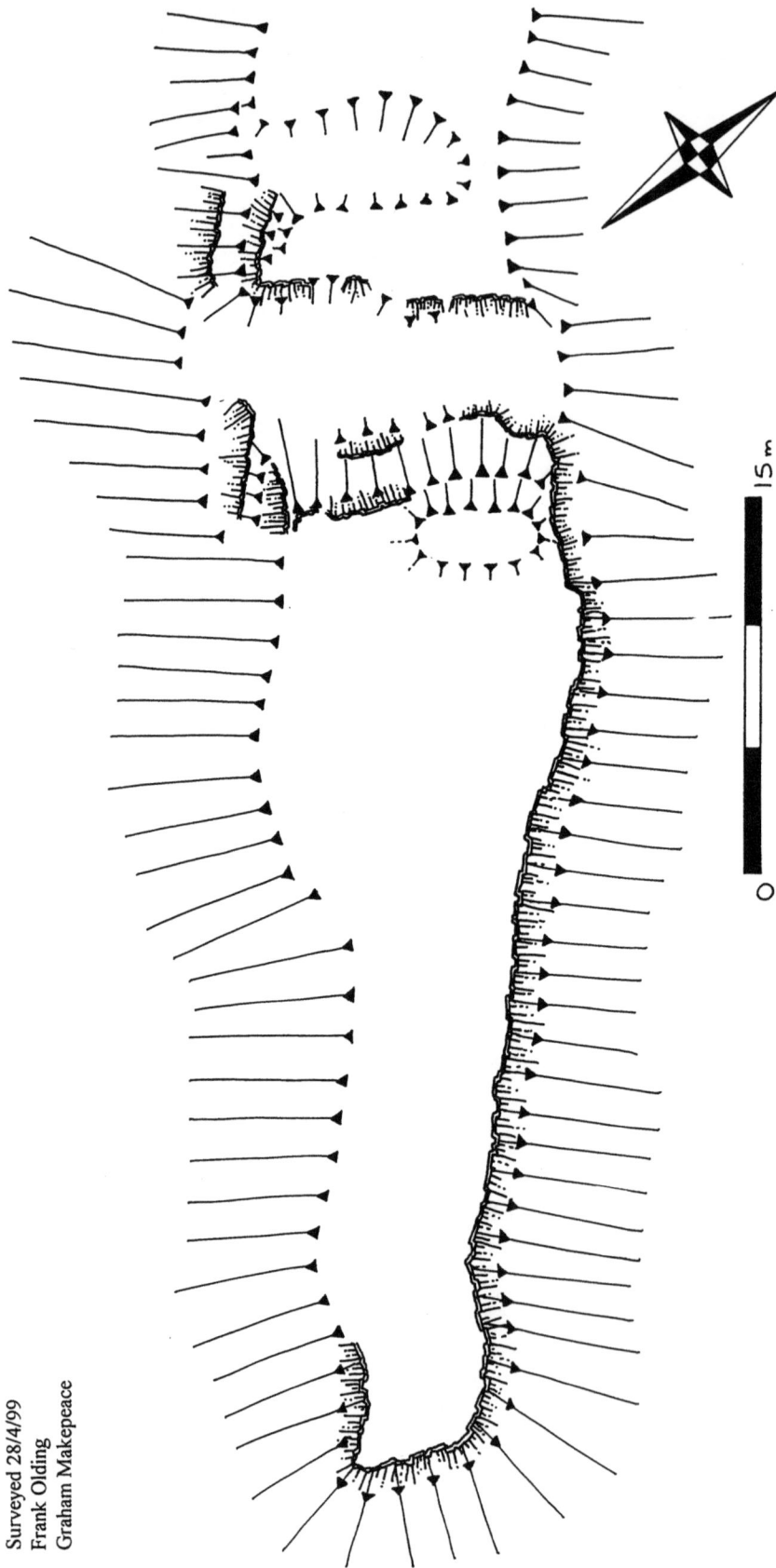

15 m

Fig. 32: The Black Darren Hill-fort (HI 4).

54

Overall, the impression created by the distribution of Middle and Late Bronze Age metalwork in the eastern Black Mountains (Fig. 31) is of a marked shift from upland to lowland activity and this goes some way to supporting the suggestion that the period saw the abandonment of the upland areas which had been so heavily exploited in the Early Bronze Age - though the leaf-shaped Ewart Park sword (B-BR 26) found some 427m above OD at Cwm Du in the western Black Mountains implies continued interest in high places in the Late Bronze Age (Stanford 1991, 32).

The presence of weaponry among both hoards and stray finds may reflect the social tension which would have resulted from increased pressure on finite resources. Burgess's Penard Period (now assigned to Needham's late Middle Bronze Age c. 1300-1150 cal. B. C.) may have seen changes in agriculture, including a switch from emmer to spelt wheat and from naked to hulled barley, as well as the earliest development of hill-forts such as Dinorben and Ffridd Faldwyn (Burgess 1980, 268-27-).

5.7 Late Bronze Age Hill-forts

It has long been accepted that eastern Wales and the Marches saw construction of hill-forts during the Late Bronze Age. At Moel y Gaer, Flintshire (NGR: SJ 211 691), a pre-existing settlement of post-ring round-houses was enclosed by a continuous free-standing palisade several metres outside a later rampart (Guilbert 1976, 317). A drastic remodelling of the whole settlement saw the construction of a large timber-framed-and-laced rampart and a radical change in the internal lay-out of the settlement with round, post-ring houses replaced by stake-wall round-houses and a grid of four-post structures (*ibid.*, 313-314). The two phases produced radiocarbon dates of 620 ± 70 b. c. and 580 ± 90 b. c. respectively (*ibid.*, 317). The excavator regarded the four-post structures as storage units (*ibid.*, 314).

Another palisaded enclosure at Dinorben, Denbighshire (NGR: SH 968 766), dated to some time after the 11th century B. C. - probably to the 10th or 9th century B. C. (Savory 1976, 245).

The Breiddin, Powys (NGR: SJ 292 144), can also certainly be regarded as Late Bronze Age in date. The first phase of enclosure at the site and was formed of an irregular double palisade (Musson 1976, 296) dated to 800 ± 41 b. c. i.e. c. 900 cal. B. C. (Stanford 1991, 49) which underlay the stone-faced Iron Age rampart. Internally, a phase of timber round-houses dated to between 479 ± 55 b. c. and 375 ± 63 b. c. was followed by the construction of four-posted rectangular structures dated to between 294 ± 40 b. c. and 238 ± 70 b. c. (Mussson 1976, 302).

Based on the results of these excavations at the Breiddin and Dinorben, the latter situated on a headland protected on three sides by crags or steep slopes, it has been suggested that at least some of the inland promontory forts in the Welsh Marches date to the Late Bronze Age (Savory 1976, 247) and it is possible that the small but spectacularly situated promontory enclosure at the Black Darren (HI 4, Fig. 32) should be assigned to this period.

6 – THE IRON AGE

6.1 Hill-forts

The paucity of Iron Age hill-forts and enclosures at high altitudes in either the Brecon Beacons or the Black Mountains (Fig. 33) implies widespread abandonment of upland areas in the Later Bronze Age and Iron Age. This was probably due to decreasing soil fertility and deteriorating climatic conditions. There is a fundamental contrast between the Bronze Age and Iron Age distributions and upland depopulation may have had important implications for farming practice and social organisation (RCAHMW 1997, 206).

In Herefordshire as a whole, over half the hill-forts are larger than 6ha in area. The largest of all, Credenhill (HI 7), covers some 20ha and has been interpreted as the tribal capital of Iron Age Herefordshire. Other large hill-forts like Midsummer Hill and Pentwyn (MI 1) are found on or near the old county boundary and Stanford has suggested that the tribal boundaries of the Iron Age corresponded roughly to those of the historic county of Herefordshire (1991, 58).

In support of this hypothesis, Stanford cites a remarkable consistency in architecture and material culture from excavated sites within the county. Similarities in defences, house types and pottery seem to link Croft Ambrey, Midsummer Hill and Credenhill (HI 7) at least from the early fourth century B. C. and, in the period c. 390 B. C.-200 B. C., all three, together with Twyn y Gaer (MI 2) and Poston Camp (HI 2) were using the duck-stamped pottery produced near the Malvern Hills (*ibid.*, 62). This pottery, now known as the Croft Ambrey-Bredon Hill style of the wider saucepan pot tradition (Gibson and Wood 1990, 133), has been classified into four distinct groups on the basis of the rock inclusions used for tempering the fabric: Group B1 is made up of cooking pots stamped with lines of arrowheads, S-stamps or zigzags and with limestone inclusions; Group D is tempered with mudstone and less crisply stamped; Group A commonly relies on linear tooled decoration forming trellis designs or crescents. A minor group, Group C, using sandstone inclusions came into production in the late Iron Age and continued into the early Roman period (Stanford 1991, 63).

Other Herefordshire sites such as Sutton Walls, Poston Camp (HI 2), Dinedor and Aconbury and the earlier phases at Twyn y Gaer (MI 2) also seem to fit the general pattern of cultural homogeneity (*ibid.*, 59) which has been seen as a reflection of a distinct Iron Age "culture" in the southern Marches (Hogg 1973, 20-21).

Monmouthshire lay firmly within the territory of the Silures. There are a few Dobunnic gold coins from sites in the county, though Stanford attributes them to losses by Roman soldiers and even offers the eccentric suggestion that the gold stater of Corio from Llanthony Priory (MI 11) may have arrived in the Black Mountains via the sister priory, Llanthony Secunda, at Gloucester (1991, 73). This seems a deliberate attempt to place the eastern Black Mountains beyond the influence of the Dobunni and to strengthen the theory that a tribe known as the Decangi inhabited Iron Age Herefordshire (*ibid.*, 75-76). This is another theory which

has not enjoyed widespread favour - some authors agree in assigning Herefordshire to the Dobunni (Cunliffe 1991, 170-179), others regard Herefordshire as Silurian territory until Roman administrative reorganisation assigned the area east of the Wye to the Dobunni in the 1st century A. D. (Manning 1981, 21-22).

Whatever, their political affiliations, the fact that all the known Iron Age settlements in the eastern Black Mountains are fairly strongly defended suggests that the risk of attack was always present (Hogg 1973, 17). At Coed y Bwnydd hill-fort, some 3km SW of the defended farmstead at Camp Hill (MI 10), there is strong evidence that the defences were destroyed by burning c. 400 b. c. and later deliberately and systematically slighted (Babbidge 1977, 172-173). The integral guard-chambers which are such a feature of the Marches hill-forts also imply that the defences and gates had to be constantly guarded, though whether by hereditary porters, as some have suggested, we will never know (Hogg 1973, 19).

The largest hill-fort in Herefordshire, Credenhill Camp (HI 7, Fig. 34) was partly excavated by Stanford in 1963 (Stanford 1970). It was significant in being the first published report of a settlement where the interior appeared to be covered with small rectangular buildings in regular arrangements. The site is on a steep hill, well-suited to defence and encloses some 20ha. Two entrances, probably with guard-chambers, survive. Excavation was restricted to an area behind the rampart just S of the E gate. Stanford interpreted the four-post structures he found there as houses and estimated a total population of some 4,000 people - in effect, the political capital of the region. It is now thought that these features are more likely to be granaries. The construction of the fort was dated to c. 390 B. C. (Hogg 1975, 184-185; Children and Nash 1994, 87-89).

Croft Ambrey, in the north of the county (NGR: SO 445 668) remains one of the most important Iron Age excavations in the UK (Stanford 1974). The site provided a fairly reliable absolute chronology based on the probable duration of the successive phases in the construction of the gateways using a thirty year life for the posts and radio-carbon controls (Hogg 1975, 99).

The earliest phase at Croft Ambrey is dated to c. 550 B. C. and saw the construction of a small dump rampart and ditch enclosing 2.2ha with a simple double portal gateway. The interior was densely covered with lines of four-posters which were rebuilt as many as six times. Ranging from between 1.8 to 3.6m square, Stanford again interpreted most of these buildings as houses and always believed the entire interior of the hill-fort to have been covered with four-posters separated by narrow paths (1991, 60). Considering the very small area of Croft Ambrey actually excavated, this seems highly unlikely. At one time, these buildings were thought to represent influence from outside Britain and Hogg (1975, 101) suggested that Croft Ambrey was built by the descendants of invaders.

The site saw a period of enlargement in the period c. 390 B. C. (Phase IV) with the building of a massive glacis-type rampart. These developments have been seen as part of a general expansion of local hill-fort construction in the 4th

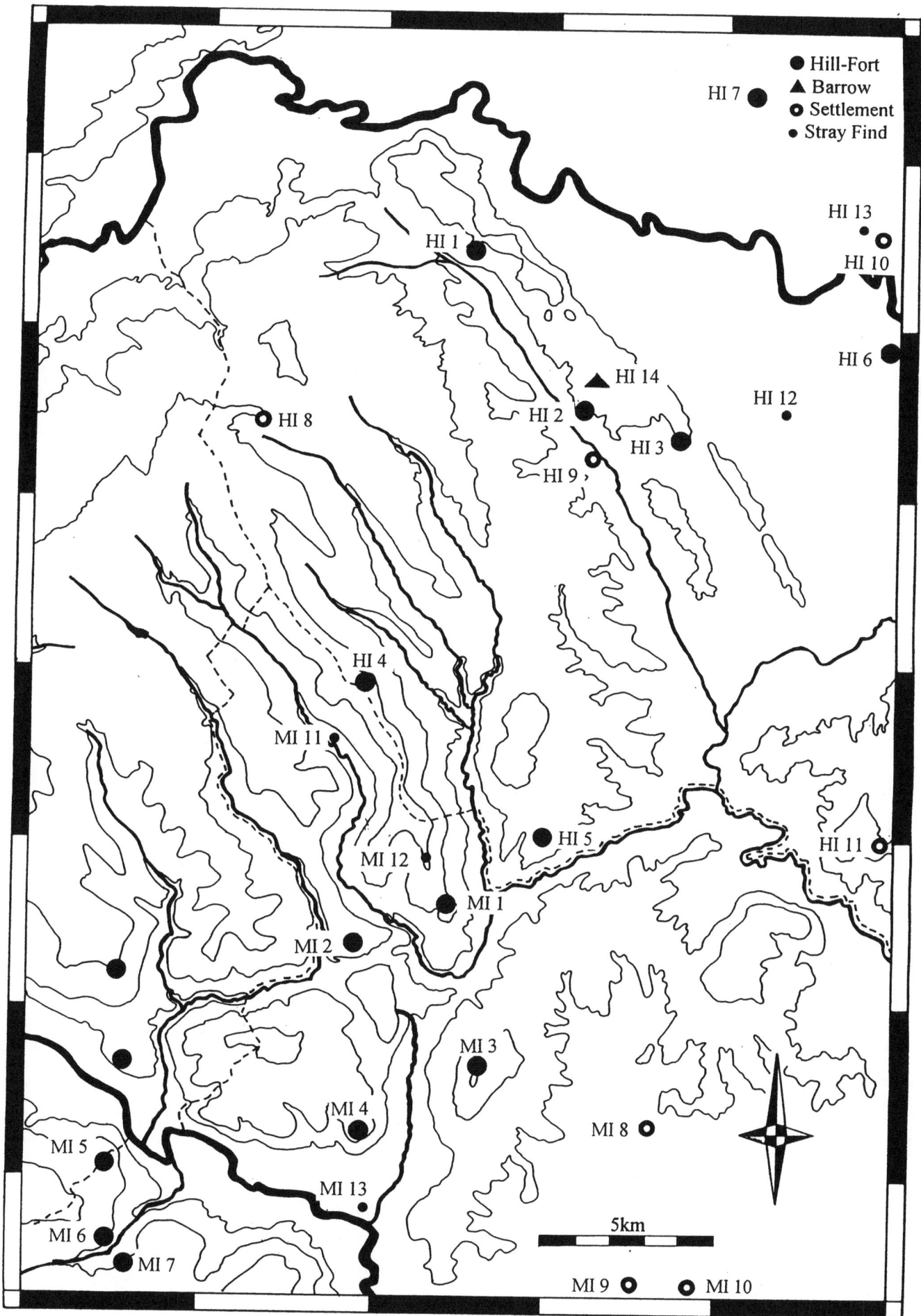

Fig. 33: Iron Age Sites and Finds.

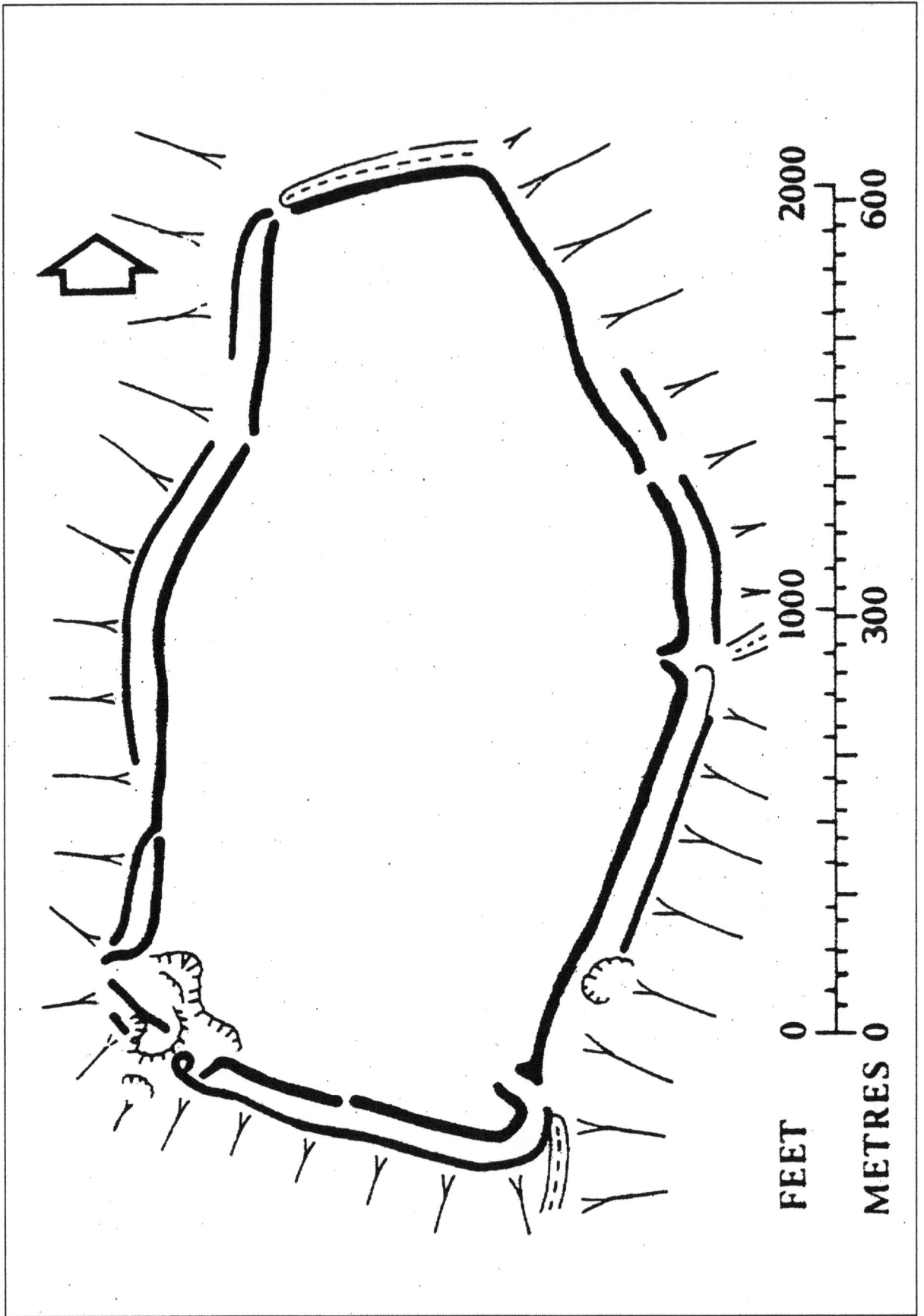

Fig. 34: Credenhill Hill-Fort (HI 7)(after Hogg 1975).

century B. C. is also represented by the fenced enclosure at Twyn y Gaer (MI 2), Phase I at Midsummer Hill and the construction of Credenhill. Other local hill-forts which may have been established c. 390 B. C. include Eaton Camp (HI 6), Aconbury, Sutton Walls and Gaer Cop. The period also saw the construction of rectangular four-post structures at Credenhill and Midsummer Hill and a vogue for markedly inturned entrances (Stanford 1991, 64).

Poston Camp (HI 2, Figs. 35, 36) was excavated in the autumn of 1932 (Marshall 1933a) and again in 1958. The earlier investigations produced evidence of Neolithic and Bronze Age occupation of the hilltop (ibid., 27; Antony 1958). Romano-British occupation was also attested. Antony pointed out similarities between the material from Poston (especially the "duck-stamped" pottery) and that from Bredon Hill, Worcs., and from the other Herefordshire hill-fort sites of Sutton Walls and Aconbury which has been dated by C-14 to the period c.390 B. C. to c.250 B. C. (Children and Nash 1994, 111). The 1958 excavations produced bronze fibulae. There was very little evidence of cereal growing and though cattle, pig and sheep bones were present, the total numbers were not great. It has been suggested that the sheep were kept mainly for wool - a suggestion backed up by the presence of no less than seven spindle whorls of various materials and a bone weaving comb (ibid., 112). There was evidence of stone revetment and timber lacing of the defences which may have undergone refurbishment immediately prior to the campaigns of Julius Frontinus in the Marches in the 70s A. D. ((ibid., 113). Antony accepted an Iron Age date and suggested a funerary purpose for the Poston mound close to the hill-fort (HI 14, Fig. 24).

Marshall, the original excavator placed Poston with Timberline Camp (HI 3) and Walterstone Camp (HI 4) in a "Monnow Basin Group" as distinct from the "Wye-Lugg Group" and suggested that they represented an imitation of the Wye-Lugg forts by a native late Bronze Age population (Marshall 1933a, 21-9). The Wye-Lugg group of hill-forts centred on Sutton Walls with satellites at Dinedor and Aconbury (Children and Nash 1994, 71)

Walterstone Camp (HI 5, Fig. 36), the only fully multivallate fort in the eastern Black Mountains, guards the lower reaches of the Monnow Valley. It is a well-preserved site of about 4 ha. with three concentric ramparts and ditches to the NW and SW and a single rampart to the E. Such defences have been assigned to the last two centuries B. C. (Savory 1976, 279) and it is possible that the construction of Walterstone should be seen against the background of the incorporation of Twyn y Gaer (MI 2) and its neighbours into the sphere of influence of the Silures in the period after c. 200 B. C. It is also possible that the element of multivallate defences and elaborate bastion and barbican at Pentwyn (MI 1) belong to the same phase (see below).

The best understood of the Monmouthshire sites is Twyn y Gaer (MI 2, Fig. 37). Excavations in the 1960s (Probert 1976) proved that the main rampart was drystone revetted with, in its later phases, a stone-built rampart-walk along the top. Probert identified six phases (Periods I - VI) in the site's development:

Period I: area A-B formed the main enclosure of a promontory hill-fort with area C as a fenced annexe. The birch-hurdle fence was replaced at least eight times, and probably enclosed an area used as paddocks for stock. The probable date for the first annexe fence is c. 470 B. C. ((ibid., 116). The final rebuilding of the fence was dated by C-14 to 392 B. C. which also provides a *terminus post quem* for the Period II defences ((ibid., 109).

Period II: the annexe was incorporated into the fort by the construction of a bank and ditch along the line of the final fence with an inturned E gate (Fig. 37). The gate (2.1m wide) had double posts set on either side of the passage connected a tranverse slot for a wooden threshold (ibid., 110). It is likely that the gate was topped by a matching lintel (ibid., 112). Parallels for the threshold slot are found at Croft Ambrey and Midsummer Hill in Herefordshire (Stanford 1974, figs. 16-18). Stanford dated these structures at Midsummer Hill to c. 332-262 B. C., though Probert argues for a recalibration to c. 404 B. C. at Midsummer Hill and c. 410 B. C. at Croft Ambrey (ibid., 116). The Twyn y Gaer slot was built immediately after the burning of the final annexe fence which produced a C-14 date of c. 392 B. C. (ibid., 117). The construction of the gate would therefore date to c. 380 B. C. which points to a widespread vogue for threshold slots in the southern March in the 4th century B. C. Twyn y Gaer's lack of guard-rooms Probert attributes to the small population postulated for the site. He speculates that the "watchman or gate-keeper was quartered in an ordinary house near the gate" (ibid., 117).

Period III: the E gate passage was reduced in width by thickening the terminals, the gate was widened to 2.7m and the tranverse slot abandoned. This phase saw the first use on the site of Malvernian Croft Ambrey-Bredon Hill style duck-stamped pottery and iron La Tène II brooches (ibid., 112). The brooches were the work of same craftsmen who supplied both Croft Ambrey and the Breidden (ibid., 115).

Period IV: the E gate terminals were extended further into the fort with a new, wider, gate (3.7m) placed at the inner end of the corridor. This phase saw the last use of duck-stamped pottery. The rectangular rampart terminals and new gate design which followed the use of threshold slots were also present at Croft Ambrey and Midsummer Hill, though the new lay-out was in use for a much shorter period at Twyn y Gaer.

Period V: c. 200 B. C., there were further significant changes to the lay-out of the E gate, the gate-posts stood in the angle formed by an offset in the now apsidal rampart terminals and would have been able to withstand considerable force from outside. These designs ceased to follow the Croft Ambrey-Midsummer Hill pattern.

Period VI: saw the reduction of the fort to area A (0.5ha) by the construction of the most westerly cross-bank with its own inturned gate. The bank was probably surmounted by a stone rampart-walk and it is possible that sporadic occupation continued near the original E gate (ibid., 114).

Hut platforms and the range of domestic objects produced by the excavations show the fort to have been permanently occupied. Probert postulated a much smaller community at

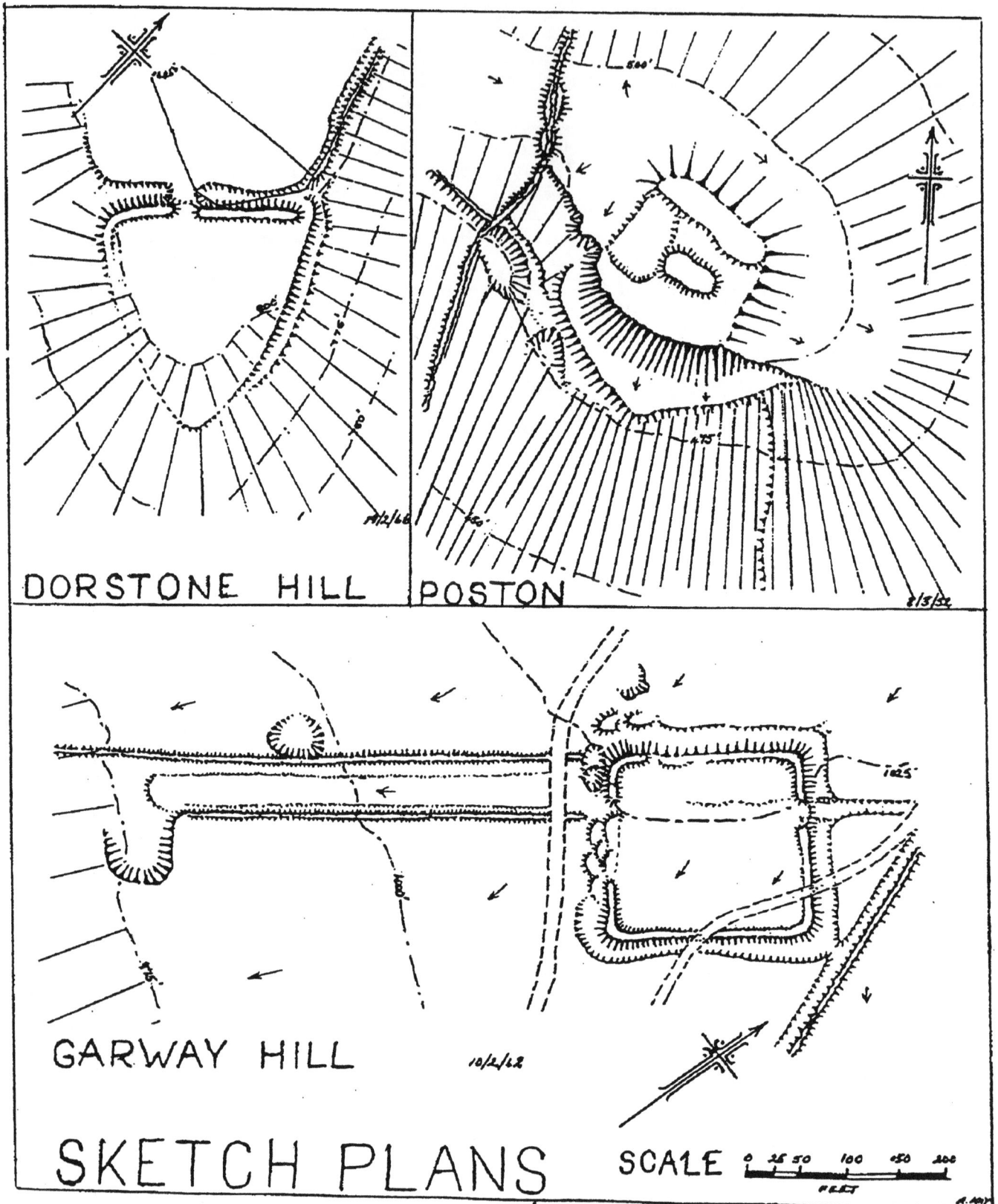

DORSTONE HILL   POSTON

GARWAY HILL   10/2/62

SKETCH PLANS   SCALE

Fig. 35: Dorstone Hill (HI 1), Poston Camp (HI 2) and
Garway Hill Enclosure (HI 11) (after Kay 1963).

60

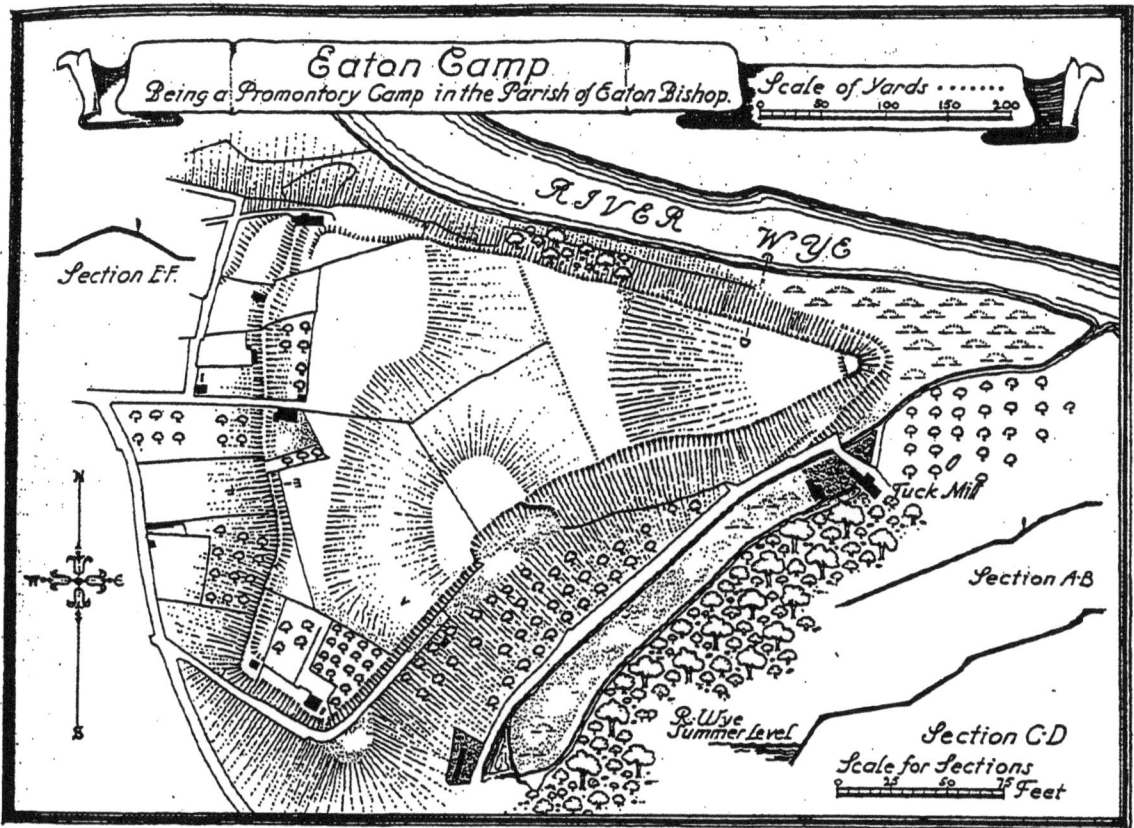

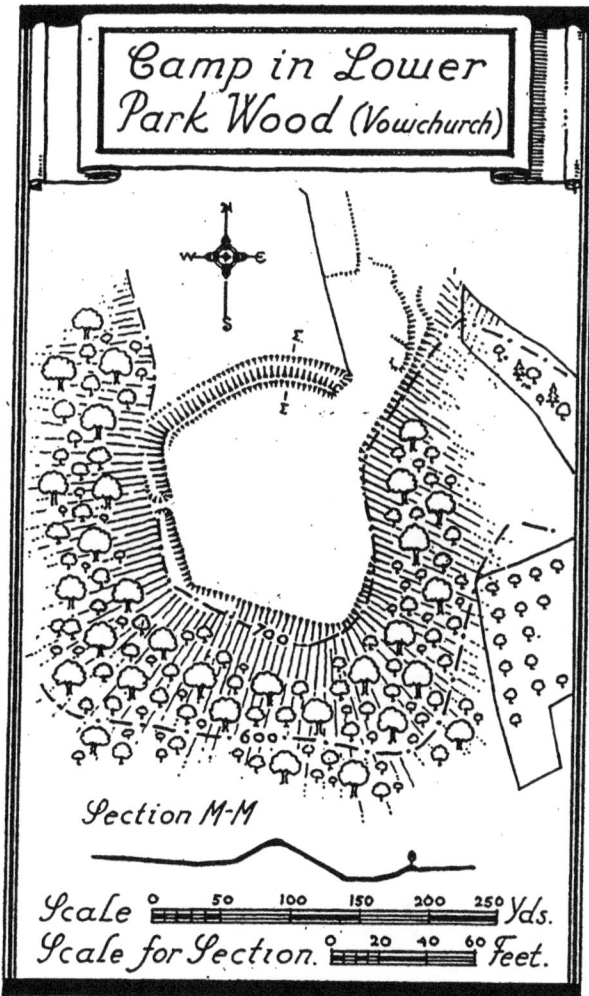

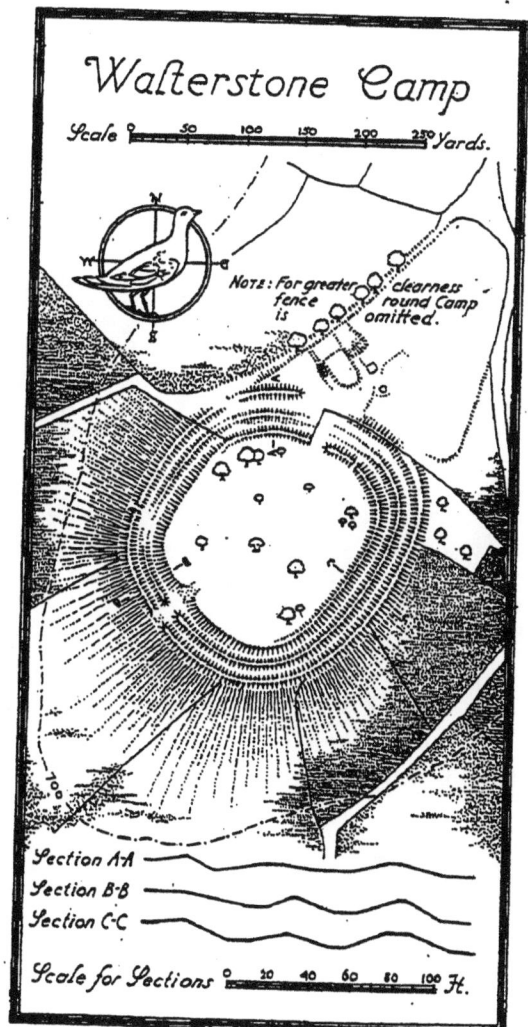

Fig. 36: Eaton Camp (HI 6), Poston Camp (HI 2) and Walterstone Camp (HI 5) (after RCHME 1931).

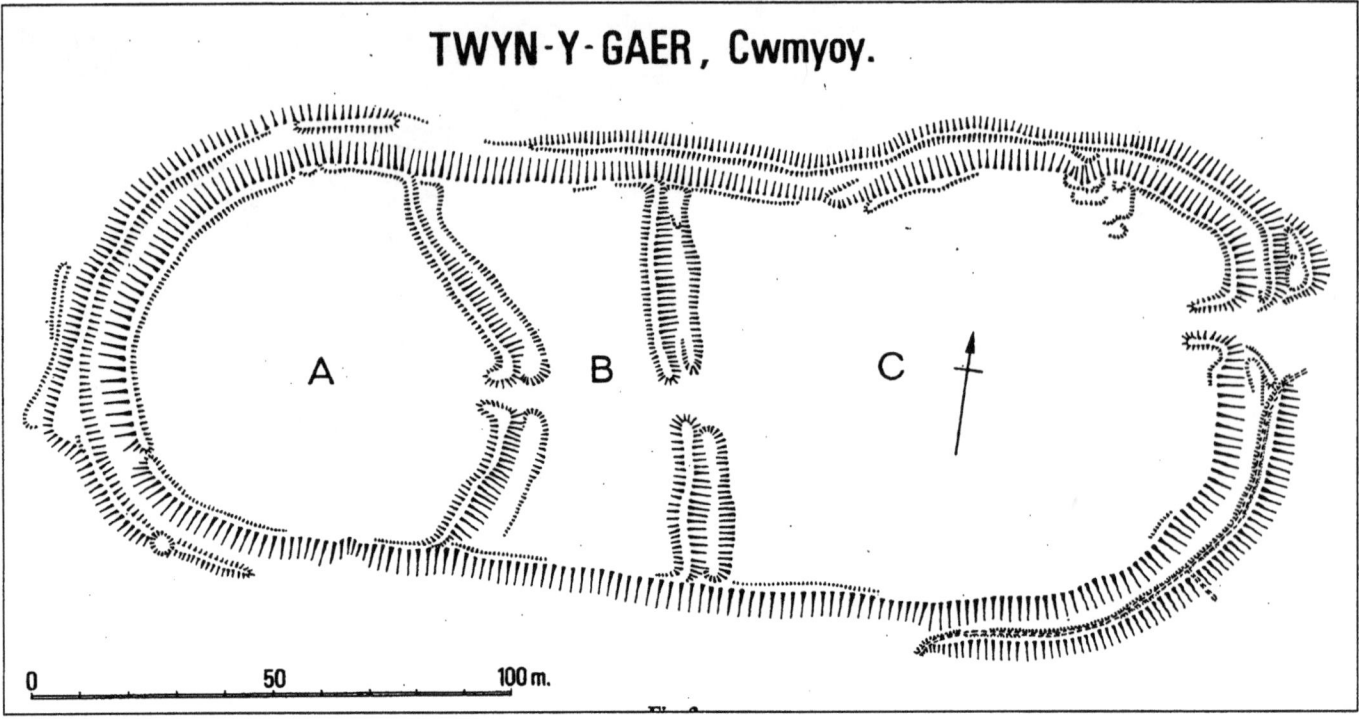

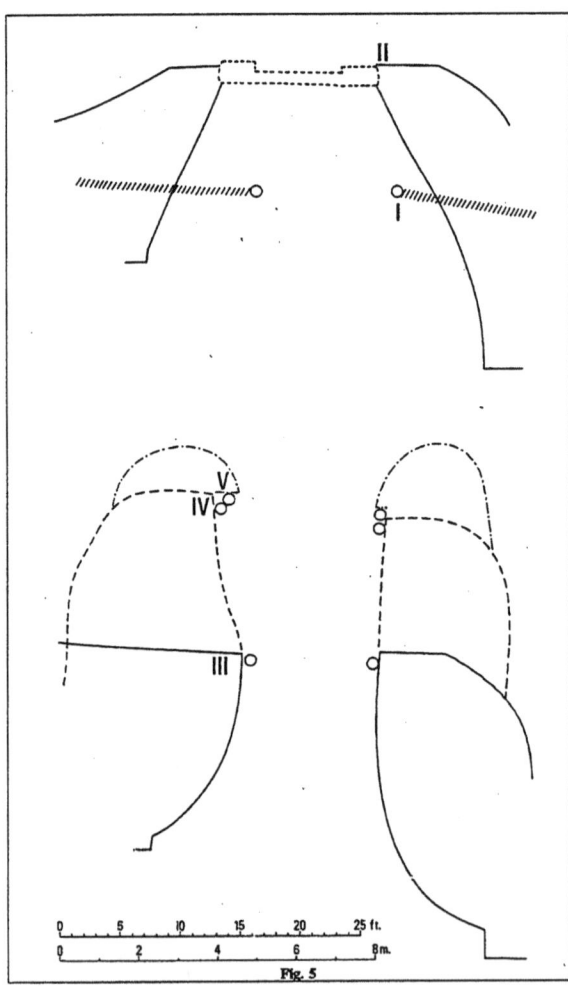

Fig. 37: Top – Twyn y Gaer (MI 2); bottom – Twyn y
Gaer E Gate Phases I-V (after Probert 1976).

Twyn y Gaer than at the Herefordshire hill-forts (Stanford 1972, 307-319). The presence of opposed pairs of post-holes were interpreted by the excavator as the door-posts of turf-built houses, though the best evidence for buildings was the presence of burnt daub with wattle marks in area C. The presence of quern stones indicates a mixed economy, with iron slag and crucibles pointing to iron working. Carpentry and smithing tools were present, but weaponry was represented only by a few curved knives, a broken spearhead and many sling-stones. Saddle-querns were in use up to Period IV but were replaced by rotary beehive querns in Periods V and VI (*ibid.*, 116).

The cultural affinities of the earlier phases at Twyn y Gaer are with the hill-forts of mid-Wales and Herefordshire. In the last phase, the material culture was heavily influenced by the Silures to the S (*ibid.*, 105-119; Whittle 1992, 43-44). Twyn y Gaer marks the southern limit of "Central Marches (i.e. Croft Ambrey-Midsummer Hill) influence" in terms of both architecture and material culture. However, Period V sees a change in material culture as well as in architecture. The Malvernian stamped ware and La Tene brooches of Periods II to IV (c. 200 B. C.) fall out of use and the parallels for the pottery of Periods V and VI lie with material from Lydney Park (Wheeler and Wheeler 1932), Llanmelin and Sudbrook (Nash-Williams 1933 and 1939; Whittle 1992, 48-49). Beehive rotary querns also make their appearance at this time. It is possible that the presence of similar querns at Parc y Meirch (HI 8) and Vowchurch (HI 9) reflects the extent of Silurian influence to the N and NE of Twyn y Gaer.

This phenomenon may represent the extension of Silurian power into the eastern Black Mountains. No similar cultural material is found at the Herefordshire sites of Poston, Aconbury or Credenhill and Twyn y Gaer may well mark the most northerly extent of the influence and power of the Silures (Probert 1976, 118). Twyn y Gaer probably stood at the boundary of the Silures and the tribe which occupied Herefordshire and Stanford has postulated that the boundary followed the Monnow and the Wye. The 10km gap in the distribution of hill-forts in the eastern Black Mountains between Walterstone (HI 5) and Poston Camp (HI 2) has been interpreted as an undeveloped buffer zone along this political boundary (Stanford 1991, 70).

Twyn y Gaer's eastern neighbour at Pentwyn (MI 1, Fig. 38) has not been excavated, but there are superficial similarities between them and the two sites may share similar histories (Whittle 1992, 42). The site commands vast views in all direction except along the ridge of Hatterall Hill to the N and is intervisible with Walterstone hill-fort to the E and Twyn y Gaer to the W.

Kay interprets the NW-SE scarp which crosses the southern enclosure as a levelled rampart which he assigns to a Phase 1 which also includes the existing northern and western defences of the rectangular northern enclosure. Phase 2 sees the fort extended to the S and SW by the construction of bivallate defences and the SE gate with its hornwork and fighting platform. Kay assigns the central cross-ditch to a Phase 3 which also sees the abandonment of the southern defences and gateway and the strengthening of the massive N rampart. He admits, however, that excavation may well modify or reverse his suggested sequence (Kay 1984, 317).

The formidable N rampart stands to height of some 5.4m from the bottom of the rock-cut ditch. Its outline on the ridge is a prominent landmark for many miles to the E. The W ditch is currently used as a road and a strong counterscarp is now obscured by dry-stone walling. The original entrance in the central cross-bank lies near its SW angle and is marked by a causeway in the ditch. This and the complex SE gate are the only original entrances (*ibid.*, 318). The inner southern rampart ends in a thickened knoll at the SE gate which may represent the remains of a fighting platform or bastion which protects an outer hornwork or barbican (Fig. 38). These arrangements may date to the last two centuries B. C. (Savory 1976, 281). In 1936, two Roman copper coins of Constans were found in the upcast of a rabbit burrow near the N rampart. They are now lost (Kay 1984, 319).

6.2 Smaller Defended Settlements

Although such sites are more common and better understood in SW and NW Wales, important examples have been excavated in the SE. At Mynydd Bychan, Glamorgan, the defences, which included a bastion and "barbican" protecting the entrance, enclosed a triangular area roughly 55m by 45m internally. The enclosure contained at least three timber-framed houses and the earliest occupation was dated by Lydney-Llanmelin pottery to the Middle Iron Age (Gibson and Wood 1990, 201). At Whitton, Glamorgan, the defences of a rectangular enclosure included a substantial structure, perhaps a bridge, over the entrance (Fig. 39). Occupation does not seem to have begun here until c. A. D. 30 (Jarrett and Wrathmell 1981, 84).

The best local evidence for defended Iron Age settlement outside the hill-forts comes from the lowland areas of NE Monmouthshire. At Camp Hill, Bryngwyn (MI 10, Fig. 40), a roughly circular enclosure some 90m in diameter with a possible entrance to the E was partially excavated in 1962 and interpreted as an Iron Age defended farmstead (Leslie 1962). The excavations traced a deep ditch and in the "fall" against the lip of the outer edge was found imitation Samian of the late 2nd century A. D. At a depth of about 30cm were sherds of 1st century A. D. pottery and a Roman black cooking pot with a lattice pattern. Prior to the excavations, the enclosure bank stood to a height of 1.2m from the bottom of the ditch. The site is now completely ploughed out and is a telling example of the alarming rate of destruction of such sites in the area.

At White Castle Farm, Llantilio Crossenny (MI 8, Fig. 41), aerial photographs show a possible Iron Age or Romano-British farmstead consisting of a sub-circular enclosure approx. 75m in diameter with an entrance again to the E. The remains of adjacent field systems and roadways have also been identified together with possible hut circles within the enclosure (Mein 1990, 52). In addition, the circular enclosure concentric with but larger than Tregaer churchyard (MI 9) and comprising a bank and ditch with a marked outer counterscarp is similar in size, aspect and elevation to Camp Hill (MI 10, Fig. 40) and is probably of similar date (Mein 1989, 48).

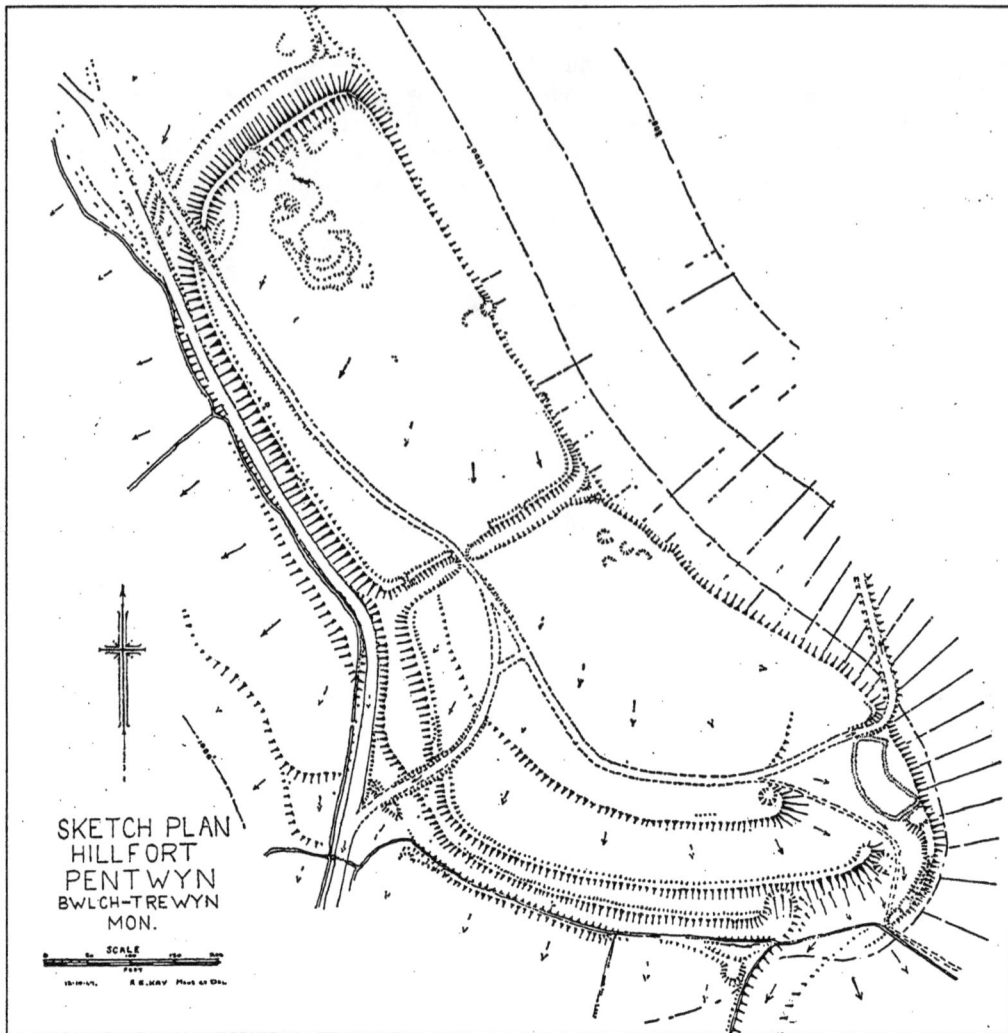

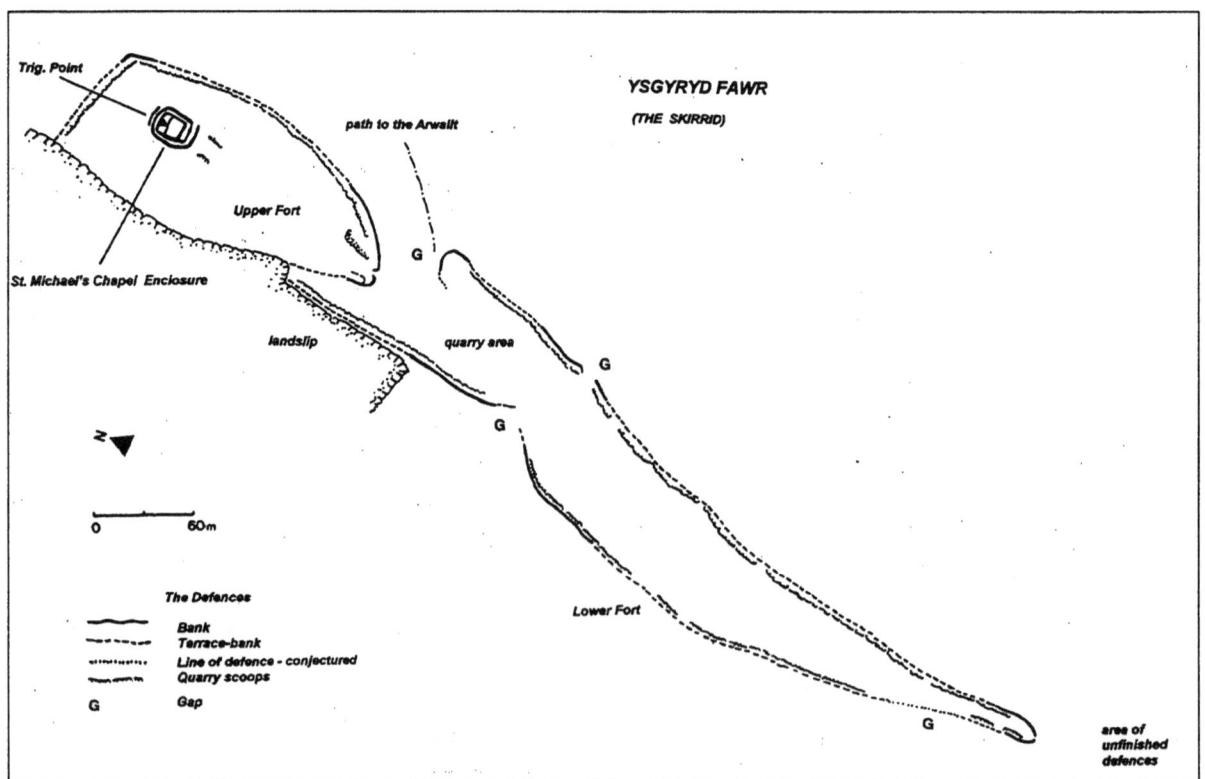

Fig. 38: Top - Pentwyn (MI 1) (after Kay 1984); bottom
Skirrid Fawr (MI 3) (after Makepeace 1996).

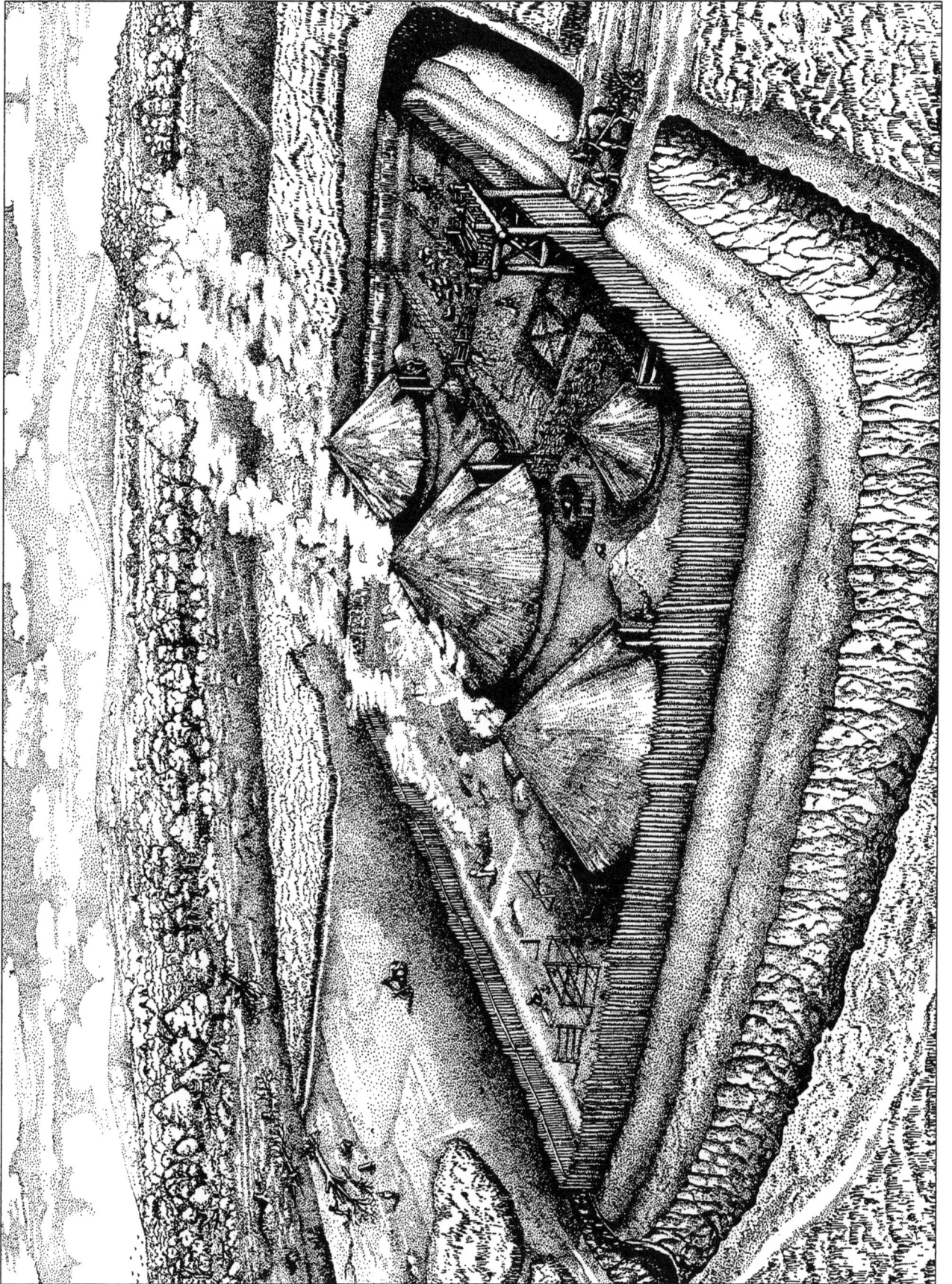

Fig. 39: Whitton Iron Age Farmstead (after Jarrett and Wrathmell 1981).

65

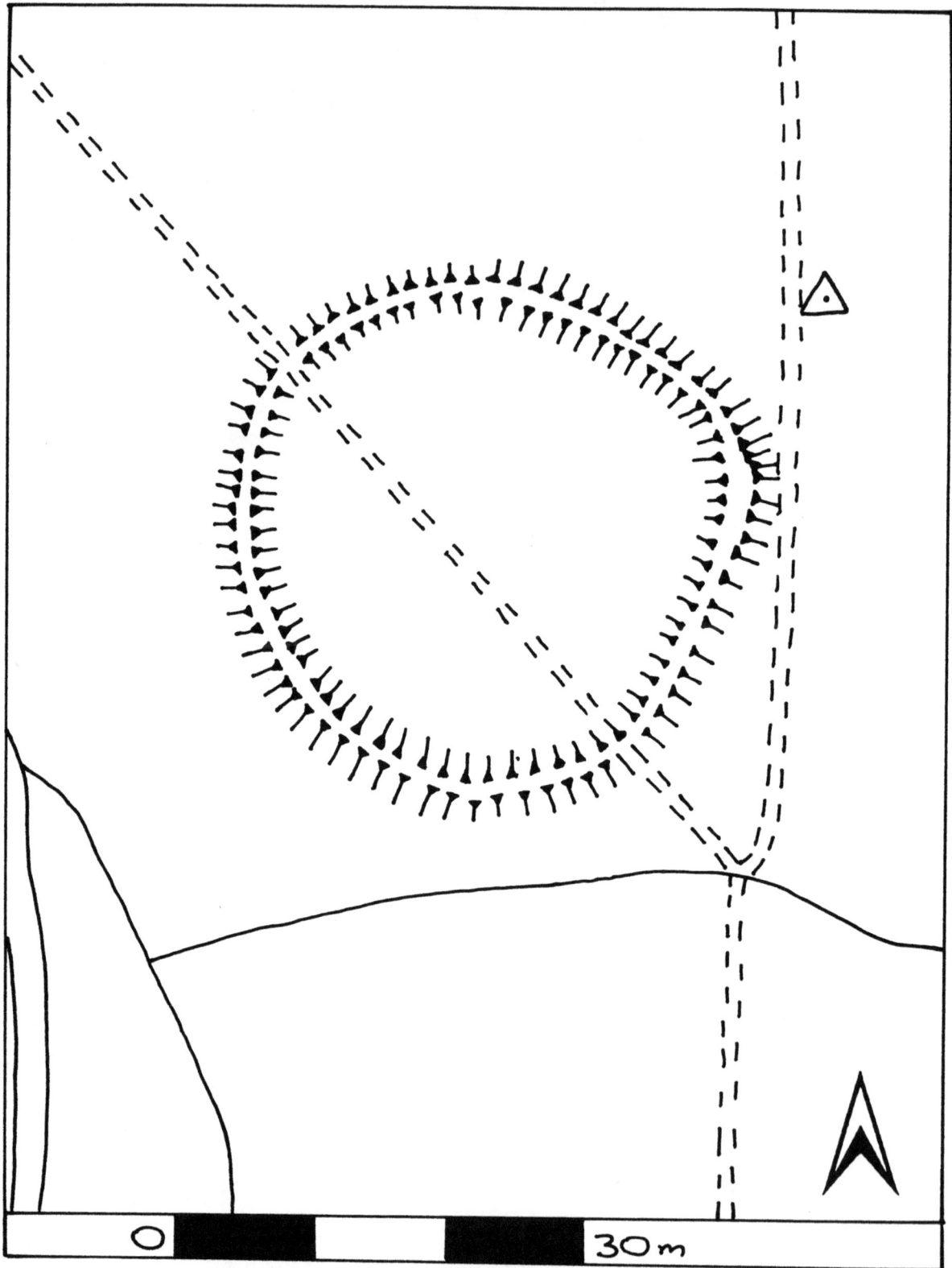

Fig. 40: Camp Hill Enclosure (MI 10).

Of the other Monmouthshire sites, Twyn yr Allt (MI 4, Figs. 42-44) fits well into Class 3 of the Welsh Royal Commission's proposed typology of the neighbouring Brecknock hill-forts (RCAHMW 1986, 14) - namely "smaller univallate enclosures in positions which are naturally strong" and is comparable in size and lay-out to several of the Brecknock sites, particularly Coed Cefn (B-HF 63) which is the site's immediate western neighbour (Fig. 43).

The Brecknock Class 3 sites range in area from 0.24 to 0.88ha and at least one of them (B-HF 1) also lacks a defensive ditch. It is probable that several of these enclosures were earlier foundations than some multi-vallate hill-forts and may be as early as the 6th century B. C. They may represent single homesteads with simple defences and generally have a single gateway. The sole excavated example, Twyn Llechfaen (B-HF31) produced pottery of a date early in the local Iron Age sequence and certainly not later than the 3rd century B. C. The site was a defended farmstead containing one or two dwellings for an extended family and some utility structures and also produced the bones of oxen, sheep and pigs (*ibid.*, 14).

The likelihood of an early date for some of the sub-rectangular Brecknock Class 3 sites is interesting when considered in the light of the sequence of development of Twyn yr Allt's larger and better studied neighbours, Twyn y Gaer and Pentwyn (Fig. 44). Both begin with sub-rectangular enclosures of similar proportions to Twyn yr Allt which undergo extension and elaboration culminating in multi-enclosure and, in the case of Pentwyn, multi-vallate hill-forts.

It seems possible, therefore, that Twyn yr Allt may represent the first stage of this sequence - an early Iron Age defended homestead which for some reason was never the subject of the process of enlargement which transformed its neighbours.

Another sub-rectangular enclosure for which a date possibly contemporary with, or earlier than, the Iron Age has been suggested (RCAHMW 1997, 199) is that in the western Black Mountains on the western slopes of Gadair Fawr (B-US 111) (*ibid.*, 269). The site has an entrance on the E side (Jones 1978e, 60) and an associated linear bank runs up the slope of Pen y Gadair Fawr for about 1km. The site may have served as animal pens or for the protection of crops (*ibid.*, 199).

The only well-preserved example of non-hill-fort Iron Age settlement in Herefordshire is the well-preserved sub-rectangular, univallate enclosure (approx. 50m by 50m and 0.25ha in area) on the E facing ridge of Garway Hill (HI 11, Figs. 35, 45). On the W and E sides, the ramparts still stand to approx. 3m in height with well-defined ditches, the N and S defences are slighter (approx. 2m high) and no ditch is visible on the S side. The E side is slightly convex. The defences are breached in six places by modern tracks but only that in the E side appears to be original. The site has outstanding views throughout the E.

Garway Hill is comparable to sites like Whitton (Jarrett and Wrathmell 1981) and also to Bromfield, the most southerly of the Severn valley ditched farmsteads. Here a defensive

ditch dating to the 3rd century B. C. enclosed a square area some 35m by 35m. Within were two four-posters, some haytrees, racks and shallow clay-lined pits. Such farms could have supported a family unit of perhaps ten people and scores have been plotted from aerial photographs in the valley of the Severn and its tributaries (Stanford 1991, 48). Such sites may have been complementary to hill-forts or periodic alternatives (*ibid.*, 55-56).

East of the Wye at Field Barn Farm, Kenchester (HI 10), excavations on a suspected Romano-British temple revealed underlying Iron Age occupation. The Iron Age phase consisted of one (possibly two) round houses surrounded by a ditch. The site produced much pottery of late Iron Age date, together with furnace fragments and two crucibles.

In addition, the presence of rotary querns at Parc y Meirch (HI 8) and Vowchurch (HI 9) may indicate the existence of more fugitive non-hill-fort settlements and may be tentatively dated to the period after c. 200 B. C. by comparison with similar finds at Twyn y Gaer (MI 2). There, such querns have been taken as evidence of the political influence of the Silures in the later phases of the hill-fort's history (see above).

Although unenclosed Iron Age settlements are known from SE Wales (Lloyd Jones 1984, 20), no sites of this type have so far been identified in the eastern Black Mountains. Similar enclosures are known near Leintwardine, but have not been excavated (Stanford 1991, 92).

6.3 Population, Economy and Territory

Stanford has estimated the total population of the Herefordshire hill-forts at about 25,000 (*ibid.*, 67), with individual population figures of about 900 at Croft Ambrey, 2,000 at Midsummer Hill and some 3,600-4,800 at Credenhill (1974, 219-230), though it should be remembered that these estimates are based on his belief that the entire interiors of the forts were occupied by densely-packed four-posters acting as dwellings - an interpretation which is far from widely accepted. On the basis of surface surveys of hill-forts with visible house remains, others have suggested populations of 20-25 people per acre or 80-100 people per hectare (Hogg 1973, 19) with a hill-fort occupied by a population of some 400-500 people requiring a block of territory of some 70 square km to support it. Based on Stanford's figures of a population of some 3600-4800 inhabitants for Credenhill, Hogg postulated an associated territory of some 100 square km of intensively cultivated land (*ibid.*, 20).

These figures must, however, be treated with extreme caution. Only 5% of the total area of Croft Ambrey and 1% of Midsummer Hill was actually excavated and the four-post structures may only have been used as granaries or stores. The interiors of the forts may well have been zoned and less closely packed circular buildings probably await discovery. More conservative estimates of hill-fort populations for Wales and the Marches suggest a rate of 30 people per hectare (Lloyd Jones 1984, 19). It is clear that the Herefordshire hill-forts represent substantial nucleations of population and that their expansion c. 390 B. C. reflects

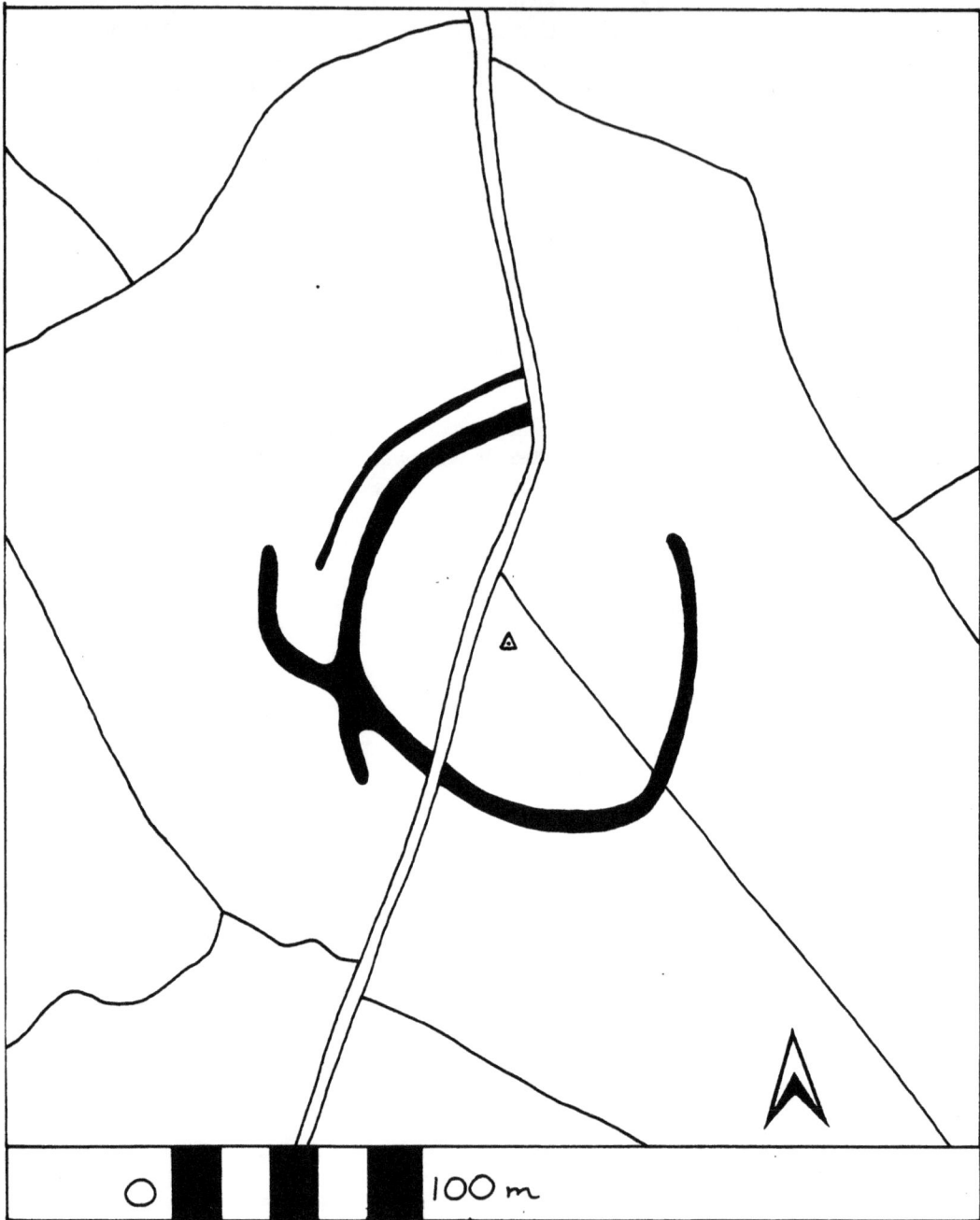

Fig. 41: White Castle Farm Enclosure (MI 8)
(transcribed from photographs taken by John Sorrell).

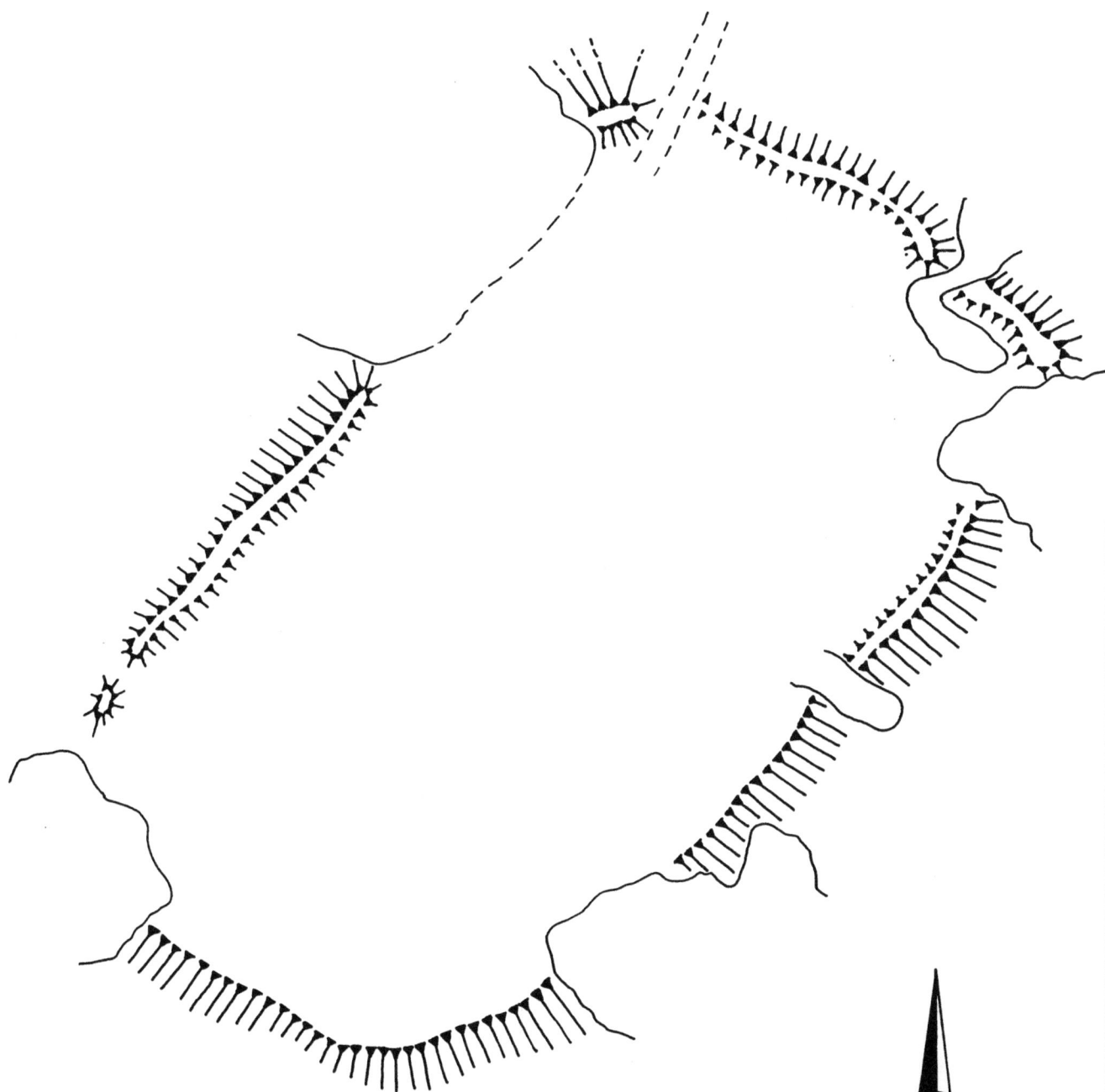

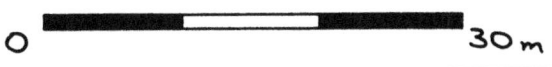

Twyn yr Allt Iron Age Enclosure
Abergavenny, Monmouthshire.
NGR: SO 2965 1628
350m above OD

Surveyed 15/12/98
Frank Olding
Neil Phillips

0   30 m

Fig. 42: Twyn yr Allt Enclosure (MI 4).

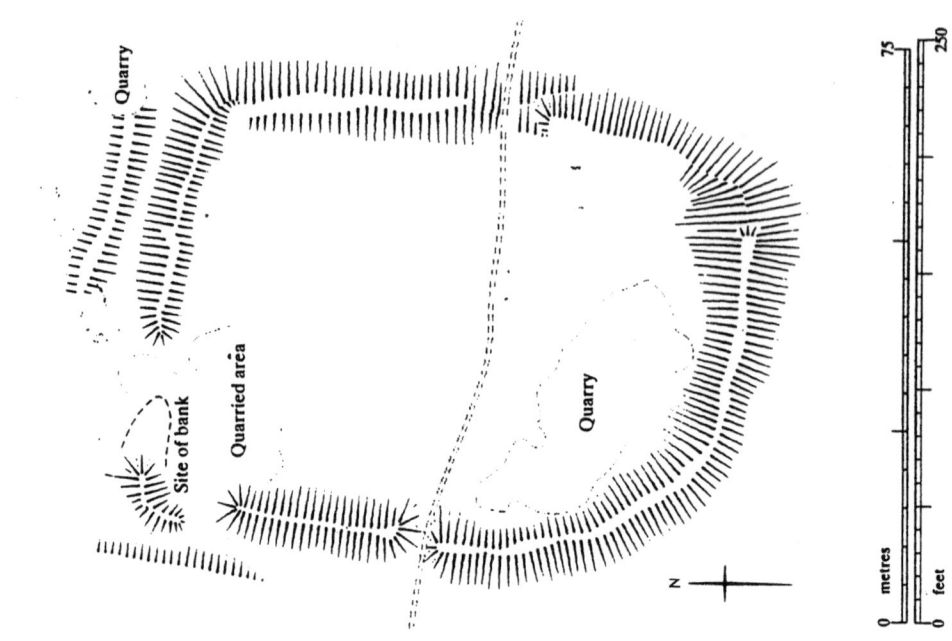

Coed Cefn (HF 63)

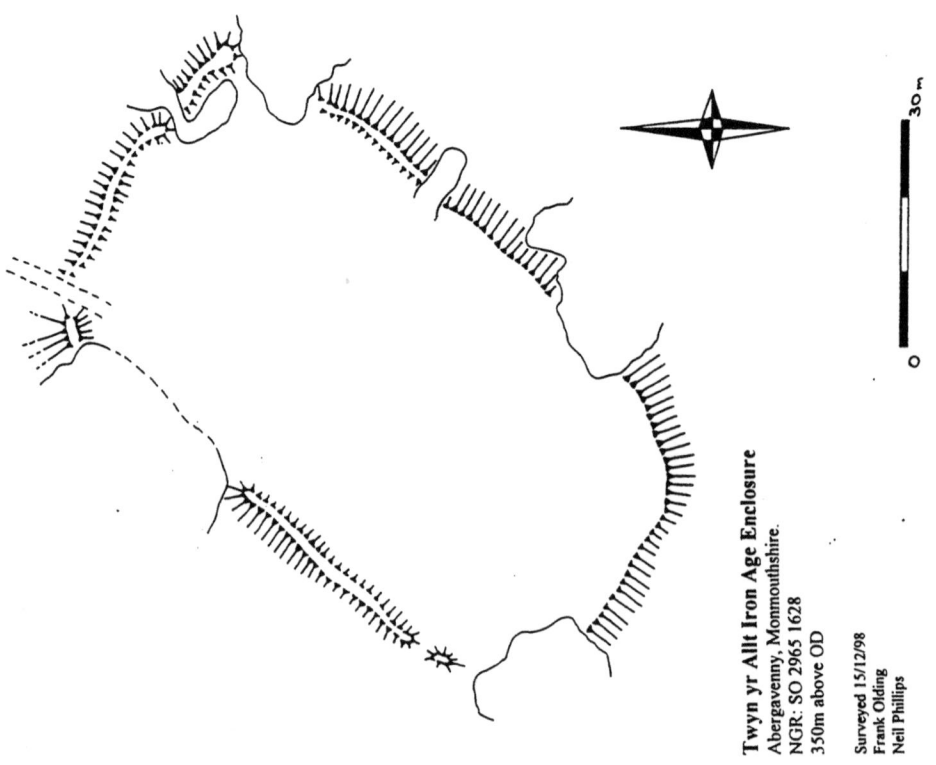

Quarry

Quarry

Quarried area

Site of bank

Quarry

N

75

250

0 metres

0 feet

Twyn yr Allt Iron Age Enclosure
Abergavenny, Monmouthshire.
NGR: SO 2965 1628
350m above OD

Surveyed 15/12/98
Frank Olding
Neil Phillips

30 m

**Fig. 43: Twyn yr Allt (MI 4) and Cefn Coed (B-HF 63)
(latter after RCAHMW 1986).**

70

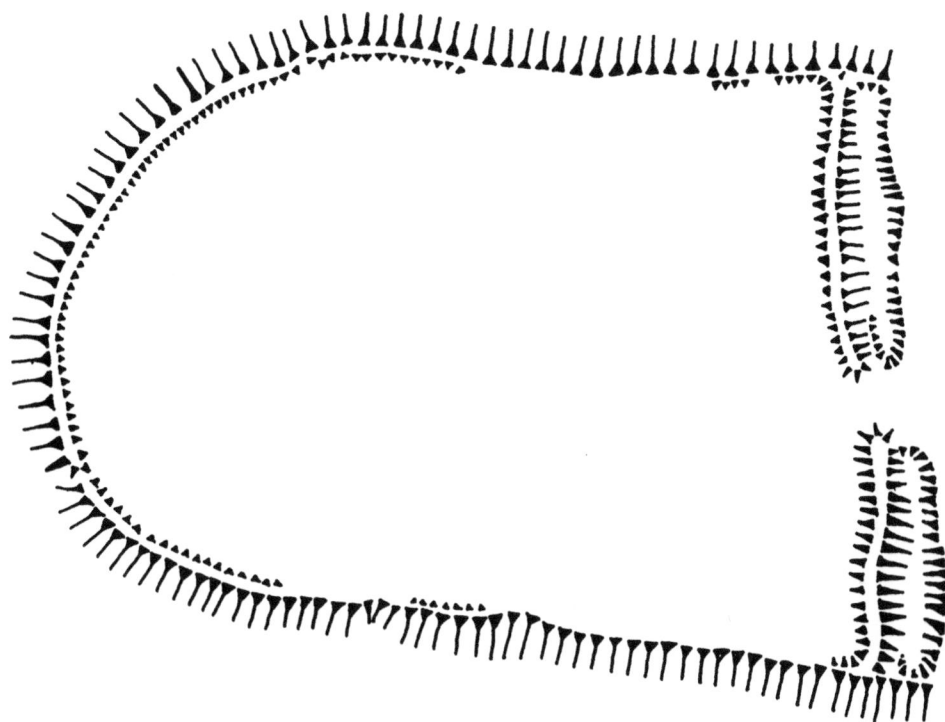

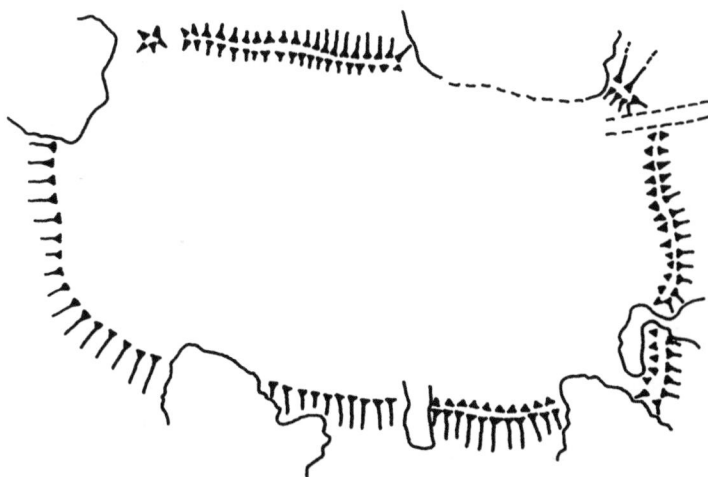

Fig. 44: Twyn yr Allt and Twyn y Gaer Phase I (latter after Probert 1976).

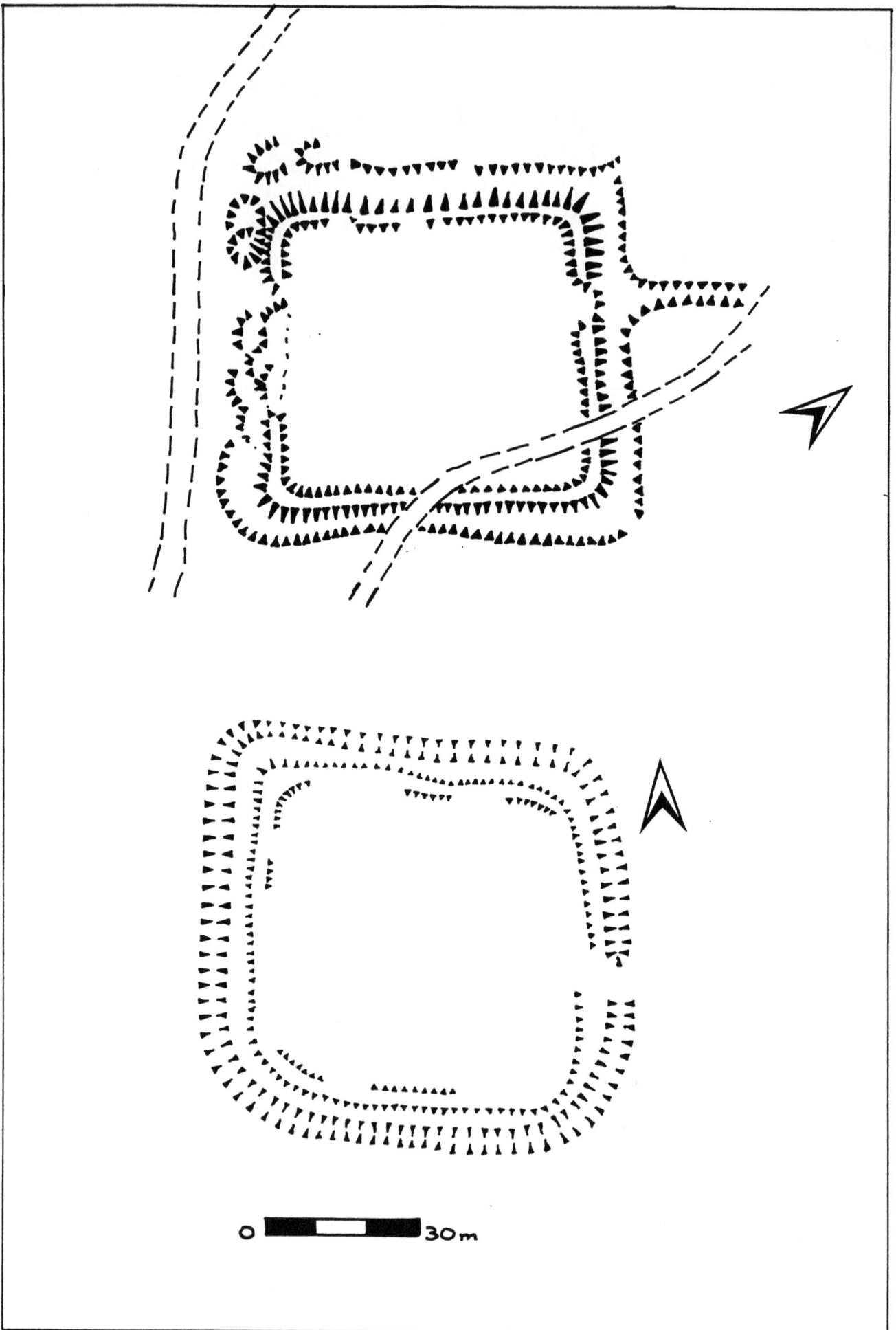

Fig. 45: Top – Garway Hill (HI 11) (after Kay 1963);
bottom – Whitton (after Jarrett and Wrathmell 1981).

either a growth in overall population levels or a process of combination of smaller units (*ibid.*, 157).

At any rate, large areas of Herefordshire must by this time have been cleared of trees for agriculture (Lloyd Jones 1984, 155) and, although the exact balance of arable to pastoral production cannot be estimated, the higher ground may well have seen greater emphasis on pastoralism (Stanford 1991, 67). Many of the four-post structures attested by excavation were probably used a granaries (Cunliffe 1993, 65-68) and this certainly implies widespread cultivation of cereals. Carbonized wheat from Caynham Camp, near Ludlow, and from the Wrekin, Shropshire (which produced radio-carbon dates of 760-530 cal. B. C. and 90 cal. A. D.) suggests that wheat remained an important crop throughout the local Iron Age (Stanford 1991, 55).

Wheat was certainly the predominant crop at Croft Ambrey and at Midsummer Hill there is evidence for emmer or spelt wheat, some barley and the cornfield weed, brome (Richardson 1992, 151). The presence of reaping hooks and rotary querns at Credenhill, sickles and querns at Sutton Walls and saddle and rotary querns at Twyn y Gaer implies a significant and widespread element of cereal production in the local economy (Lloyd Jones 1984, 287; 430). In Herefordshire as a whole, 42% of the known hill-forts lie on the leached brown soils of the Bromyard, Middleton and Eardiston series which are excellent for corn crops (*ibid.*, 155). Iron Age climatic conditions were cooler and wetter than previous periods and seem to equate fairly closely to modern conditions. A wetter climate favours the production of cereals and Iron Age farms would almost certainly have been capable of producing a surplus. It should be remembered that both grain and cattle were listed among exports from Britain in the mid-1st century B. C. (Richardson 1992, 146).

The proportions of domesticated animal bone at Croft Ambrey saw 29% cattle, 37.5% sheep and 33.5% pigs. At Sutton Walls, cattle accounted for 52.7%, sheep 32.1% and pigs 15.2%. The high proportion of pigs at Croft Ambrey may have been due to the presence of more forest for pannage. The majority of the sheep on site had been over-wintered at least once and their primary function may have been wool production (Stanford 1991, 68). It has also seems likely that lambing took place within the hill-fort (Richardson 1992, 150). Cattle at Croft Ambrey were also over-wintered, a fact which implies the presence of enclosed paddocks, cattle-houses or shelters and the ability to provide adequate fodder. The manure accumulated was probably used to fertilise arable fields (*ibid.*, 151). It is also possible that pigs were herded onto arable fields after the harvest to consume the last of the fallen grains, weed seeds and plant roots with the added advantage of their manure and the partial turning over of the soil (Stockley 1998, 92).

Richardson has compared hill-fort distributions in Herefordshire against modern agricultural land classifications (Grades 1-5). Thus, the land around Croft Ambrey is mainly Grade 3 with some Grade 2, while Sutton Walls has mainly Grade 2 with some Grade 3 (1992, 151). This may imply a greater proportion of woodland to field at Croft Ambrey and may account for the higher proportion of pigs among the domesticated animals there (see above).

It has been suggested that the economic base of a given hill-fort, combined with the need to guard both agricultural land and its produce, may be reflected in the type of defences constructed. Thus, multiple enclosures may reflect greater commitment to animal husbandry, while a single enclosure might imply short-term penning of animals and longer-term storage of grain (*ibid.*, 146). Rivers could have acted as territorial boundaries, but could also have served a highways and certainly as food resources (*ibid.*, 147).

With the important caveat that it is uncertain which of Herefordshire's hill-forts were occupied simultaneously (*ibid.*, 145), some attempts at estimating potential territories have been made. Each of the county's hill-forts would almost certainly have drawn upon the resources of an extensive hinterland and theoretical territories of some 60-65 km could be attributed to each one. However, their average internal area stands at 5.23ha and, for every hectare enclosed within hill-forts, there is only 12.89 square km of land outside. If each hill-fort had a territory proportional to its internal area, that of the average hill-fort would stand at 4.5km in radius, rising to 9.0km for Credenhill. It has also been suggested, on analogy with medieval sites, that the maximum area occupied by a hill-fort represents 7% of its arable land (Lloyd Jones 1984, 25). Stanford has proposed territories for the Herefordshire and Monmouthshire hill-forts in direct proportion to the size of their enclosures (1972, 312-314; 1991, 58) and, apart from Credenhill, none of these territories are too large to have been farmed by communities resident in the forts themselves (Fig. 46). Credenhill may well have fulfilled functions other than the home of a farming community (Lloyd Jones 1984, 156-157).

A more recent study of hill-fort territories in Herefordshire based firmly on agricultural practicalities suggests that each hill-fort on the Woolhope Dome, east of the Wye, had access to a range of agricultural land with widely varying characteristics and potential, from the level and fertile river valleys to the poorer soils of the higher slopes. The poorer soils and steeper slopes may been utilized as managed woodland, providing fuel, building materials and pannage for pigs. The network of streams in the area also assured ease of access to water for livestock (Stockley 1998, 93-94).

Such waterways also provide convenient boundaries which may or may not represent barriers to movement. They are certainly valuable common resources to the communities living either side of them (*ibid.*, 80). Thiessen polygons constructed for the Woolhope hill-forts were indeed found to correspond remarkably well with topographical features - mainly significant waterways ((*ibid.*, 81).

On the basis of a detailed analysis of the agricultural potential of each of the territories identified in this way, Stockley argues that estimates of population at 10 people per one square kilometre (Hogg 1973, 14-21) are far too low. Either the populations of the Woolhope hill-forts combined to construct the forts and manage their territories, or the population was considerably higher, or both (Stockley 1998, 98).

When plotted on distribution maps, the various models proposed make for interesting viewing. However, bearing in

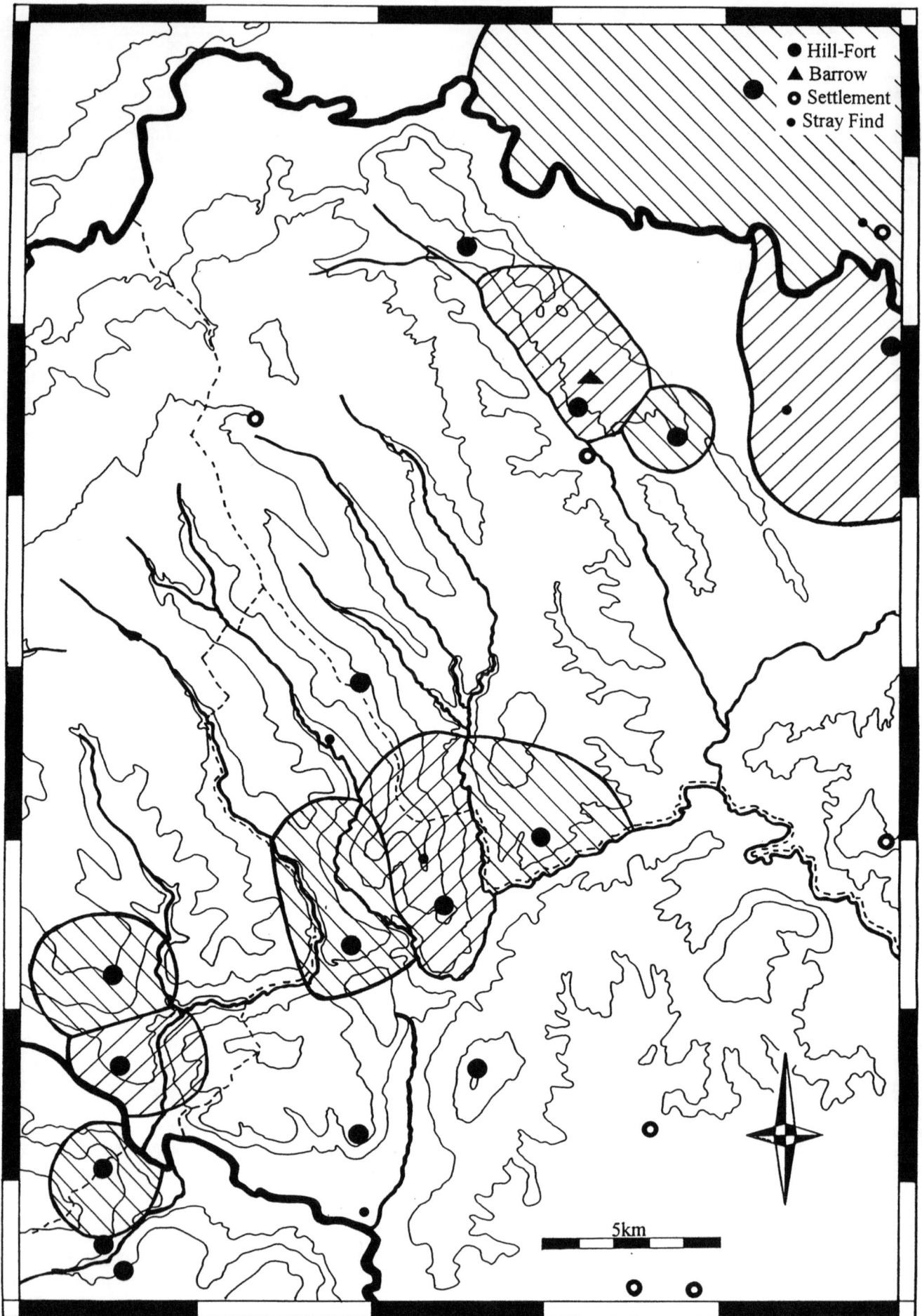

Fig. 46: Hill-Fort Territories (after Stanford 1991).

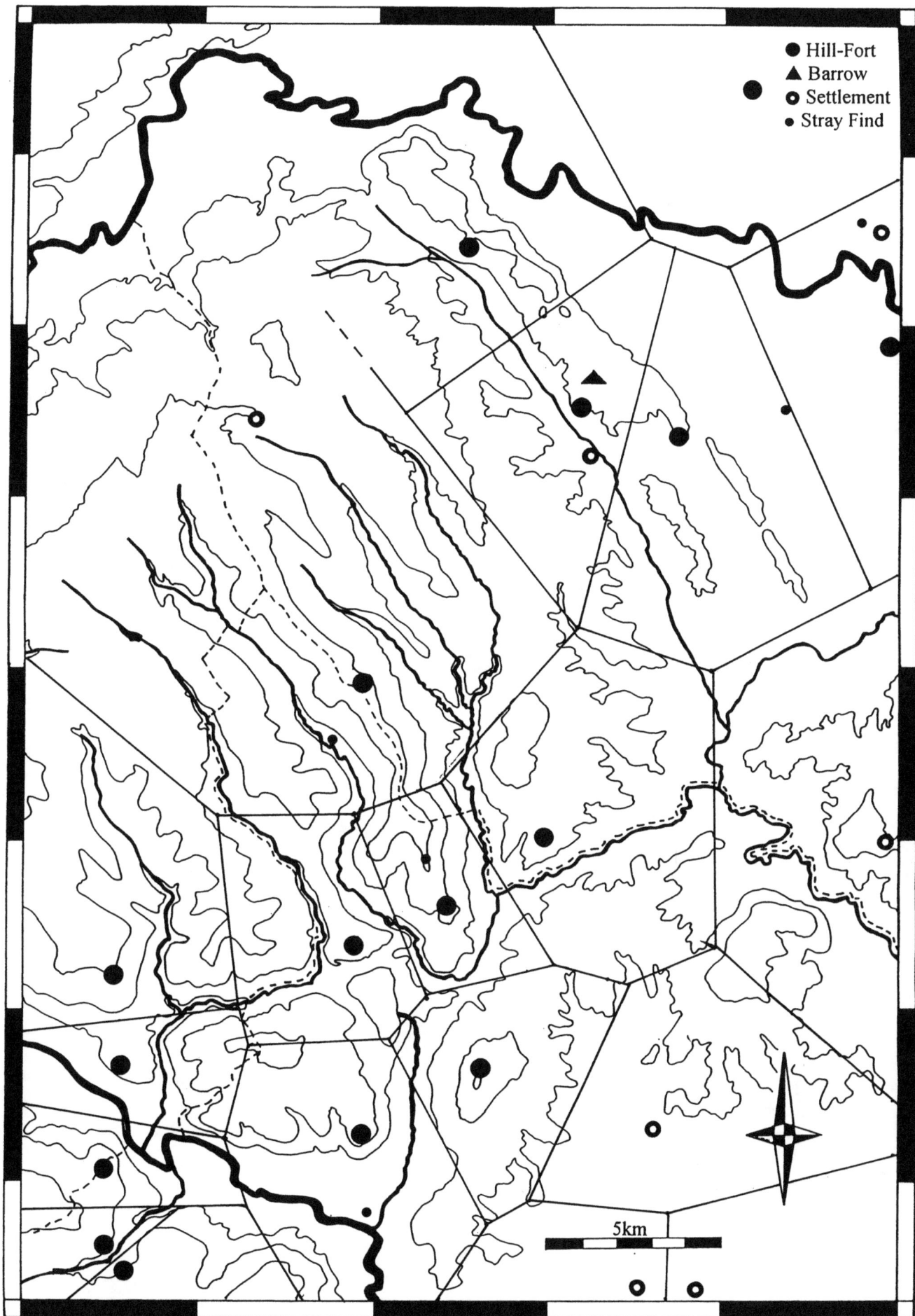

Fig. 47: Thiessen Polygons for the Hill-Forts of the eastern Black Mountains.

Hill-Fort

Barrow

Settlement

Stray Find

5km

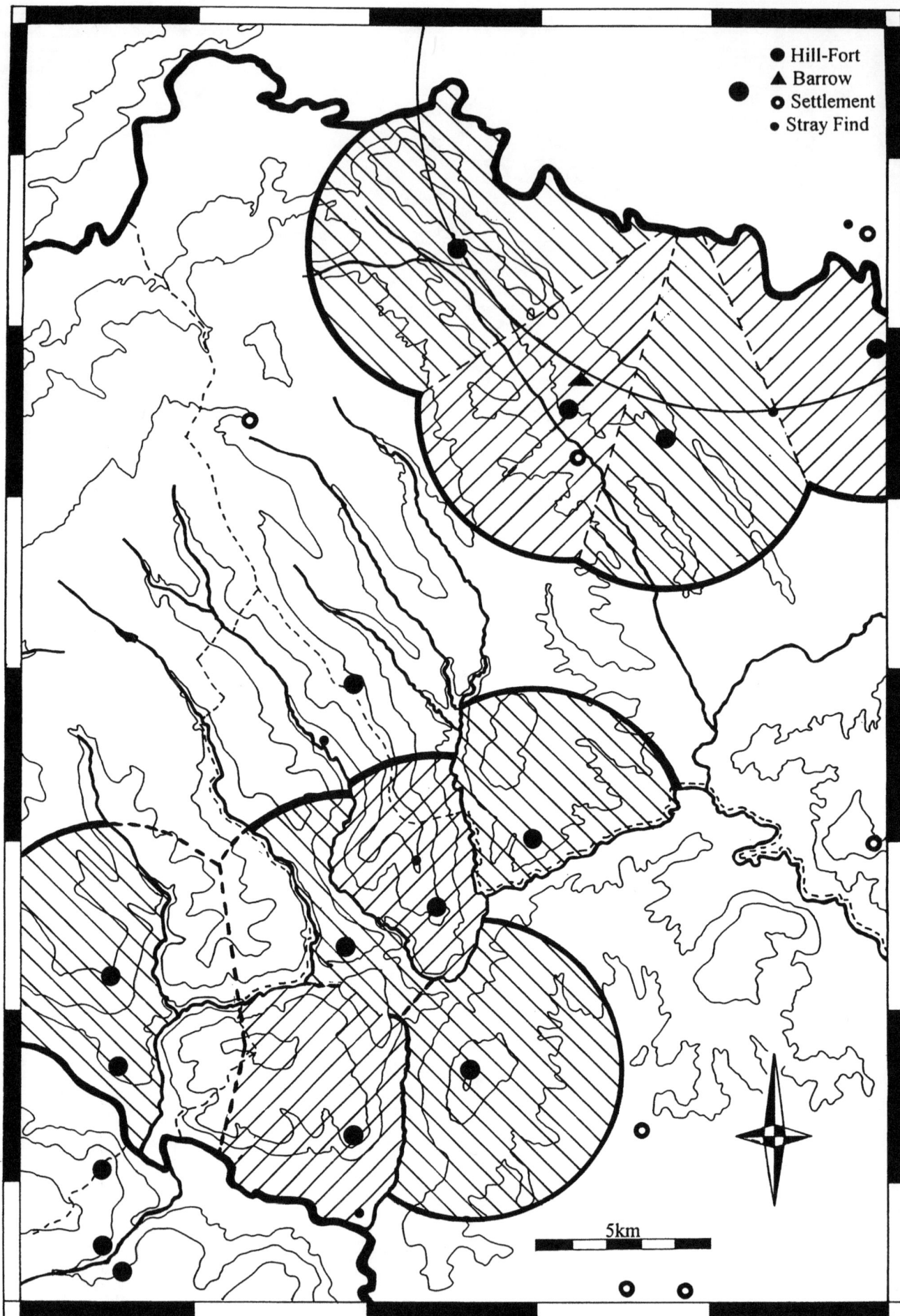

Fig. 48: Hill-Fort Territories for the eastern Black Mountains.

Hill-Fort
Barrow
Settlement
Stray Find

5km

mind Stockley's analysis, and by combining Thiessen polygon projections (Fig. 47) with Richardson's site catchment estimates, more organic territories can be postulated for the hill-forts of the eastern Black Mountains (Fig. 48). It is clear that the Dorstone (HI 1), Poston (HI 2), Timberline Camp (HI 3) and Eaton Bishop (HI 6) fall within the sphere of influence of Credenhill (HI 7). The gap in hill-fort distribution recognised by Stanford (see above) between Walterstone (HI 5) and Timberline (HI 3) may well reflect the final tribal affiliations of the area.

It seems fairly obvious that Twyn y Gaer (MI 2), Pentwyn (MI 1) and Walterstone (HI 5) form a coherent defensive and territorial pattern. It seems unlikely that their territories were exclusive and they probably controlled a common resource base, worked and defended by all three in concert. If Walterstone is indeed later than the other two (see above), can its construction be taken as a consolidation of newly extended Silurian territory in the period after c. 200 B. C.? As in earlier times, Skirrid Fawr (MI 3, Fig. 38) may well have occupied a prime position to exploit both the Gavenny Valley and the lowland area to the E and may have acted as a focus for the defended farmsteads scattered there (MI 8-10). To the W, it seems likely that the sites at Llanelli (MI 5) and at the bottom of the Clydach Gorge (MI 6-7) may also have formed a grouping centred on the gorge and its iron deposits.

6.4 Iron Age Ritual

Very little is known of Iron Age ritual in the eastern Black Mountains and only one site has been assigned a ritual purpose. Prior to excavation in 1932 (Marshall 1933b), the enigmatic mound in Bradley's Wood close to the hill-fort at Poston, was some 21m in diameter and 2.30m high (HI 14, Fig. 24). A trench through the centre failed to find any sign of a central burial, but did produce the remains of nine hearths, five flints and five pieces of pottery (ibid., 31). The flints included an Earlier Neolithic leaf-shaped arrowhead which was originally thought to have been brought to the site with the fine soil which formed the base of the mound (ibid., 33). At the base were found two pieces of pottery which Marshall dated to the period c. 50-100 A. D. (loc. cit.) and upon which his assignment of the site to the Iron Age rested.

The structure of the Poston mound was of exceptional interest. The base consisted of a ring-bank of fine soil some 16.5m in diameter and about 1.2m in height. This was then covered with a carefully constructed cairn of small, flat, sandstone slabs tipping steeply inwards (ibid., 32). Although Marshall assumed that the cairn's structure represented a single phase of construction, it is possible that an earlier ring-bank was incorporated in a later cairn.

Antony also suggested an Iron Age date and a funerary purpose for this site. However, the excavation of a similar feature at Croft Ambrey demonstrated ritual use (but not burials) throughout the late Iron Age and Romano-British periods (Stanford 1974, 132-143). In about 75 A. D., a raised ceremonial floor was constructed into which were dug several fire-pits. Also found were numerous fragments of the bones of sheep, goats and cattle together with much broken pottery. This has been taken as evidence of ritual animal sacrifice and feasting (Children and Nash 1994, 95). It seems

likely that the Poston mound fulfilled a similar function. Until the 1950s, the mound and its excavation trench survived intact but both have since been destroyed by ploughing (Brown 1972, 315).

7 - CONCLUSIONS

Gwernvale, the sole Palaeolithic site in the eastern Black Mountains, has also been claimed as the first Late Upper Palaeolithic open site in Wales has been seen as forming part of a pattern of "bi-polar" settlement which saw seasonal movement from home-bases in the lowland coastal areas towards temporary inland encampments in pursuit of migrating herds of larger herbivores.

Some Mesolithic clearances of woodland in the Black Mountains may have been aimed at the creation of new settlement sites. Other, more widespread burning was probably used to manage animal and plant resources by increasing grazing potential, as well as flushing animals from forests and increasing visibility for hunters under the canopies and from nearby ridge-tops.

Early Mesolithic activity is attested at Gwernvale (B-MS 15) and Cefn Hill (HM 7) and represents the repeated use of favourable places to intercept the seasonal movements of ungulates. Later Mesolithic hunting may have been increasingly centred around small task-groups actively searching for their prey and would have involved a more general use of the landscape. The more widespread representation of sites for the Later Mesolithic in the eastern Black Mountains accords with the expected pattern (Fig. 49).

Possible Later Mesolithic summer base camps have been identified at Merbach Hill (HM 3), Arthur's Stone Ridge (HM 5), Dorstone Hill (HM 6) and Woodbury Hill (HM 11); a larger summer base camp at Hill Farm (HM 22), a small winter or autumn task-group camp at Cothill Farm (HM 18) and a winter domestic camp at Lower Blakemere Farm (HM 20). Lower Blakemere Farm may have acted as a winter base for the groups exploiting the summer camps on the eastern ridge of the Golden Valley (HM 3, 5, 6, 11, 22). It is also possible to postulate a similar relationship between the Cothill Farm task-group camp and the single find-spots on Vagar Hill and Urishay Common (HM 9, 10, 14-16).

It is possible, therefore, that the Later Mesolithic communities of the Golden Valley exploited two distinct territories meering along the river Dore itself.

In Monmouthshire, similar relationships may have existed between the winter base camps at Abergavenny (MM 9) and Blaengavenny (MM6) and the flake-blade scatters on the Sugar Loaf (MM 10) and the Llwygy (MM 11) respectively. Here, winter base-camps cluster closely in the confined terrain of the Gavenny and Usk valleys. It is possible that the groups involved were smaller than those of their Herefordshire neighbours, or that the major food resource of the river Usk attracted more Mesolithic people to the area.

Fourteen local Mesolithic sites have also produced Earlier Neolithic material. Clearings made by hunter-gatherers for management of game may have been attractive to early farmers. Neolithic patterns of movement obviously included places that had been important for centuries.

Neolithic agricultural activity (Fig. 49) seems to have been small in scale and clearances short-lived. The Black Mountains chambered tombs are mainly sited on the boundary between good, freely-drained soils and wetter soil and it has been suggested that the valleys may have supported cattle and pigs, with sheep on the lower hill-slopes. In summer, both cattle and sheep would have moved to the better-drained soils adjacent to the tombs.

In Brecknock, individual Neolithic farmsteads are represented by Gwernvale and Cefn Cilsanws. Excavations at the former clearly illustrated the establishment of local arable and pastoral systems by about 3100 b. c. (c. 3900 cal. B. C.). Cereals were cultivated locally and processed for consumption on site and domesticated cattle, sheep and pigs also played a part in the local economy, though the total assemblage was too small to assess the relative importance or function of each species.

In Herefordshire, possible Neolithic settlements have been identified at Cefn Hill (HN 10) and Abbey Farm (HN 10), though there is more convincing evidence for long-term activity and actual structures at Dorstone Hill (HN 8). Parallels may be drawn between this site and the causewayed enclosures of the Cotswolds and Dorstone may have played an analogous role in the local Neolithic landscape. In Monmouthshire, it is possible that the earlier Neolithic lithic scatters at Pen y Clawdd (MN 20) and Skirrid Fawr (MN 21) represent the residue of periodic visits to significant places by essentially mobile earlier Neolithic groups.

The local distribution of axes reflects areas of Earlier Neolithic clearance in the Golden Valley, the Gavenny Valley and the lowlands of NE Monmouthshire. The exchange of Group XXIII and Group VIII axes probably served to maintain contact between people in different areas of southern and central Wales.

Overall, the pattern suggests that the axe finds and flint scatters reflect the areas of most intense Neolithic activity and it is possible to suggest the existence of eight Neolithic territories in the eastern Black Mountains based on the Golden Valley (A), Urishay Common-Cefn Hill (B), Grey Valley (C), Garway Hill-Monnow Valley (D), the Gavenny Valley (E), north-east Monmouthshire (F), the Usk Valley-Gilwern (G) and Gwernvale-Grwyne Fawr (H) (Fig. 49).

The Black Mountains chambered tombs form an isolated and compact inland group. Excavations at Mynydd Troed showed that in Neolithic times the monuments were set in clearings in open, dry, climax oak forests in areas which would have served as summer pastures. Within the group, two different principles regarding the alignment of the tombs' long axes have been identified - those which run parallel with the major rivers or their tributaries and those which are orientated towards particularly prominent points on the escarpment edges of the Black Mountains. River valleys, prominent hills and spurs, paths and landmarks whose ancestral significance had already been established during the Mesolithic were monumentalised during the Earlier Neolithic by the construction of megalithic tombs. Repeated visits to a tomb fixed a routine in the use of the surrounding landscape - ancestral worship at these sacred monuments and sacred areas served to attach people very closely to particular places in their landscapes, they fixed a sense of place.

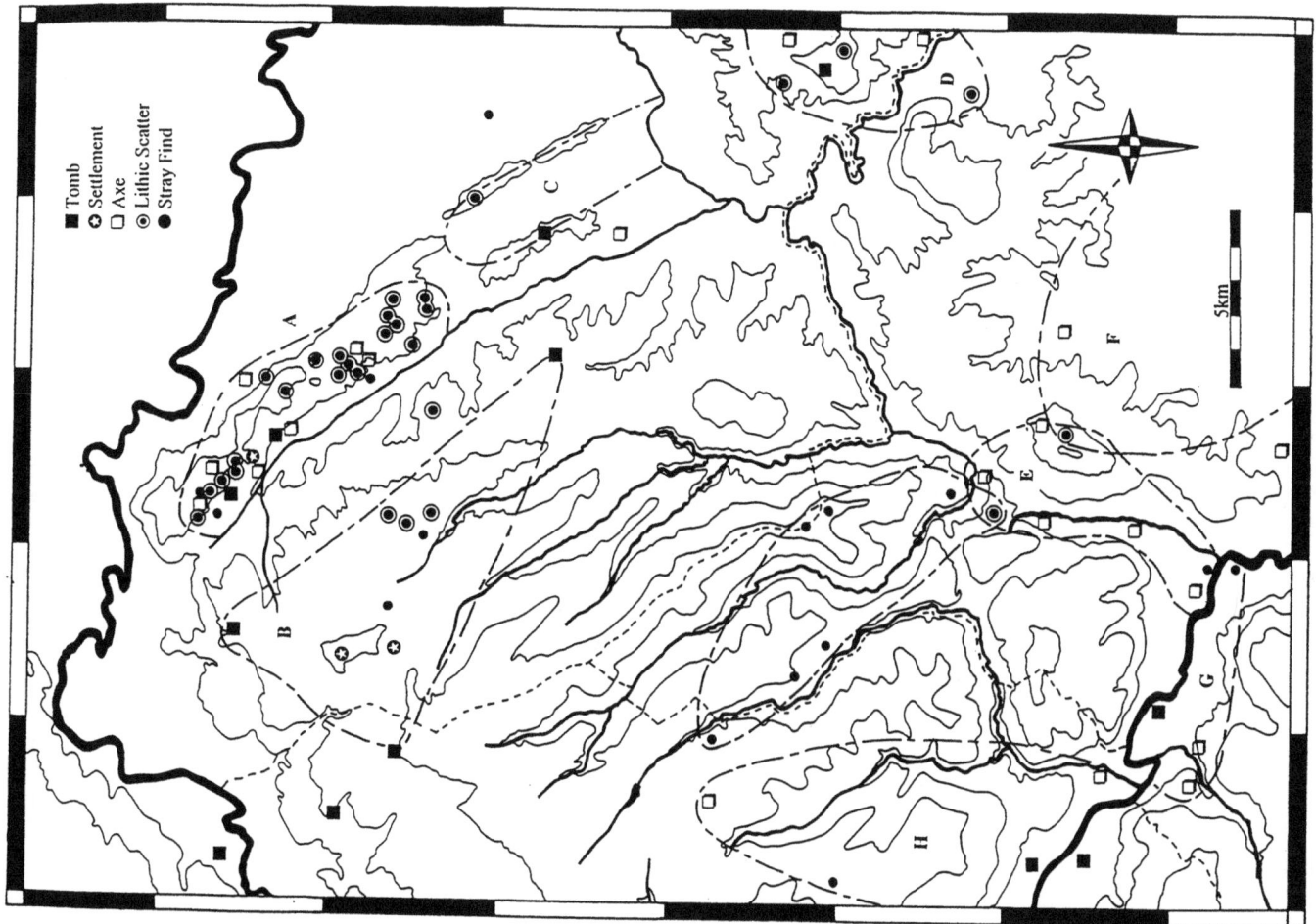

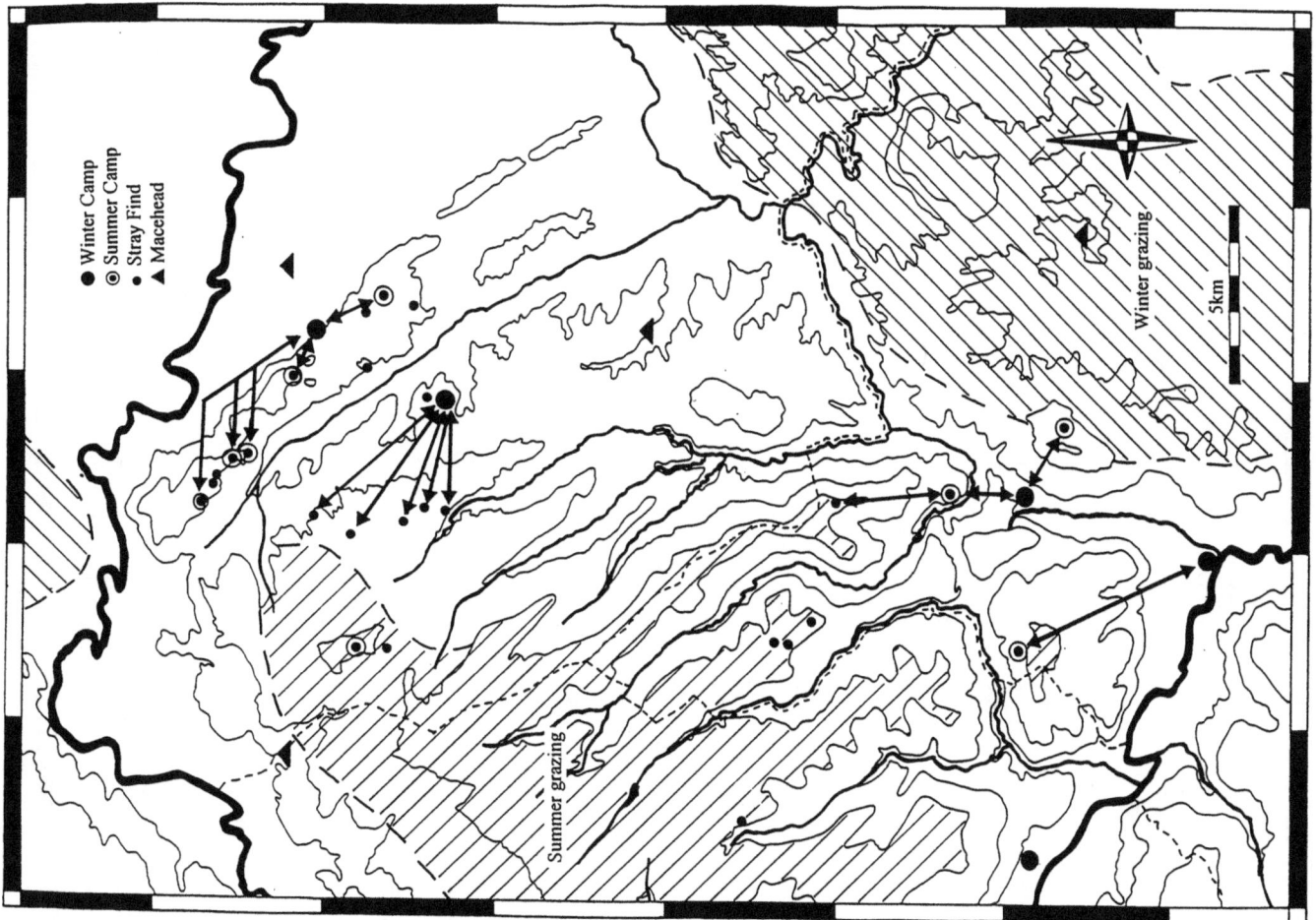

Fig. 49: The Mesolithic (bottom) and Earlier Neolithic (top) Landscapes.

Legend (top map):
▲ Round Cairn or Barrow
○ Ring-Ditch
■ Standing Stone
✪ Stone Circle or Ring-Bank
☐ Metalwork
● Stray Flints
◉ Lithic Scatter

Legend (bottom map):
✪ Ring-Bank
● Flints
☐ Axe
■ Pottery

5km

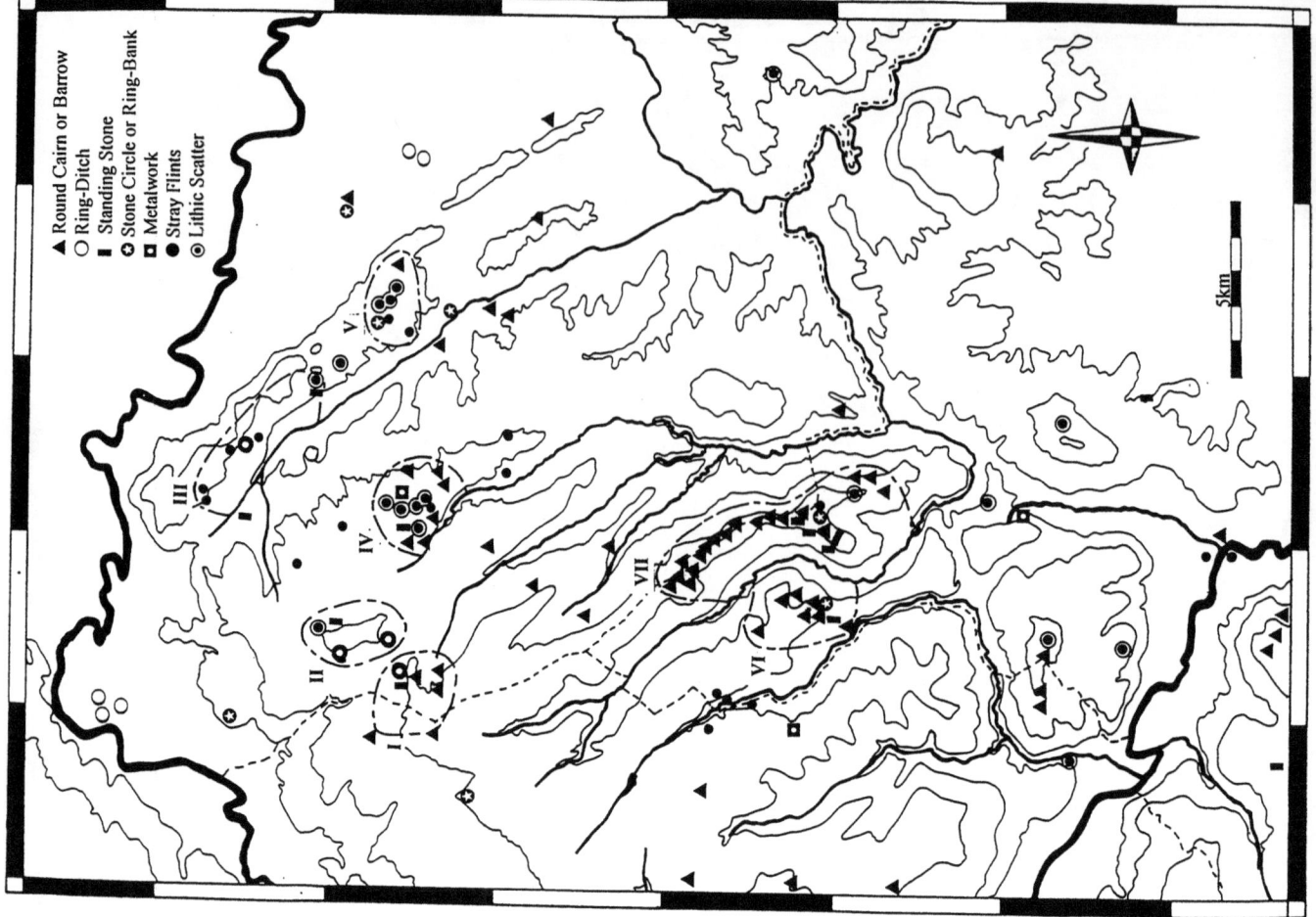

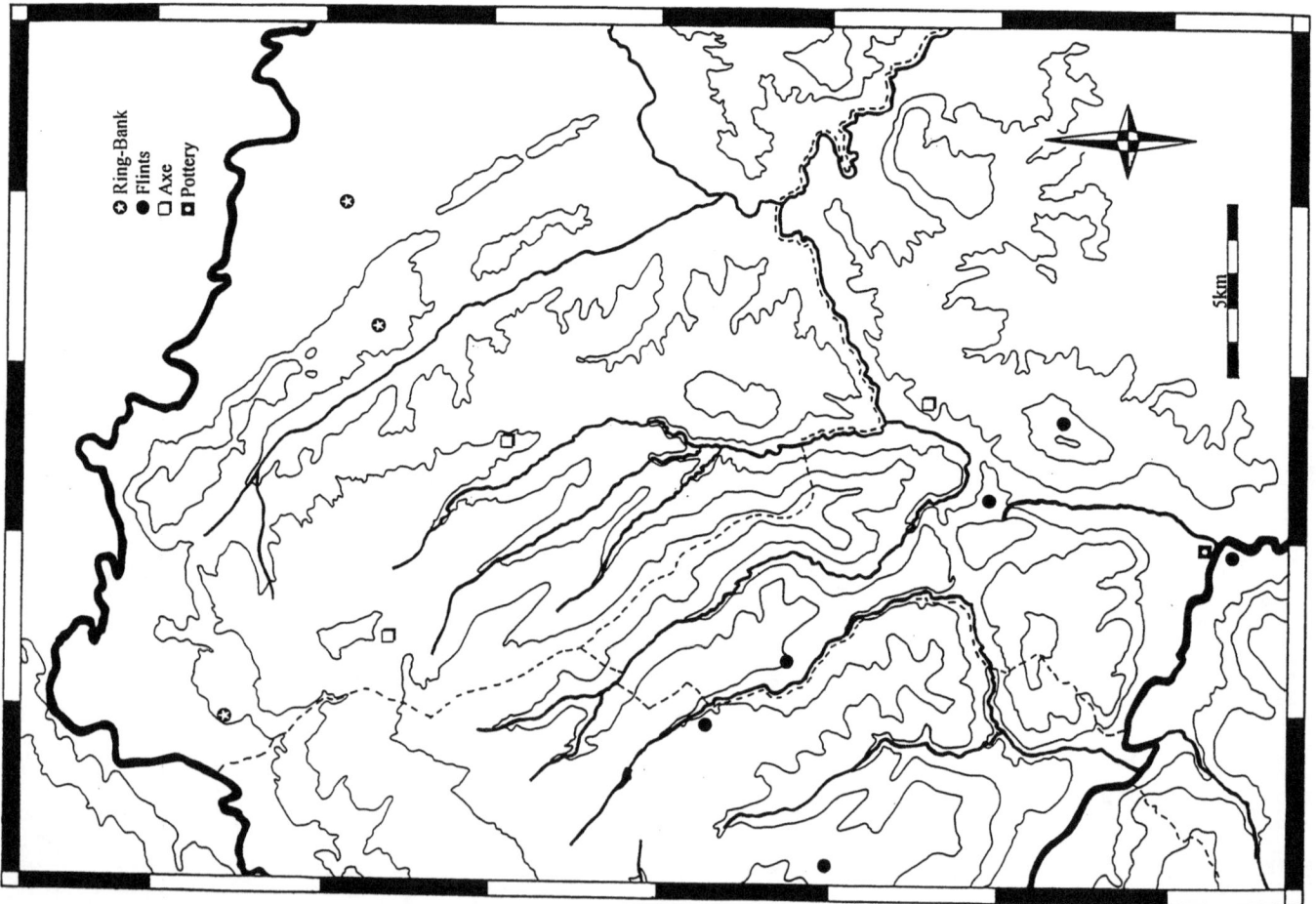

Fig. 50: The Later Neolithic (bottom) and Early Bronze
Age (top) Landscapes.

No Later Neolithic element has yet been identified in the Herefordshire lithic assemblages and the evidence for Later Neolithic activity in Monmouthshire is also scanty (Fig. 50). A great deal of effort was put into the final closure of the tomb at Gwernvale (dated by two radiocarbon dates of c. 2440 b. c. and c. 2640 b. c.), implying that it retained ritual or symbolic meanings apart from burial, possibly still connected with the ownership of territory. There is also a strong possibility that some at least of the Herefordshire ring-banks date to the Later Neolithic period.

The distributions of Neolithic and Early Bronze Age flint sites show a considerable amount of overlap and apparent continuity between the two periods. Two of the Herefordshire Neolithic scatters have also produced Bronze Age material and seven of the Herefordshire sites produced Mesolithic, Earlier Neolithic and Early Bronze Age flint. In Monmouthshire, the same chronological depth of prehistoric activity from the Mesolithic through to the Bronze Age is evident at Abergavenny (MN 24) and at Skirrid Fawr (MM 7-MN 21-MB 53). There was both Neolithic and Bronze Age material among the lithic scatter at Pen y Clawdd (MN 20-MB 52), in the Grwyne Fawr valley (MN 14-MB 47), on Hatterall Hill (MN 18-MB 52) and at Llanfoist (MN 23-MB 58).

The Early Bronze Age saw widespread upland forest clearances in search of cultivable soil. Territories which had kept mainly to the lower ground during the Neolithic expanded onto the adjoining uplands (Fig. 50) becoming geographically more diverse in the process. The distribution of dated Early Bronze Age burials gives some indication of the chronology of the colonisation of upland areas. This points to the exploitation of the lower slopes in the early Beaker period c. 2500-2300 cal. B. C., some movement onto the higher ground in the later Beaker phase c. 2300-2050 cal. B. C. and intensive exploitation of the highest land during the full Early Bronze Age c. 2050-1500 cal. B. C.

The only site with good evidence of Early Bronze Age settlement is Dorstone Hill (HB 43), though other sites at Abbey Farm (HB 45), Cefn Hill (HB 44) and Birches Farm (HB 46) may also represent Early Bronze Age settlements. There seems to be a clear territorial role for both burial cairns/barrows and standing stones in marking ritual and social foci or "core areas" for seven Early Bronze Age territories centred respectively on Parc y Meirch (I), Cefn Hill (II), Dorstone Hill (III), Urishay Common (IV), Stockley Hill (V), Garn Wen (VI) and Garreg Las (VII) (Fig. 50).

In Herefordshire, round barrows and cairns occur both on hill tops and on valley floors. Many are not actually visible from the surrounding countryside and they seem to have been sited with reference to what may be seen from them rather than to their own visibility. The two major Monmouthshire concentrations of round cairns occur on Hatterall Ridge-Loxidge Tump (MB 9-22) and the ridge of the Ffawyddog (MB 1-7). It seems likely that these sites situated on the highest ridges date to the full Early Bronze Age (c. 2050-1500 cal. B. C.) and reflect the intensive exploitation of the uplands in this period.

A new group of ring-bank monuments has been recognised in Herefordshire for the first time, with examples at Clifford (HB 33), Poston (MB 34) and Upper Chilstone (HB 35). These sites may belong to the Later Neolithic or represent a lowland version of Early Bronze Age ring-cairns. Only two stone circles are recorded for Herefordshire, on Stockley Hill (HB 36) and Loxidge Tump (HB 37) - both are doubtful. In Monmouthshire, the Garreg Las ring-cairn (MB 29) and Garn Wen circle (MB 28) form part of extensive Early Bronze Age ritual complexes which also include standing stones and round cairns.

In Herefordshire, some standing stones (MB 38-40) marked the core areas or boundaries of Early Bronze Age territories. Others are ideally placed to act as way-markers along paths from the valley bottoms to the ridge tops (MB 32-34) or through the high moorland (HB 41-42). Other Black Mountains standing stones are found in obvious association with Early Bronze Age ritual monuments and form an element in ritual complexes.

Overall, the impression created by the distribution of Middle and Late Bronze Age metalwork (Fig. 51) is of a marked shift from upland to lowland activity and this goes some way to supporting the suggestion that the period saw the abandonment of the upland areas which had been so heavily exploited in the Early Bronze Age. The presence of weaponry among both hoards and stray finds may reflect the social tension which would have resulted from increased pressure on finite resources and it is possible that the small promontory fort at Black Darren (HI 4) should be assigned to this period.

During the Iron Age, there is a remarkable consistency in architecture and material culture from excavated hill-forts within the area. Similarities in defences, house types and pottery seem to link Croft Ambrey, Midsummer Hill and Credenhill (HI 7) at least from the early fourth century B. C. and, in the period c. 390 B. C.-200 B. C., all three, together with Twyn y Gaer (MI 2) and Poston Camp (HI 2) were using the duck-stamped pottery produced near the Malvern Hills. Other Herefordshire sites such as Sutton Walls, Dinedor and Aconbury also seem to fit the general pattern of cultural homogeneity which has been seen as a reflection of a distinct Iron Age "culture" in the southern Marches.

In its earlier phases, Twyn y Gaer (MI 2) marks the southern limit of this phenomenon. However, from c. 200 B. C. onwards, the site's material culture was heavily influenced by the Silures to the S. This may reflect an extension of Silurian power into the eastern Black Mountains. It is possible that the construction of the neighbouring Walterstone Camp (HI 5), the only fully multivallate fort in the eastern Black Mountains, should be seen against this background.

Conservative estimates of hill-fort populations for Wales and the Marches suggest a rate of 30 people per hectare and it is clear that the Black Mountains hill-forts represent substantial nucleations of population. The exact balance of arable to pastoral production in the local economy cannot be estimated, though the higher ground may well have seen greater emphasis on pastoralism. Many of the four-post structures attested by excavation were probably used a granaries and this certainly implies widespread cultivation of

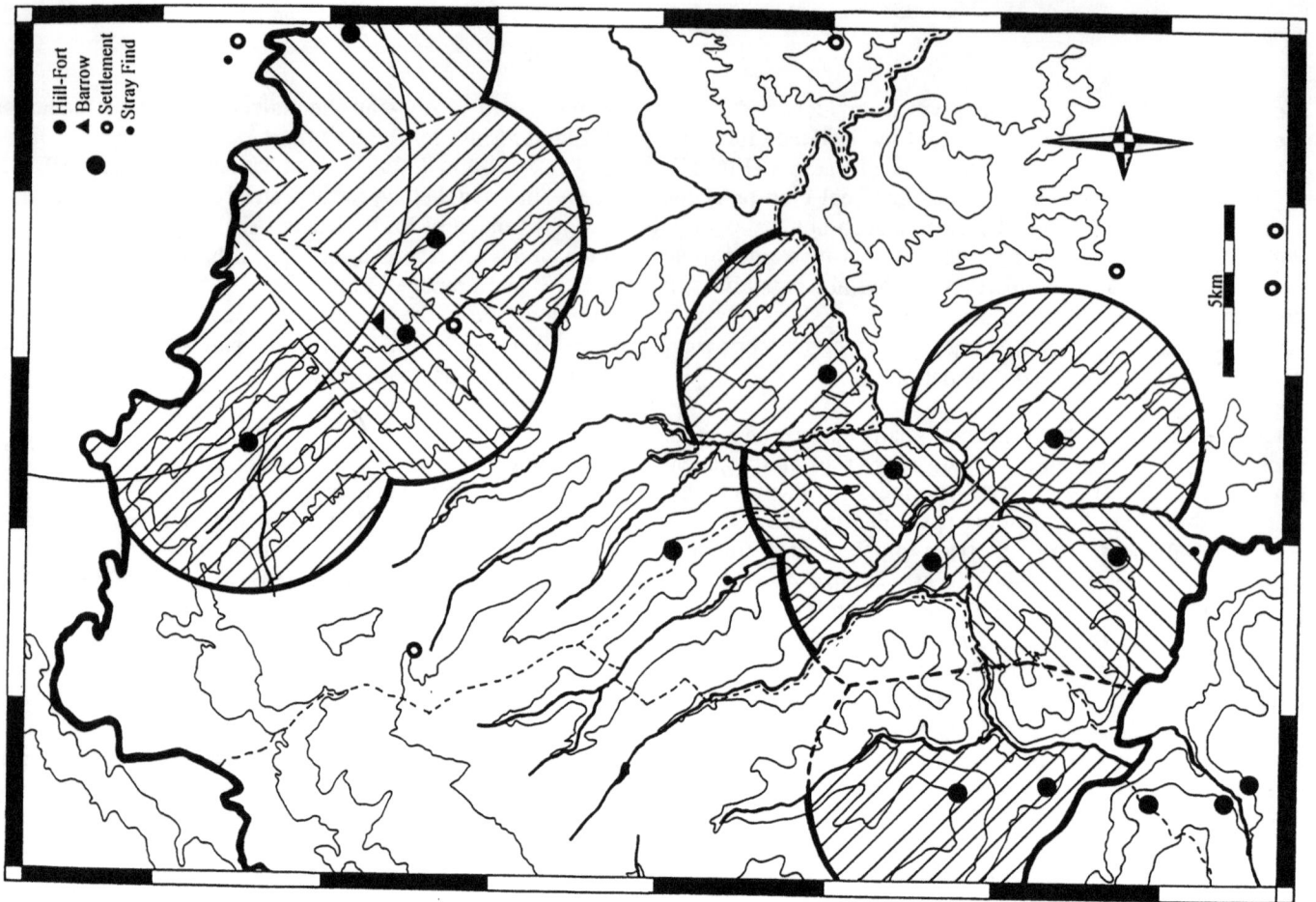

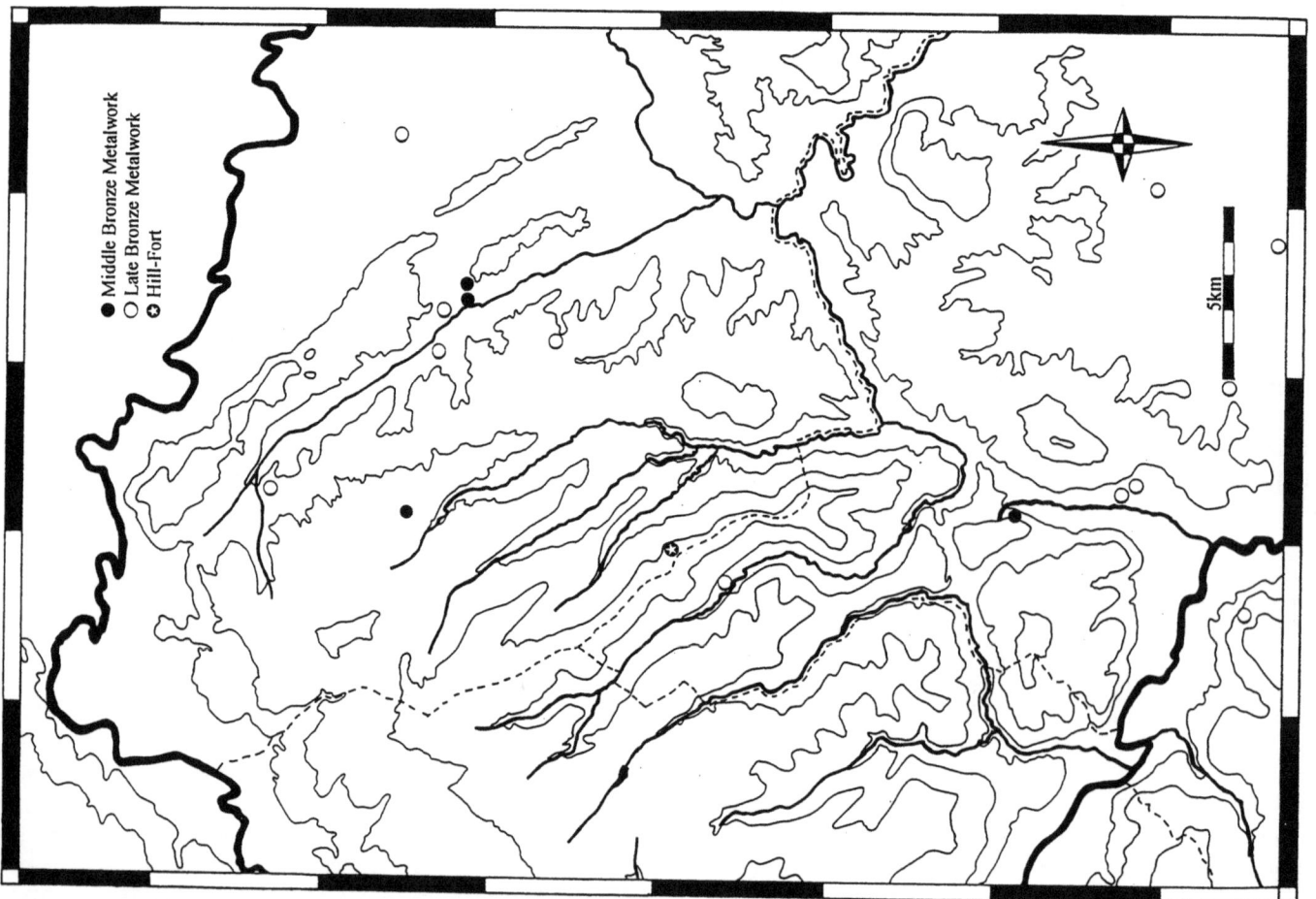

Fig. 51: The Middle-Late Bronze Age (bottom) and Iron Age (top) Landscapes.

cereals. There is evidence for emmer or spelt wheat and some barley and the Iron Age farms were certainly capable of producing surpluses.

The primary function of local flocks of sheep may have been wool production and it seems likely that lambing took place within the hill-forts. Cattle were over-wintered, a fact which implies the presence of enclosed paddocks, cattle-houses or shelters and the ability to provide adequate fodder. The manure accumulated was probably used to fertilise arable fields. It is also possible that pigs were herded into forests for pannage and onto arable fields after the harvest to consume the last of the fallen grains.

As well as hill-forts, smaller defended sites have been identified at Camp Hill, Bryngwyn (MI 10), White Castle Farm (MI 8) and Field Barn Farm, Kenchester (HI 10). Larger rectangular sites, possible of higher status, also existed at Twyn yr Allt (MI 4) and Garway Hill (HI 11).

Various models have been proposed for Iron Age territories in the area, but it is clear that the Dorstone (HI 1), Poston (HI 2), Timberline Camp (HI 3) and Eaton Bishop (HI 6) fell within the sphere of influence of Credenhill (HI 7). It seems fairly obvious that Twyn y Gaer (MI 2), Pentwyn (MI 1) and Walterstone (HI 5) form a coherent defensive and territorial pattern (Fig. 51). It seems unlikely that their territories were exclusive and they probably controlled a common resource base, worked and defended by all three in concert. As in earlier times, Skirrid Fawr (MI 3, Fig. 38) may well have occupied a prime position to exploit both the Gavenny Valley and the lowland area to the E and may have acted as a focus for the defended farmsteads scattered there (MI 8-10).

Very little is known of Iron Age ritual in the eastern Black Mountains and only one site, the enigmatic mound at Poston (HI 14), has been assigned a ritual purpose.

One of the most striking results of this survey has been the remarkable longevity of land-use patterns. The Mesolithic territories postulated for the Golden Valley correspond with Earlier Neolithic territories A and B, while possible relationships between Mesolithic sites in Monmouthshire prefigure Earlier Neolithic territories E, F and H (Fig. 49).

The Earlier Bronze Age core areas I, II and IV are contained within the larger Earlier Neolithic territory B, while areas III and V correspond to Earlier Neolithic territory A. The Honddu Valley hinterland of Earlier Neolithic territory E is, in turn, covered by Early Bronze Age areas VI and VII (Fig. 50). These are almost identical to the Iron Age territories postulated for the Twyn y Gaer and Pentwyn hill-forts (Fig. 51). Those for the hill-forts at Dorstone Hill and Poston are represented in the Earlier Bronze Age by core areas III and V respectively.

An exception to this Bronze Age-Iron Age continuity is the Parc y Meirch, Cefn Hill, Urishay Common area covered in the Earlier Neolithic by territory B and in the Earlier Bronze Age by core areas I, II and IV. This area has produced very little evidence for Iron Age settlement.

In short, there appears to be a large measure of continuity in patterns of land-use and territoriality in the eastern Black Mountains from the Mesolithic period through to the Iron Age.

Gazetteers

The gazetteer entries include the unique county/period number assigned to each site (e.g. MM 4, HB 75), followed by the name, in bold type, of the parish for the sites in Herefordshire (e.g. **Dorstone, Peterchurch**) and of the community council areas for those in Monmouthshire (e.g. **Crucorney Fawr, Grosmont Fawr**). This is followed by the site's County Sites and Monuments Record (SMR) number, National Monuments Record (NMR) number (when available) or Brecon Beacons National Park (PRN) number and, finally, by the site's National Grid Reference (NGR).

The county/period numbers (e.g. HM 11, MI 13) prefixed by the letter *M* refer to Monmouthshire sites, those with *H* to those in Herefordshire. The numbers also indicate period i.e. MM - Monmouthshire Mesolithic, MN - Monmouthshire Neolithic, MB - Monmouthshire Bronze Age, MI - Monmouthshire Iron Age, HM - Herefordshire Mesolithic etc.

8 Monmouthshire Gazetteer

8.1 Mesolithic Sites
    Lithic Finds: MM 1-13   86
8.2 Neolithic Sites
    Chambered Tombs: BN 1-MN 1   87
    Axes: MN 2-13   87
    Lithic Finds: MN 14-25   87
8.3 Bronze Age Sites
    Round Cairns and Barrows: MB 1-27   89
    Stone Circles and Ring-Cairns: MB 28-29   90
    Dykes: MB 30   91
    Standing Stones: MB 31-36   91
    Metalwork: MB 37-45   91
    Lithic Finds: MB 46-58   92

8.4 Iron Age Sites
    Hill-forts: MI 1-7   93
    Smaller Defended Settlements: MI 8-10   93
    Stray Finds: MI 11-14   94

8.1 Mesolithic Sites (MM 1-13, Figs. 3, 4)

MM1, Llanbedr Ystradwy (not on SMR) NGR: SO 2236 2771
From Penmaen Hir - a Mesolithic or Earlier Neolithic flint blade. National Museum of Wales acc. no. 83.51H.

MM2, Crucorney Fawr (SMR 06183G) NGR: SO 2740 2680
On Bâl Bach - a retouched flint flake, possibly Mesolithic.

MM3, Crucorney Fawr (SMR 02298G; NMR SO 22 NE 18) NGR: SO 273 263
From the Ffawyddog Ridge S of Bâl Bach - flint flakes, including a micro-core and a burnt flake (Palmer and Tucker 1978, 40).

MM4, Crucorney Fawr (SMR 06184G) NGR: SO 2801 2579
At Garn Wen - fourteen pieces of burnt flint, three pieces of waste brown flint and one Mesolithic point with ventral retouch.

MM5, Crucorney Fawr, (not on SMR) NGR: SO 314 250
From Hatterall Hill - six flakes, a scraper fragment and an exhausted core from the footpath. Also a microlith from SO 313 251 (Dorling 1991, 21).

MM6, Llantilio Pertholey (SMR 03634G; NMR SO 31 NW 31) NGR: SO 317 194
At Blaengavenny - three Mesolithic flakes and a fragmentary blade found in ploughsoil (Palmer 1980, 33).

MM7, Llantilio Pertholey (SMR 03637G; NMR SO 31 NW 32) NGR: SO 336 183
The debitage among the Skirrid Fawr assemblage (see MN 21 and MB 30 below) included 12 cores some possibly Mesolithic (Palmer and Jones 1980, 34).

MM8, Llantilio Crossenny (SMR 05636G) NGR: SO 3915 1785
A core trimming from near the find spot of a Mesolithic macehead (Makepeace 1997, 58) found in a stream near to Little Berth-Glyd Farm, Llantilio Crossenny . Abergavenny Museum acc. no. A.20.1961.

MM 9, Abergavenny (SMR 03277G) NGR: SO 2987 1417
Mesolithic material found during excavations at Flannel Street 1962-1969 - four minute blades, six coarser blades, two cores and a grey chert flake - represented a microlithic chipping floor (Probert et al. 1968-69, 170-73) which, taken together with Later Neolithic and Early Bronze Age finds, demonstrated the chronological depth of the prehistoric use of the site (Gibson 1995, 30).

MM 10, Llanfoist Fawr (not on SMR) NGR: SO 2730 1970
From near a denuded cairn base on the northern face of the Sugar Loaf - six Mesolithic flint flakes and a blade (Palmer 1980, 33). See MB 8.

MM 11, Crucorney Fawr (SMR 03633G; NMR SO 32 SW 37) NGR: SO 318 217
Found on recently cleared scrub on the Llwygy - ten Mesolithic flakes and a possible Earlier Neolithic serrated blade (Palmer 1980, 33). See MN 19.

For the sake of completeness, other Mesolithic find spots within the county, but outside the scope of this study, include:

MM 12, Llanbadoc Fawr (not on SMR) NGR: SO 3610 0070
From Cefn Ila - surface finds of two unretouched blades and flakes and one microlith. The site also produced much Neolithic and Bronze Age flint. In the D. P. Webley Collection (Wymer 1977, 202).

MM 13, Usk NGR: (not on SMR) NGR: SO 3780 0050
Found during excavations on the Roman fort of Burrium sealed below Roman features - a number of cores, unretouched blades and flakes, microliths and other flint fragments. Now in the National Museum of Wales (donated by Monmouth District Council (Wymer 1977, 202).

8.2 Neolithic Sites (MN 1-25)

Chambered Tombs (BN1, MN1, Fig. 7)

BN 1, Llanigon/Hay Rural (not on SMR) NGR: SO 2414 3810 (Fig. 14)
A previously unrecorded long cairn at Maes Coch-Twyn y Beddau below Hay Bluff. The trapezoidal cairn measures 29.5m in length, 1.5m in height at its higher SW end and 14.5m at its widest narrowing to approx. 6m at its tail. The cairn is aligned SW-NE and is undisturbed and in excellent preservation.

MN 1, Llanelli (SMR 1958G) NGR: SO 2469 1561
Battle Tump - a possible long cairn some 57.5m long with a maximum width of 30.5m and maximum height of 4.6m. The site is situated on the flat valley bottom and is aligned NW-SE along the valley. The site has also been described as a glacial kame or drumlin.

Axes (MN 2-13, Figs. 9, 10)

MN 2, Llanelieu (NMR SO 22 NW 1) NGR: SO 230 287
Found on a rock floor in cutting through peat containing oak and birch, approx. 300m SE of summit of Y Gadair - a chert plano-convex adze, blunt butt (125mm x 55.5mm x 34.5mm), National Museum of Wales acc. no. 35.482 (Grimes 1951, 148).

MN 3, Crucorney Fawr (not on SMR) NGR: SO 340 223
From Penbidwal - a fragment of a Graig Lwyd Group VII polished stone axe. In private hands (Clough and Cummins 1988, 252).

MN 4, Crucorney Fawr (not on SMR) NGR: SO 324 208
Found in a wall at Nant-y-felin, Llanfihangel Crucorney - a polished stone axe (10 x 5.6 cm) with a flattened oval section. The shape and form is comparatively rare for Wales being short and plump and is probably early in date. The rock is an acid tuff of Welsh origin although the location of its source is uncertain (Clough and Cummins 1988, 252). Abergavenny Museum acc. no. A.12.1965.

MN 5, Crucorney Fawr/Llantilio Pertholey (SMR 03840G) NGR: SO 3107 1928
Found at Llwyn Gwyn on the site of a levelled section of the Llanfihangel tramroad - a Group VIII polished axe (L 138mm, W 52mm, T 25mm). National Museum of Wales acc. no. 81.109H (CBA: M17).

MN6, Crucorney Fawr (not on SMR) NGR: SO 339 190
Found in a field at the rear of Pen-y-Parc Farmhouse, Llanfihangel Crucorney - a Group VIII flaked stone axe, possibly a "rough-out". Some retouch and polishing near the blade (Clough and Cummins 1988, 252). Abergavenny Museum acc. no. AL.5.1964.

MN 7, Grosmont Fawr (SMR 03240G; NMR SO 31 NE 40) NGR: SO 3666 1844
Found on the W bank of the Full Brook in 1963 - a polished quartzite axe (L 146mm, W 61mm, T 37mm). Now in Newport Museum - acc. no. 71.268 (*Mon. Antiq.* 1, 127).

MN8, Llanofer Fawr (NMR SO 31 SW 30) NGR: SO 338 118
From Tre Saeson, Llanddewi Rhydderch - a Group VIII polished stone axe, blunt butt, pointed oval section (140mm x 71m x 37mm), National Museum of Wales acc. no. 20.11 (Grimes 1951, 143-4; Clough and Cummins 1988, 252).)

MN 9, Llantilio Pertholey (SMR 03975G) NGR: 3117 1626
From the garden of Glebe Cottage - a polished stone axe. The blade (13 x 5.6 cm) is thin and the rock from which it has been made is either a fine-grained siliceous mudstone or possibly a fine grained basic igneous rock. Abergavenny Museum acc. no. A.336.1984.

MN 10, Abergavenny (not on SMR) NGR: SO 2910 1445
From the garden of 10 Hatherleigh Road, Abergavenny - a broken polished stone axe (7.4 x 6.8 cm). Abergavenny Museum acc. no. A.76.1988.

MN 11, Llanelli (SMR 03212G; NMR SO 21 SW 25) NGR: SO 24 14
Found "in a new housing estate" - a small, reworked, partially polished axe head (Savory 1971, 7-8).

MN 12, Llanelli (SMR 03211G; SO 21 SW 24) NGR: SO 23 14
Found in 1909 - a chert axe, flaked all over, thin butt (butt itself missing) pointed oval section (126mm x 57mm x 17mm). National Museum of Wales acc. no. 30.340.I (Grimes 1951, 145).

MN 13, Llangenny (not on SMR) NGR: SO 24 17
From Upper Paper Mill - a hoard of four axes - one of polished grey flint from S England, thin butt, pointed oval section (124mm x 67mm x 38mm), three of grey argillite, ground and polished, thin butt, flattened oval section (137mm x 64mm x 31mm; 131mm x 63mm x 28mm; 102mm x 56mm x 26mm) National Museum of Wales acc. no. 18.152.1-4 (Grimes 1951, 149).

Lithic Finds (MN 14-25, Fig. 8)

MN 14, Crucorney Fawr (not on SMR) NGR: SO 247 286
From west of the footbridge at the bottom of Cwm Trethiw, only two flints have been found here, a Later Neolithic scraper and an Earlier Bronze Age slug knife. The Ken Palmer Collection - catalogue and drawings at Abergavenny Museum.

MN 15, Crucorney Fawr (not on SMR) NGR: SO 265 262
On the open mountain on the southern slopes of B□l Mawr. Diagnostic tools include an Earlier Neolithic knife and two Later Neolithic scrapers. The rest of the collection includes 1 scraper, 1 blade, 1 awl and 10 flakes. The Ken Palmer Collection - catalogue and drawings at Abergavenny Museum.

MN 16, Crucorney Fawr (not on SMR) NGR: SO 254 274
To the north-west of Tŷ Isaf Farm, this site has produced twenty pieces of flint the majority of which are of a bluish type. The collection includes two Earlier Neolithic cores and one Earlier Bronze Age thumbnail scraper. The rest of the

collection is comprised of two cores, 11 flakes, 1 notched flake, 2 core rejuvenation flakes and 1 chipped nodule. The Ken Palmer Collection - catalogue and drawings at Abergavenny Museum.

MN 17, Crucorney Fawr (SMR 02300G; SO 32 SW 32) NGR: SO 308 260 to 315 239
Found on the footpath on Hatterall Hill between these two points - over 40 flint artefacts and flakes including a broken leaf-shaped arrowhead, a knife and utilised flakes and two burnt flakes (Jones, Palmer and Tucker 1978, 40).

MN 18, Crucorney Fawr (SMR 02315G; NMR SO 32 NW 14) NGR: SO 313 253
On the crest of Hatterall Hill near the footpath - five flint flakes including a Neolithic scraper, and snapped Neolithic blade of trapezoidal section with heavy marginal retouch. Now at National Museum of Wales (Dunn 1970, 12).

MN 19, Crucorney Fawr (SMR 03633G; NMR SO 32 SW 37) NGR: SO 318 217
Found on recently cleared scrub on the Llwygy - a possible Earlier Neolithic serrated blade. The site also produced ten Mesolithic flakes (Palmer 1980, 33).

MN 20, Llantilio Pertholey (SMR 03635G; NMR SO 32 SW 36) NGR: SO 313 205
From Pen y Clawdd - a total of 34 flakes, tools, retouched flakes, representing 17% of the total assemblage, were found by Mr. J. Davies of Pen y Clawdd Court Farm on ploughed fields. They include 6 scrapers, one knife, two possible piercers, two core fragments, one core rejuvenation flake, one base of an arrowhead (or flake from a polished axe), a broken flint pebble and 20 flakes (Palmer 1980, 33). The other material in the assemblage represents stray finds from the slopes of Bryn Arw, the prominent hill immediately to the west of Pen y Clawdd Court.

The total assemblage (183 flints) is comprised of 39 scrapers, 9 blades, 5 blade fragments, 6 awls, 8 retouched flakes, 1 fabricator, 3 cores, 90 flakes, 4 core rejuvenation flakes, 8 chipped nodules, 1 broken flint pebble, 1 flint hammer stone and 8 pieces of burnt flint.

The diagnostic retouched tools in the collection which can be assigned to Earlier Neolithic traditions include two endscrapers (nos. 78 and 88), two narrow blades; one awl, three retouched flakes, one core and one flake. There are also two sub-circular scrapers of Later Neolithic date (nos. 14a and 15) and eight Earlier Bronze Age thumbnail scrapers. The Ken Palmer Collection - catalogue and drawings at Abergavenny Museum.

MN 21, Llantilio Pertholey (SMR 03637G; NMR SO 31 NW 32) NGR: SO 336 183
From Ysgyryd Fawr. There are 228 flints in the assemblage as a whole, of which 77% were discovered in two discrete scatters. A total of 132 flakes and tools picked up on two ploughed fields at c. 320m above OD. The retouched artefacts included the Later Neolithic oblique arrowhead described below, seven Early Bronze Age scrapers, two burnt fragments of bifacially flaked implements, two serrated pieces, one knife and 15 retouched/utilised blades and flakes. The debitage included 12 cores (some possibly Mesolithic), 6 core rejuvenation pieces, 80 flakes/blades/spalls and two struck pieces of greensand chert. Preliminary analysis was undertaken by Dr. S. H. Aldhouse Green Mrs. E. Henley of the National Museum of Wales.

A further 44 flakes and retouched fragments were subsequently found on an adjacent field. These include the transverse and leaf-shaped arrowheads described below, a scraper, a core, a core fragment and six blades (Palmer and Jones 1980, 34). The remainder were stray finds numbered by the finders in the order in which they were found with no reference to the exact site or of any associations between finds.

Within the collection as a whole, the diagnostic retouched tools of Earlier Neolithic date include scrapers, one core, two blades, a very fine ogival leaf-shaped arrowhead and a knife point. There is also a Later Neolithic transverse arrowhead, a Later Neolithic oblique arrowhead, an Earlier Bronze Age knife fragment and four Earlier Bronze Age thumbnail scrapers.

The rest of the collection includes three scrapers, 5 blades and a blade fragment, 3 awls, 11 retouched flakes, 7 cores, 141 flakes, 12 core rejuvenation flakes, 1 hammerstone, 8 chipped nodules and 21 pieces of burnt flint. The Ken Palmer Collection - catalogue and drawings at Abergavenny Museum.

MN 22, Llangattock Vibon Avel (SMR 03864G) NGR: SO 433 212
At Blackbrook - a Neolithic flint scatter (Darvill, T. *Monmouth Archaeology Group. Newsletter* **13**, 1; Clarke, S. *ibid.* **11**, 18; **14**, 2).

MN 23, Abergavenny (SMR 05989G) NGR: SO 2980 1330
From the Abergavenny Sewage works - Later Neolithic and Bronze Age flints.

MN 24, Abergavenny (SMR 03277G) NGR: SO 2987 1417
Found during excavations at Flannel Street 1962-1969 - four minute Mesolithic blades, six coarser blades including two with hinge fractures, two cores, a worked chert flake, two coarse Later Neolithic convex scrapers and an Earlier Bronze Age barbed and tanged arrowhead (Probert et al. 1968-69, 170-173). Also a sherd of Peterborough Ware (Gibson 1995, 30). Excavated prehistoric finds were found in the Roman and later levels and therefore were not stratified.

MN 25, Pen Allt Mawr (not on SMR) NGR: SO 206 250
From Pentwyn Glas - a Later Neolithic transverse flint arrow head. National Museum of Wales acc. no. 91.11H.

8.3 Bronze Age Sites (MB 1-58)

Round Cairns and Barrows (MB 1-27, Figs. 23, 29)

MB1, Crucorney Fawr (SMR 01753G; NMR SO 22 NE 7) NGR: SO 2759 2720 (Fig. 29)
At Cwm Bwchel - a badly damaged round cairn and cist. The mound (original diameter approx. 14.5m) has only partly survived on the N side and is only faintly visible on the other sides. Two side slabs of the cist still stand (internal dimensions 1.8m by 0.9m) aligned 65° magnetic (Jones 1978a, 40). The cairn stands on a SE facing shelf of Bâl Mawr and only has extensive views to the SE. It is not visible from the valley floor. Visited 16/03/99.

MB 2, Crucorney Fawr (SMR 01751G; NMR SO 22 NE 14a) NGR: SO 284 264 (Fig. 29)
Three cairns have been reported as visible in the immediate area of the Craig Ddu cairn (see MB 3 below) (Jones 1978b, 40). However, no evidence of these could be seen when the site was visited (16/03/99).

MB 3, Crucorney Fawr (SMR 01751G; NMR SO 22 NE 14b) NGR: SO 2845 2624 (Fig. 29)
At Craig Ddu - a round cairn (c. 15.5m in diameter and 1.5m in height) situated on a spur of the Ffawyddog Ridge. The cairn's central cist (1.56m by 0.8m internally) is described on the SMR as having been dug in antiquity. It was actually dug in 1980 and produced the rim of a large vessel with incised decoration, a barbed and tanged arrowhead, a few small particles of bone and some potsherds. There were no floor slabs (the original surface being brown boulder clay) and no capstone. Heather was removed from the cairn surface in order to examine the construction. This proved to be a random piling of sandstone boulders and there was no evidence of a kerb.

The published account of this episode of fossicking is very inadequate (Jones, Tucker and Palmer 1980, 35-36) but it seems likely that the cist contained the remains of .a collared urn and should be assigned to the Early Bronze Age c. 2050-1500 cal. B. C. (Needham's Periods 3 and 4). As far as is known, the finds have not been deposited with any public institution.

The cairn stands on a S facing shelf of Craig Ddu with extensive views to the S and SE over the Dyffryn Ewias. It is intervisible with the large cairn at Garn Wen, but is not visible from the valley floor. Visited 16/03/99.

MB 4, Crucorney Fawr (SMR 06187G) NGR: SO 2801 2565 (Figs. 28, 29)
At Garn Wen - a small round cairn, approx. 8m in diameter and 0.5m high. Visited 16/03/99.

MB 5, Crucorney Fawr (SMR 01755G; NMR SO 22 NE 2a) NGR: SO 2806 2561 (Figs. 28, 29)
At Garn Wen - a heather-covered round mound, probably a cairn, though no surface stone is visible. It is approx. 12m in diameter and 0.8m in height. Visited 16/03/99.

MB 6, Crucorney Fawr (SMR 01754G; NMR SO 22 NE 2) NGR: SO 2802 2553 (Figs. 28, 29)
At Garn Wen - a large, partly heather-covered round cairn, approx. 27m in diameter and standing to a height of some 2m on the W side. A small circular drystone "turret" (SMR) has been built on its top.

MB 7, Crucorney Fawr (not on SMR) NGR: SO 2787 2495 (Figs. 28, 29)
On Garn Wen approx. 265m SW (205°) of the Garn Wen standing stone - a previously unrecorded small round cairn discovered by Mr. Aidan McCooey (16/03/99). The cairn is approximately 6.5m in diameter and 0.5m high to the S. The cairn is almost completely denuded on its N side and with a pit at the centre. Extensive views to S and SW.

MB 8, Llanfoist Fawr (NMR SO 21 NE 11) NGR: SO 2730 1970
A denuded cairn base on the northern face of the Sugarloaf. The site also produced Mesolithic flints (MM 10) (Palmer 1980, 33).

MB 9, Crucorney Fawr (SMR 02303G, PRN 2989, NMR SO 22 NE 20) NGR: SO 289 297 (Fig. 29)
W of Black Darren - a large cairn with a cist at its centre. A recumbent stone lies nearby (Jones 1976b, 25).

MB 10, Crucorney Fawr (PRN 4712) NGR: SO 2895 2950 (Fig. 29)
On Loxidge Tump - a small, neat cairn (3.50m dia. x 0.50m high) in area of heather free grassland on Loxidge Tump, cairn itself is bilberry covered. Constructed of "large-ish" (>0.40m length) (*sic*) stones.

MB 11, Crucorney Fawr (SMR 01748G, PRN 3012, NMR SO 22 NE 8) NGR: SO 2887 2922 (Fig. 29)
On Loxidge Tump approx. 1.4km N of Llanthony Priory and 570m above OD - a small grass-covered cairn, approx. 6.5m in diameter and 0.7m high. The centre appears to have been robbed out. Both Jones (1978c, 40) and the SMR record the presence of a residual kerb, though this was not visible when the site was visited (11/01/99).

MB 12, Crucorney Fawr (SMR 03081G, PRN 3027, SO 22 NE 9) NGR: SO 2933 2943 (Fig. 29)
On Loxidge Tump - a cairn some 16.5m in diameter and 1.0m high with an exposed cist slightly north of the centre. The cist is 1.5m long, 0.5m wide and 0.3m deep, stands in the body of the cairn above ground level and is oriented NE-SW. Two sheep shelters have been built into the cairn (Lillie 1991, 56).

MB 13, Crucorney Fawr (SMR 03081G/PRN 3027) NGR: SO 2934 2937 (Fig. 29)
On Loxidge Tump - a large (approx. 20m in diameter and 1.5m high) prominent round cairn with outstanding views to the NE especially of the Black Hill and Olchon valley. A circular shelter some 6m in diameter has been erected on top of the cairn. Visited 02/02/99.

MB 14, Crucorney Fawr (not on SMR, PRN 3013) NGR: SO 297 288 (Fig. 29)
E of the footpath on Hatterall Ridge - a grassed-over cairn, 10m in diameter with a 1m wide depression at its centre (Jones 1978d, 40).

MB 15, Crucorney Fawr (not on SMR) NGR: SO 302 282 (Fig. 29)

A grass-covered mound 7m to the E of the footpath on Hatterall Ridge (Jones and Palmer 1983, 24).

MB 16, Crucorney Fawr (not on SMR) NGR: SO 3065 2720 (Fig. 29)
On Hatterall Ridge adjacent to and W of the Offa's Dyke footpath- a previously unrecorded round cairn approx. 9m in diameter. Outstanding views in all directions except N and S along the ridge. Discovered 02/02/99.

MB 17, Crucorney Fawr (not on SMR) NGR: SO 3075 2685 (Fig. 29)
On Hatterall Ridge - a previously unrecorded round cairn approx. 17m by 10m transected on its E side by the Offa's Dyke footpath. Outstanding views in all direction except directly along the ridge to N and S. Discovered 02/02/99.

MB 18, Crucorney Fawr, (not on SMR, PRN 3970) NGR: SO 307 267 (Fig. 29)
On Hatterall Ridge - a small round cairn, approx. 2.0m in diameter and 0.3m high, with an internal kerb of orthostats, exposed by erosion in the centre of the Offa's Dyke footpath (Dorling 1990, 52).

MB 19, Crucorney Fawr (PRN 4549) NGR: SO 3091 2573 (Fig. 29)
On Hatterall Hill - an irregular mound (10.0m diameter 0.40m high) some stone visible in the surface, heather cover obscures the exact form.

MB 20, Crucorney Fawr (SMR 01600G, PRN 3000) NGR: SO 3076 2554 (Figs. 27, 29)
About 50m W of the ring-cairn (MB 29) on Hatterall Hill, stands a small cairn (12m diameter) and some 600m to the SW a large reeve-like rubble cross dyke bank (approx. 15m wide and 1.5m in height) cuts across the promontory of the N arm of Hatterall Hill.

MB 21, Crucorney Fawr (not on SMR) NGR: SO 3163 2446 (Fig. 29)
On Hatterall Hill - a previously unrecorded pair of small round cairns (both approx. 5.5m in diameter and 0.5m high) adjacent to and E of the Offa's Dyke footpath. Outstanding views in all directions except to the N along the ridge. Discovered 02/02/99.

MB 22, Crucorney Fawr (PRN 4567) NGR: SO 3157 2370
On Hatterall Hill - a roughly circular grass and heather-grown mound (8.0m dia. x 0.3m h). Two small stones visible.

MB 23, Grosmont (not on SMR) NGR: SO 413 202
NE of Cross Ash - a large grass-covered mound at the upper margin of a field (Jones 1981, 30).

MB 24, Abergavenny (not on SMR) NGR: SO 3045 1323
"The Recollections of Abergavenny by an Octogenarian", published in the Abergavenny Chronicle in about 1884 records the early 19th century discovery of a cist inhumation at Ysbyty Farm on the southern outskirts of the town:

John Price, who then kept the Foresters' Arms in Tudor-street, and who worked on the roads, while engaged in obtaining gravel in the Spitty (sic)

gravel pit, came upon a kind of rude stone coffin, and on removing the stone slab which covered it, the skeleton of a man in a good state of preservation was disclosed to view. The edges of the coffin consisted of paving slabs placed on edge, the bottom being made of large stones, and the whole indicating that some troubled care had been taken in making the arrangements.

In local trade directories, John Price is recorded as the landlord of the Foresters' Arms between 1853 and 1865.

MB 25a and b, Llanfoist Fawr (NMR SO 20 NE 7) NGR: SO 2706 0997
Carn y Defaid South (MB 25a) stands at NGR: SO 2706 0997, c. 485m above OD on a false crest. It is a large, conical cairn (11m in diameter, 0.9m in height uphill and 1.5m downhill) with a central crater.
Carn y Defaid North (MB 25b) stands on the same ridge some 30m NE of MB 25a at NGR: SO 2708 1003, c. 490 m above OD on a false crest. It is a large, conical cairn (13m in diameter, 1.2m in height) also with a central crater.

MB 26, Llanfoist Fawr (NMR SO 21 NE 13) NGR: SO 2698 1185
On the summit of the Blorenge - a round cairn which the NMR dubs Carn Blorenge South. It stands at NGR: SO 2698 1185, c. 555m above OD with wide views in all directions. It is a large, conical mound (14.5m in diameter and 1.8m in height) crowned by two pyramid-shaped piles of stones. A cist is visible some 3.0m from the NE edge of the cairn, aligned NW-SE, 1.4m long x 0.7m wide x 0.9m deep. The displaced capstone measures some 1.5m long x 1.1m wide x 0.3m thick. The cairn was opened in 1873 but no details are recorded.

MB27, Llanfoist Fawr (NMR SO 21 NE 10) NGR: SO 2735 1226
On the NE edge of the summit of the Blorenge in an extensive limestone exposure some 500m NE of MB 26 at c. 555m above OD - a small round cairn (5.5m in diameter) which the NMR refers to as Carn Blorenge North.

Stone Circles and Ring-Cairns (MB 28-29, Fig. 26)

MB 28, Crucorney Fawr (SMR 01752G; NMR SO 22 NE 5) NGR: SO 2807 2545 (Fig. 28)
Some 90m SE (150°) of the Garn Wen cairn - four large, earthfast stones in an arc NE-SE with an overall length of some 29.5m. This site has been described as a possible stone circle and stone alignment (Jones 1972, 18) and would form an open circle some 50m in diameter. Visited and surveyed 21/01/00.

MB 29, Crucorney Fawr (SMR 01600G) NGR: SO 3076 2554 (Fig. 27)
At Garreg Las on Hatterall Hill some 525m above OD - a large ring-cairn, 57m in diameter consisting of a rubble bank some 7m wide and standing to an average height of approx. .75m. The entrance at the E is overlain by a small modern cairn (3m diameter) and there is a smaller, irregular ring-cairn approx. 17m in overall diameter some 50m to the SE. The enclosure has no visible ditch and has panoramic views

in every direction except E and NE. Visited 13/3/98, surveyed 2/2/99.

About 50m SW of the enclosure stands a small cairn (12m diameter) and some 600m to the SW a large reeve-like rubble cross dyke bank (approx. 15m wide and 1.5m in height) cuts across the promontory of the N arm of Hatterall Hill.

Dykes (MB 30, Fig. 26)

MB 30, Crucorney Fawr (SMR 04513G) NGR: SO 3029 2520 to 3038 2510 (Fig. 27)
On the N arm of Hatterall Hill - a massive drystone cross-dyke approx. 6.0-8.0m wide which terminates at NW and SE at the edge of a very steep natural slope. The dyke incorporates a natural scarp approx. 1-1.5m high but has no visible ditch. This is of similar construction to the ring-cairn and may be contemporary (APs 106G UK 1652 2075-2077 7/1946 and 540/42 5177-5179 5/1948).

Standing Stones (MB 31-36, Fig. 26)

MB 31, Crucorney Fawr (SMR 03214G, NMR 22 NE 15) NGR: SO 2796 2518 (Fig. 28)
An isolated standing stone some 350m SSW of the Garn Wen cairn, discovered in 1976 (Jones 1976a, 17). The published NGR (SO 278 252) is inaccurate. The stone is 90cm high at its highest (northern) point and is aligned NW-SE (300°). The stone is roughly rectangular in section some 60cm long by 45cm wide along its NW face, narrowing to 30cm at the SE.

MB 32, Crucorney Fawr (not on SMR, PRN 3029) NGR: SO 3061 2602 (Fig. 29)
On the N slope of Hatterall Hill - a large upright stone c. 1.0m in height (Jones 1976c, 25).

MB 33, Crucorney Fawr (PRN 4650) NGR: SO 3039 2550 (Fig. 29)
Upright stone (0.90m long x 0.20m wide x 1.10m high) possibly natural but looking set, it is on a natural route (desire line) along the hillslope and may be route marker.

MB 34, Crucorney Fawr (PRN 4651) NGR: SO 2987 2500 (Fig. 29)
Small, single, edge-set stone (0.36m long x 0.06m wide x 0.30m high) possibly boundary marker, possibly path route marker on mid slope path/desire line.

MB 35, Llanddewi Ysgyryd (not on SMR) NGR: SO 344 156
The former presence of a standing stone at Parsonage Farm is indicated by the "Maen Llwyd" marked on the 1956 OS 1: 25000 map.

MB 36, Llanelli/Llanfoist Fawr (NMR SO 21 SW9) NGR: SO 2382 1133
On the boundary of the historical ecclesiastical parishes of Llanelli and Llanwenarth and the modern communities of Llanelli, Llanfoist Fawr and Blaenafon - the Carreg Maen Taro standing stone.

MB 36a, Crucorney Fawr (NMR SO 22 NE 22) NGR: SO 260 276
NW of Bâl Mawr - a roughly shaped vertical orthostat, c. 1.0m in height (Jones 1980, 20).

Metalwork (MB 37-45, Fig. 30)

MB 37, Crucorney Fawr (NMR SO 22 NW 6) SO 247 252
On the upper reaches of Cwm Ddeunant - an Early Bronze Age haft-flanged axe ploughed up during forestry work in 1968 (Savory 1980a, 102, 166). Assigned by Savory to the end of his Early Bronze Age III c. 1450 B. C. (1980a, 45) - now Needham's Early Bronze Age (Period 3) c. 1700 cal. B. C.

MB 38, Crucorney Fawr (SMR 01742G, NMR SO 22 NE 3) NGR: SO 2885 2785
From near Llanthony Priory - a Late Bronze Age (Needham's Period 7 c. 950-750 cal. B. C.) Llantwit-Stogursey looped, socketed axe with three converging ribs on each face. Now in the National Museum of Wales, acc. no. 20.358 (Grimes, 1951, 249; Savory 1980a, 49, 109, *103)

MB 39, Llantilio Pertholey (SMR 04925G) NGR: SO 311 196
Acton Park shield pattern palstave, now assigned to the second half of the Early Bronze Age (i.e. Needham's Period 4) c. 1700-1500 cal. B. C. Found during ploughing at Blaengavenny Farm. It appears to have been lost or buried without ever being used. There is some recent damage to the blade. On fieldwalking the site a number of unworked flint flakes were found. Now in Abergavenny Museum (loan: Mr. P. Jones) (Burns 1995, 44-45).

MB 40, Llantilio Pertholey (not on SMR) no NGR cited
An Early Bronze Age flint scraper (90.57) and a hoard of six Late Bronze Age (Needham's Period 7, c. 950-750 cal. B. C.) socketed axes (90.2). A hoard of other Late Bronze Age metalwork (MB 41) was also discovered here (Trett and Hudson 1989, 48) and replicas are now in Newport Museum (Trett and Hudson 1990, 53). A Late Bronze Age gouge (91.72) additional to the hoard found at the same location. Now in Newport Museum (Trett and Hudson 1991, 22).

MB 41, Llantilio Pertholey (not on SMR) exact location confidential
A Late Bronze Age (Needham's Period 7, c. 950-750 cal B.C) hoard consisting of two South Wales socketed axes, one plain socketed axe, one socketed spear (deliberately broken into two pieces), one fragment of a pegged socketed spear blade typical of the Llantwit-Stogursey tradition (Burgess 1980, 272) and the tip of a rapier blade. In private hands, replicas at Newport Museum (Trett and Hudson 1989, 48).

MB 42, Llantilio Crossenny (SMR 02289G/03315G, NMR SO 41 NW 28) NGR: SO 40 15
Found near the park gate at Llantilio Court, Llantilio Crossenny - a fragmentary Late Bronze Age (Needham's Period 7, c. 950-750 cal. B. C.) Llantwit-Stogursey leaf-shaped riveted spearhead. National Museum of Wales acc. no. 26.3 (Grimes 1951, 182; Savory 1980a, 51, 112).

MB 43, Llanarth (SMR 03247G, NMR SO 31 SE 46) NGR: SO 387 114
From a deep drain, 300m E of Tŷ Newydd. A rare, imported Late Bronze Age three ribbed socketed axe not belonging to South Welsh, Yorkshire or Irish types, c. 8th-4th centuries B. C. (Burgess 1963, 22). See also HB 54.

MB 44, Llanofer Fawr (SMR 01360G, NMR SO 31 SW 31) NGR: SO 3480 1310
From Church farm, Llanddewi Rhydderch - a hoard of twelve Late Bronze Age (Needham's Period 7, c. 950-750 cal. B. C.) Llantwit-Stogursey socketed axes ploughed up in 1902. Two are now in the National Museum of Wales - acc. no. 20.528.1-2 (Grimes 1951, 187; Savory 1980a, 40, 120, 189*). Interpreted as a founder's hoard (Stanford 1991, 31).

MB 45, Llanfoist Fawr (not on SMR/NMR) SO 280 120
Found along with two others in the roots of a tree on the Tramroad incline at Glebe Wood, Llanfoist - a Late Bronze Age (Needham's Period 7, c. 950-750 cal. B. C.) Llantwit-Stogursey socketed axe with 3-rib decoration. Now in Abergavenny Museum acc. no. A.3.1959.

Lithic Finds (MB 46-58, Fig. 19)

MB 46, Crucorney Fawr (not on SMR) NGR: SO 254 274
One Earlier Bronze Age thumbnail scraper. The site also produced Neolithic material (see MN 16 above).

MB 47, Crucorney Fawr (not on SMR) NGR: SO 247 286
West of the footbridge at the bottom of Cwm Trethiw, an Earlier Bronze Age slug knife. The site also produced a Later Neolithic scraper (see MN 14 above).

MB 48, Crucorney Fawr (not on SMR) NGR: SO 257 284
A ploughed forestry area to the east of Blaen y Cwm Farm and sometimes referred to as the "Eithon" which produced 1 large worked flake of high quality flint which may be a crude Earlier Bronze Age knife. The Ken Palmer Collection - catalogue and drawings at Abergavenny Museum.

MB 49, Crucorney Fawr (not on SMR) NGR: SO 255 281
South-east of Blaen y Cwm Farm - an Early Bronze Age plano-convex knife, found here during the cutting of a roadway in 1970 and now in the possession of Abergavenny Museum (acc. no. A.17.1970) (Burns 1995, no. 12).

MB 50, Crucorney Fawr (not on SMR) NGR: SO 3130 2545
A barbed and tanged flint arrowhead and a flint scraper washed out of peat at the edge of the Offa's Dyke footpath on Hatterall Hill (Dorling 1990, 52).

MB 51, Crucorney Fawr (SMR 03828G) NGR: SO 3124
S of Hatterall Hill - a surface stray find of a barbed and tanged flint arrowhead, two scrapers, a broken blade and twenty other flint and chert artefacts and flakes found at the same site as an Iron Age bead (see below) (Jones and Palmer 1992, 49).

MB 52, Llantilio Pertholey (SMR 03635G) NGR: SO 313 205
From Pen y Clawdd - eight Earlier Bronze Age thumbnail

scrapers. The site also produced Neolithic material (see MN 20).

MB 53, Llantilio Pertholey (SMR 03637G) NGR: SO 336 183
From Skirrid Fawr - an Earlier Bronze Age knife fragment and four Earlier Bronze Age thumbnail scrapers. The site also produced Neolithic material (see MN 21).

MB 54, Llanfoist Fawr (SMR 03636G) NGR: SO 2730 1870
From near a denuded cairn base at the southern end of the Sugar Loaf - six flint flakes and a blade (Palmer 1980, 33).

MB 55, Llangenny (SMR 05641G) NGR: SO 2400 1820
At Llangenny - one small thumb scraper, one broken blade with retouch along one edge, one broken blade with retouch along both sides.

MB 56, Abergavenny (SMR 05635G) NGR: SO 271 165
On the Sugarloaf - small thumb scraper, a broken point with secondary retouch on one side and a waste chip (Makepeace 1997, 57).

MB 57, Abergavenny (03277G) NGR: SO 2987 1417
Found during excavations at on the site of the Roman fort of *Gobannium* at Flannel Street 1962-1969 (Probert et al. 1968-69, 17-173) - a barbed and tanged arrowhead (Abergavenny Museum acc. no. A.312.0). The site also produced Mesolithic and Neolithic material.

MB 58, Llanfoist Fawr (SMR 03974G) NGR: SO 298 133
At Abergavenny Sewage Works - six flints found during the construction of the works including a petit tranchet derivative arrowhead. The site also produced Neolithic material.

8.4 Iron Age Sites (MI 1-14, Fig. 33)

Hill-forts (MI 1-7)

MI 1, Crucorney Fawr (SMR 01607G, PRN 2905, NMR SO 32 SW 6) NGR: SO 3211 2303 (Fig. 38)
Pentwyn hill-fort (2.8ha) on the southern end of Hatterall Hill at 332m above OD - a large rectilinear hill-fort with extensive views over Herefordshire to the E and the ridges of the Black Mountains to the W. The rectangular enclosure to the N with its massive N rampart and ditch is probably the earliest phase. The later southern defences are multivallate with an elaborate SE entrance with a projecting hornwork matched by a high knoll (a fighting platform or bastion) on the main southern rampart. There are superficial similarities between Pentwyn and the better studied Twyn y Gaer and the two sites may share similar histories (Whittle 1992, 42).

MI 2, Crucorney Fawr (SMR 01713G, NMR SO 22 SE 5) NGR: SO 2940 2195 (Fig. 37)
Twyn y Gaer hill-fort (1.8ha) occupies a knoll at the S end of the Ffawyddog Ridge at 426m above OD with spectacular views in all directions. The site is intervisible with Pentwyn to the E and Crug Hywel to the W. A bank, rock-cut ditch and counterscarp enclose a roughly elliptical area. Two internal cross banks with eastern ditches divide the interior into three areas. A well-preserved inturned entrance guards the eastern approach. To the W, the defences are bi-vallate. Twyn y Gaer (MIA 2) is divided into three enclosures (A of 0.5ha, B of 0.3ha and C of 0.9ha) by univallate cross-banks and ditches. The W end of the fort, where the final approach is more gradual is bi-vallate. The earthworks rarely stand more than 1m in height and are diminutive compared with the Herefordshire forts. Originally the ramparts were faced with dry-stone revetments topped, in the latest phase (see below) by a stone rampart-walk (Probert 1976, 107).

Excavations in the 1960s (Probert 1976) proved that the main rampart was drystone revetted with, in its later phases, a stone-built rampart-walk along the top. The site's first phase consisted of the area enclosed by the central cross-bank. The eastern area, enclosed by fencing, probably acted as an annexe serving as an animal pen. There is a radiocarbon date of c. 400 B.C. for the end of this phase. In the next development, the eastern area was brought within the defensive circuit and the east gate constructed with a gateway at its inner end. In its final phase, the fort contracted to the area enclosed by the western cross-bank (Whittle 1992, 43).

Hut platforms and the range of domestic objects produced by the excavations show the fort to have been permanently occupied. The evidence indicates a mixed economy, with querns, and evidence of iron working. The cultural affinities of the earlier phases are with the hill-forts of mid-Wales and Herefordshire. In the last phase, the material culture was heavily influenced by the Silures to the S (Probert 1976, 105-119; Whittle 1992, 43-44).

MI 3, Llantilio Pertholey (SMR 01497G) NGR: SO 331 183 (Fig. 38)
Ysgyryd Fawr (Skirrid Fawr) Hill-fort. This long, prominent ridge is occupied by two hill-forts. The upper fort is a univallate contour fort some 21m by 90m surrounding the highest (western) summit of the hill. The defences follow the 475m contour. It takes advantage of the natural defence provided by the huge landslip which marks the western side of the hill, giving it both its characteristic outline and its name Ysgyryd Fawr ("The Big Broken Hill"). There is a simple, slightly inturned entrance at the S.

The lower fort is long and narrow (approx. 480m by 60m) with its univallate defences following the 450m contour line. There is a simple entrance at the southern extremity. At the southern end of the ridge is a prominent detached knoll which has undergone some modification to its sides and top. Between the knoll and the ridge itself is a double dyke and it seems reasonable to interpret both these and the knoll itself as part of the defensive system of the lower fort (Makespeace 1996, 66-68).

MI 4, Llantilio Pertholey/Abergavenny (SMR 04356G) NGR: SO 296 163 (Figs. 42-44)
On Twyn Yr Allt - a small (86m by 46m, approx. 0.39ha), sub-rectangular univallate Iron Age enclosure sited at 341m above OD on a prominent knoll at the southern end of the Deri ridge between the valleys of Afon Cybi and the Gafenni. To the S, W and E, the site is surrounded by the oak woodland which gives both the ridge (deri= "oak wood") and the knoll (twyn yr allt = "the knoll on the steep, wooded hill") their names.

At the S and SSE, where the slope of the hill falls steeply away to the valley floor, the defences consist only of an outward-facing dump-built scarp. To the NW, N and NE, where the slopes are considerably less precipitous, a low rampart survives to a height of approx. 0.5m. There is no ditch. Approx. 10% of the circuit has been destroyed by quarrying and virtually all of the interior of the enclosure has been disturbed by the same activity. A modern track breaches the defences at the N corner, but no original entrance can now be identified.

MI 5, Llanelli (SMR 01958G) NGR: SO 2248 1530
At Y Gaer - a small, univallate enclosure at 290m above OD covering 0.45ha and easily approached from all directions (RCAHMW 1986, 116-117).

MI 6, Llanelli (SMR 02499G) NGR: SO 2234 1326
Craig y Gaer hill-fort had good natural defences to the N and E but was weak elsewhere. Destroyed by quarrying (RCAHMW 1986, 115).

MI 7, Llanelli (SMR 02474G) NGR: SO 228 125
Twyn y Dinas hill-fort (not "Trwyn y Ddinas" as listed by the Royal Commission) stood on a prominent limestone spur with strong natural defences. All traces have been destroyed by quarrying (RCAHMW 1986, 115).

Smaller Defended Settlements (MI 8-10, Fig. 33)

MI 8, Llantilio Crossenny (not on SMR) NGR: SO 3805 1650 (Fig. 41)
Aerial photographs by John Sorrell show a possible Iron Age or Romano-British farmstead on White Castle Farm. A sub-circular enclosure approx. 75m in diameter with an entrance to the E. The remains of adjacent field systems and roadways have also been identified together with possible hut circles within the enclosure (Mein 1990, 52).

MI 9, Mitchell Troy United (NMR SO 41 SW 16) NGR: SO 4180 1035

Hedge removal near Tregaer church in 1989 revealed a curving, earthen bank and ditch with a marked outer counterscarp. The bank stands 0.6m in height from the bottom of the ditch and forms an enclosure concentric with the circular churchyard. The site is similar in size, aspect and elevation to Camp Hill at Bryngwyn (MI 10) and is probably of similar date and represents an Iron Age farmstead enclosure (Mein 1989, 48).

MI 10, Llanarth Fawr (NMR SO 30 NE 56) NGR: SO 391 078 (Fig. 40)

Camp Hill, Tir y Mynach Farm, Bryngwyn - a roughly circular enclosure some 90m in diameter with a possible entrance to the E. The site was partially excavated in 1962 and is thought to be an Early Iron Age A defended farmstead. The excavations traced a deep ditch and in the "fall" against the lip of the outer edge was found imitation Samian of late 2nd century A. D. - at a depth of about 30cm were sherds of 1st century A. D. pottery and a Roman black cooking pot with a curved lid (in three pieces) with a lattice pattern (Leslie 1962, 5). In 1962, the bank stood to a height of 1.2m from the bottom of the ditch. The site is now completely ploughed out.

Stray Finds (MI 11-14, Fig. 33)

MI 11, Crucorney Fawr (SMR 01741G, NMR SO 22 NE 4) NGR: SO 2885 2785

At Llanthony Priory - a Dobunnic gold stater of Corio. Now in the British Museum.

MI 12, Crucorney Fawr (SMR 03828G?) NGR: SO 3124

S of Hatterall Hill - a surface stray find of a small, dark blue glass bead of Iron Age date and similar to excavated examples from Twyn y Gaer. Also a barbed and tanged flint arrowhead, two scrapers, a broken blade and twenty other flint and chert artefacts and flakes (Jones and Palmer 1992, 49).

MI 13, Abergavenny (SMR 03277G) NGR: SO 2987 1417

Found during the Flannel Street excavations - a fragment of an Iron Age glass bead of 1st century A. D. but pre-Conquest date (Guido, P. pers. comm.). Original dimensions: diameter 17mm, height 8mm, perforation diameter 7mm. Abergavenny Museum small finds no. F166.

MI 14, Mitchel Troy United (NMR SO 41 SW 4) NGR: SO 4474 1106

From Old House Farm, Dingestow - a 1st century A. D. Dobunnic gold stater (BBCS 13 (1950), 113).

9 Herefordshire Gazetteer

9.1 Mesolithic Sites
    Lithic Finds: HM 1-23   96
9.2 Neolithic Sites
    Long Barrows and Cairns: HN 1-7   98
    Settlement Sites: HN 8-10   99
    Axes: HN 11-22   99
    Lithic Finds: HN 23-54   100
9.3 Bronze Age Sites
    Round Barrows and Cairns: HB 1-26   103
    Ring-ditches: HB 27-32   104
    Stone Circles and Ring-banks: HB 33-37   105
    Standing Stones: HB 38-42   105
    Settlement Sites: HB 43-46   106
    Metalwork: HB 47-56   106
    Lithic Finds: HB 57-79   107
9.4 Iron Age Sites
    Hill-forts: HI 1-7   109
    Smaller Defended Settlements: HI 8-11   109
    Stray Finds: HI 12-13   110
    Barrows: HI 14   110

9.1 Mesolithic Sites (HM 1-23, Figs. 3, 4)

HM 1, Cusop (not on SMR) NGR: SO 2400 4100
From 460m/500 yards ESE of Birches Farm - an hour-glass perforated pebble macehead (Shotton 1959; Wymer 1977, 124). Now in private hands.

HM 2, Bredwardine (SMR 12085) NGR: SO 3180 4320
From the opposite side of the road to Arthur's Stone - two undiagnostic flints found by A. E. Brown. The same site has also produced one unretouched Mesolithic blade/flake which is now in the W. R. Pye Collection (Wymer 1977, 124).

HM 3, Dorstone NGR: SO 3130 4360
From Merbach Hill - eleven unretouched blades and flakes and one microlith. Now in Hereford Museum (Wymer 1977, 124).

HM 4, Dorstone NGR: SO 3190 4310
From Arthur's Stone No. 2 - one microlith. Now in Hereford City Museum (Wymer 1977, 124).

HM 5, Dorstone (SMR 01547) NGR: SO 3250 4270
From Arthur's Stone Ridge - an obliquely blunted microlith point, broken at the top, with cloudy blue patination (Brown 1961, 80). Also from Bodcotte Farm (same NGR) - 17 unretouched blades and flakes, 2 microliths and 2 microburins. Now in Hereford City Museum (Wymer 1977, 124). See HN 29.

HM 6, Dorstone (SMR 01551/07179/07524) NGR: SO 3260 4230
Dorstone Hill Neolithic settlement - eleven Mesolithic flints from the main site indicate a Mesolithic or very Earlier Neolithic origin for the settlement. The assemblage includes a four microlithic blades three microlithic flakes (Pye 1958, 80, Fig. 3). In private hands (W. R. Pye Collection). See HN 8.

HM 7, Dorstone (SMR 00164) NGR: SO 2710 3900
From Cefn Hill, "Site A" (field no. Dorstone 1118)(Robinson 1946) - 1 scraper, 6 microliths and a number of other flints pieces. Now in Hereford City Museum (Wymer 1977, 124). These flints have been identified as Earlier Mesolithic (obliquely blunted points and isosceles triangles) which raises the possibility that exploitation of upland Wales began in the Earlier Mesolithic (Jacobi 1980, 193).

HM 8, Craswall (SMR 00162) NGR: 2715 3816
On Cefn Hill, Abbey Farm, Craswall (N of Craswall Priory) - a backed microlithic blade (Brown 1973, 116).

HM 9, Peterchurch (SMR 07597) NGR: SO 3030 3920
From Sawpit Wood - a Mesolithic core in the W. R. Pye Collection.

HM 10, Peterchurch (SMR 01538) NGR: SO 3090 4030
From Snodhill - a flint point.

HM 11, Peterchurch (SMR 08449) NGR: SO 3490 4090
From Woodbury Hill - a collection of Mesolithic flints now in Hereford City Museum (acc. no. 7172). More recent finds (not on the SMR) include a triangular backed microlith from SO 343 408 (Brown 1973, 116; Wymer 1977, 126).

HM 12, Peterchurch (SMR 01126) NGR: SO 3670 3880
From Stockley "Site 1" - one microlith. Now in Hereford City Museum (Wymer 1977, 126).

HM 13, Peterchurch (SMR 01514) NGR: SO 3510 3870
Near Wellbrook Farm - a microlithic blade with some cortex (Brown 1961, 78). Later material was also discovered in this field, together with a large number of chips, burnt flints and debitage.

HM 14, Peterchurch (SMR 01111) NGR: SO 3070 3770
From Robinson's "Pucha No. 1", Tanners Place, Michaelchurch Escley, field 220, 1,074 ft (326m) above OD (Robinson 1934, 61-2) - a grey microlithic blade with carefully trimmed back; a broken microlithic point trimmed along one edge with cloudy blue patina. The same field produced Neolithic material, together with chips, burnt flints and debitage (Brown 1961, 81).

HM 15, Michaelchurch Escley NGR: SO 3110 3710
From "Pentwyn 3" - a microburin. Now in Hereford City Museum (Wymer 1977, 125). See HN 34.

HM 16, Michaelchurch Escley (SMR 01116) NGR: SO 3100 3650
From Pentwyn - an unretouched blade or flake. Now in Hereford City Museum (Wymer 1977, 125). See HN 34.

HM 17, Turnastone (SMR 01109-10) NGR: SO 3430 3700
From Shegear Farm - one microlith. Now in Hereford City Museum (Brown 1962; Wymer 1977, 126). Although listed by Wymer under "Peterchurch/Vowchurch", Shegear Farm is actually in the parish of Turnastone. SMR 08476, 08477 and 08482 (SO 3440 3630) record flint tools and flakes site found here by R. S. G. Robinson (Hereford City Museum acc. no. 7172).

HM 18, Turnastone (SMR 01107) NGR: 3430 3650
From Cothill Farm - a scatter of flint flakes, chips and scrapers from the W edge and E central area of field 9 at 675ft (185m) above OD. Robinson's Site 20 (Robinson 1934, 62). Miss P. Wood, of Ladywell House, Vowchurch, also recovered a large number of flakes, cores, and scrapers from the east central area (Robinson 1934, 63). Wymer identified five of the flints as microliths, but the NGR he gives (SO 357 365) actually refers to Turnastone village - he seems to have been unaware of the original find-spot (Wymer 1977, 127). Now in Hereford City Museum.

HM 19, Dulas NGR: SO 3630 3050
From a barn at Middle Cefn Farm - an hour-glass perforated pebble macehead (Wymer 1977, 124). The implement shows signs of heavy wear but may have been used as a rick-weight in recent times. The circumstances of the find are unknown, but it is certainly local (Norwood 1963, 346; Fig. 1). Shotton identified the source of the stone as "probably Lake District" (*loc. cit.*). Hereford City Museum acc. no. 7804.

HM 20, Blakemere (SMR 07598) NGR: SO 3620 4020
Seven Mesolithic blades or flakes and one other worked piece. In the W. R. Pye Collection.

HM 21, Preston on Wye (SMR 01079) NGR: SO 3870 4150

From Lower Farm - a hourglass perforated stone now in Hereford City Museum (acc. no. 7069). This implement has been interpreted as an adziform pick and displays evidence of much use. The rock has been identified as coming from a source in north Wales, though not Group VII (Norwood 1959, 235; Fig. 6). The NGR given on the SMR (SO 3800 4100) is incorrect and should read SO 387 415.

HM 22, Vowchurch (SMR 01128/01532) NGR: SO 3720 3830

From Hill Farm - one microlith in Hereford City Museum Robinson Collection. Also forty unretouched blades and flakes and one microlith in the private collection of W. R. Pye (Wymer 1977, 127).

HM 23, Vowchurch (SMR 01513) NGR: SO 3690 3740
From Vowchurch Common - a Mesolithic blade.

9.2 Neolithic Sites (HN 1-54)

Long Barrows and Cairns (HN 1-7, Fig. 7)

Definite Sites

HN 1, Clifford (SMR 04202) NGR: SO 2765 4287 (Fig. 13)
Llannerch y Coed Farm, Clifford, at the southern edge of Newhouse Wood, c. 260m above OD - a small, wedge-shaped cairn some 1.0m in height, 10.5m long, 11.5m wide at its northern end, tapering to 5m wide at the south. A recent survey (Fig. 13) has demonstrated that the axis is almost exactly N-S, not E-W as stated by Nash (1997, 25). Dry stone walling is clearly visible in an area of damage at the northern end. This is Grinsell's "Clifford I" (1993, 306) and Children and Nash's "Bach Long Barrow" (1994, 26) but should more properly be referred to as "Mynydd Bach", the correct name of the hill on which it stands.

HN 2, Dorstone (SMR 01528) NGR: SO 3189 4312 (Fig. 13)
Arthur's Stone - a mound of indeterminate form, at present oval and some 26m x 20m x 1.9m high, axis NNW-SSE, c. 280m above OD, the internal structure consists of a short passage opening from the NW leading into an antechamber and a long polygonal chamber aligned NNW-SSE (Corcoran 1969, 288 HRF1; Hemp 1935). Grinsell's "Dorstone I" (1993, 307).

HN 3, Dorstone (SMR 01529) NGR: SO 3325 4168 (Fig. 16)
At various times over the past 30 years, this site has formed part of the property of Cross Lodge Farm, Great Llanavon Farm and, more recently, the Wilmaston Estate. This has led to a certain amount of confusion over its name and also to its being mistaken for HN 6 below. Accounts of the site have been published under the names "Great Llanavon" (Corcoran 1969, 288 HRF4 - where the NGR is incorrectly given as SO 3230 4170), "Dorstone II" (Grinsell, *loc. cit.*) and "Cross Lodge" (Children and Nash 1994, 27-8). The monument is a long mound, 18m x 11m x 2.4m high, E-W axis, c. 175m above OD and apparently undisturbed. In 1952, it was described as "a long barrow with some small stones visible". The farmer had attempted to level the mound but found it too stony after removing a few barrow loads. At the time, it was intended to dig "an exploratory trench" - though whether this was actually done is not clear (Cohen 1952, 31). Grinsell published a photograph of this site in mistake for his "Peterchurch i" (see HN 6). Visited 26/01/99.

HN 4, Abbey Dore (SMR 01504) NGR: SO 3911 3381
S of Dunseal Wood, Abbey Dore - a possible long barrow in excellent condition, 27m x 14m, oval in shape, built on a N-S axis and approx. 2m high at the north end, c. 189m above OD. This is Grinsell's "Abbeydore i" and, due to its position in a natural dip, he considered the site doubtful (Grinsell 1993, 306). However, the site is not in a dip and actually occupies the highest part of a prominent ridge with excellent views to the W towards Skirrid Fawr and the Black Mountains and to the S along Grey Valley towards Garway Hill. Dunseal and the Garway Hill barrow are intervisible. Visited 26/01/99.

HN 5, Garway (SMR 21669) NGR: SO 4395 2550 (Fig. 15)
Near the TV mast on Garway Hill, c. 335m above OD - a well-preserved oval long barrow, 30m long by 16m wide and 2m high at its highest (western) end, aligned W-E. The site enjoys outstanding views in all directions except the SW and commands all of the eastern Black Mountains from Dorstone Hill in the N to Skirrid Fawr in the W. Visited 26/01/99.

Doubtful and Destroyed Sites (HN 6-7)

HN 6, Peterchurch (SMR 08451) NGR: SO 3440 4140
On Woodbury Hill, Peterchurch – the SMR records a possible long barrow, 1.8m high, c. 287m above OD. This appears to be the barrow discovered by R. S. G. Robinson in 1936 (Robinson 1936, 49). This barrow is Grinsell's "Peterchurch i" - though the photograph he published of it under this name is actually of HN 3 - Great Llanavon-Cross Lodge (Grinsell 1993, 307; Plate XXII). The SMR records finds of undiagnostic flint in the vicinity (SMR 08450). The manager at the Wilmaston estate (which farms the land) informs me that the field recorded in the SMR as the site of this barrow is currently under cultivation and that no visible remains survive. Visited 26/01/99.

HN 7, St. Margarets (SMR 01492) NGR: SO 3565 3347
In Park Wood, St. Margarets, c. 210m above OD, the site of a possible long barrow. In 1854, there was "flat, horizontal slab of limestone like the upper stone of a cromlech" measuring some 27'6"x 9'6"x 2'6" thick (8.38m x 2.9m x 0.75m) (Crawford 1925, 149). The 1854 account goes on:

> *Half a century ago . . . it stood wholly free from the ground on certain upright stones . . .*

By 1921, the monument had entirely disappeared (*loc. cit.*; Corcoran 1969, 288 HRF2). Grinsell makes no reference to this barrow in his list and mistakenly applies its SMR number to Wergin's Stone (Grinsell 1993, 307). Any remains at this site have been totally destroyed by the existing forestry plantation. Visited 26/01/96.

Rejected Sites

Dorstone (SMR 13003) NGR: SO 3360 4160
At Cross Lodge Farm - the SMR records the remains of a possible long barrow about 150m NE of Cross Lodge farmhouse, c. 190m above OD. Not listed by Grinsell. When the site was visited (26/01/99), no visible remains of anything resembling a long borrow could be located except a clearance cairn in the S corner of the field immediately N of Cross Lodge.

Pipe and Lyde (SMR?) NGR: SO 5296 4397
The Wergins Stone - the remains a possible megalithic chamber (Corcoran 1969, 288 HRF3; Crawford 1925, 206; Grinsell 1993, 307).

Settlement Sites (HN 8-10, Fig. 7)

HN 8, Dorstone (SMR 01551/07524) NGR: SO 3260 4230
In 1958, two acres of ploughed ground in a field on a broad, flat-topped S-facing spur of Dorstone Hill (which is only 150m wide at its neck) produced eleven complete or fragmentary leaf-shaped arrowheads, four fragments of axe heads, twelve implements of shale and chert, three strike-a-lights, 291 blades and blade fragments, 456 utilized flakes and 384 unworked flakes. With eleven Mesolithic flints, this gave a total of 1,290 artefacts from the hill (Pye 1958, 82).

By the early 1960s, the same field had yielded 3,000 surface flints. These included many Neolithic leaf-shaped arrowheads and 50 fragments of polished stone axes and seemed to indicate an extensive Neolithic settlement. A two day excavation in 1965 found an old ground surface with traces of burning covered by a collapsed rough sandstone wall, 2'6" (0.75m) wide and probably not more than 2ft (0.60m) high originally. This had been built to consolidate a line of stakes 5" (13cm) in diameter. An undisturbed occupation soil behind this wall contained waste flint, a polished axe fragment and Western Neolithic pottery. A trench through the site of the densest flint scatter yielded more pottery (Houlder 1965, 10).

Further excavations in 1967 in the interior of the promontory fort produced definite evidence of Neolithic occupation. A layer which produced two leaf-shaped arrowheads and a Neolithic sherd sealed a storage pit. The pit contained a scraper and other unworked flints, charcoal and a few sherds of Western Neolithic pottery (Pye 1967, 8).

More evidence of Neolithic occupation was discovered in 1968 in part of the adjoining Forestry Commission woodland. A ditch and slight bank were located and some very abraded pottery and a few flints were recovered from the primary silt. A hearth some 6ft (2.0m) across (which produced a fragment of pottery and some flint flakes) had been constructed on top of the silted ditch. The hearth was overlain by a hut-floor and post-hole - this layer produced an arrowhead made from a flake of polished axe. Another hut-floor, of different plan, was located some distance away and a scatter of flints found in its floor (Pye 1968, 8-9).

In 1969, a total of five phases were noted on the site of the bank and ditch examined the previous year. Charcoal from a fireplace of Phase III (which immediately preceded a possible house site) was dated A. D. 40-90. The bank and ditch had been levelled and a sub-rectangular house built on the site. This area represents extra-mural settlement of the small promontory hill-fort (HI 1) some 200m to SE. Some 70 flints were found in the derived soil, including a leaf-shaped arrowhead and a crescentic microlith indicating intense Neolithic occupation (Pye 1969, 11). The site also produced Mesolithic, Bronze Age, Iron Age and Roman material.

HN 9, Craswall (SMR 00164) NGR: SO 2690 3960
Cefn Hill, Craswall (Robinson's "Cefn Hill Site A") - a flint scatter on the plateau of Cefn Hill near the highest point in the SW corner of Dorstone field no. 1118, at 1,563 ft (515m) above OD. There was evidence of a fairly extensive swampy area on the edge of the S slope. The flint scatters which Robinson regarded as "living floors" covered an area of some 2 acres with several discrete, dense clusters which he identified as hut sites (Robinson 1946, 34-35). No evidence of actual dwellings was discovered but various patches of

darkened soil were also thought to represent hut sites. The site produced 5 scrapers, a chip from a polished stone axe and a shale or mudstone spindle whorl (Robinson 1946, 37). Although listed on the SMR under Craswall, the site is actually in the parish of Dorstone. Interpreted by Robinson as a Neolithic settlement site.

HN 10, Craswall (SMR 00162) NGR: SO 2715 3816
On Cefn Hill, Abbey Farm, Craswall (Robinson's Abbey Farm Site "A") - a ploughzone flint scatter discovered in 1950 on a site which had not previously been cultivated. The discrete scatter consisted of a large number of flint flakes, scrapers and chips covering an area of about a quarter of an acre (0.10ha)(Robinson 1950, 112). There were also stone "rubbers or hones" and, outside the immediate scatter, there only a "few flakes scattered here and there over the ploughed field". Several areas of blackened soil in the area were interpreted as the result of medieval charcoal burning by the monks of Craswall Priory as there were no flints found in association with them. A piece of grooved sandstone was tentatively identified as a Bronze Age loom-weight (*ibid.*, 113).

In the same field, but not within the scatter, were found two complete Neolithic polished stone axes (*ibid.*, 115). The site also produced a fragment of Graig Lwyd axe re-used as a spokeshave or hollow scraper, a narrow blade and another fragment of rhyolite or rhyolitic ash, a fragment of a polished flint axe possible re-used as a sickle and a backed microlithic blade (Brown 1973, 115-116).

Axes (HN 11-22, Figs. 9, 10)

HN 11, Craswall (SMR 00162) NGR: SO 2715 3816
In the same field as the flint scatter at Abbey Farm Site "A" (see HN 10 above), were found two complete Neolithic polished stone axes (Robinson 1950, 115). The site also produced a fragment of Graig Lwyd axe re-used as a spokeshave or hollow scraper, a narrow blade and another fragment of rhyolite or rhyolitic ash, a fragment of a polished flint axe possible re-used as a sickle and a backed microlithic blade (Brown 1973, 115-116).

HN 12, Dorstone (SMR 08327) NGR: SO 3110 4370
Two damaged flint axes.

HN 13, Dorstone (SMR 01548) NGR: SO 3190 4310
From the flint scatter SE of Arthur's Stone (see HN 27 below) - two fragments of polished stone axes (Brown 1961, 80). Jenkins (1957, 322) also records the find of a burnt chip from the blade of polished flint axe with a wide facet at the end of the cutting edge at SO 318 432.

HN 14, Dorstone (SMR 01551/07524) NGR: SO 3260 4230
From the Dorstone Hill Neolithic settlement (see HN 8 above) - four fragments of polished axe heads, three of flint and one of stone. The flint fragments include the complete cutting edge of an axe, part of the blade and facet of another axe and a small chip from the side of another. The stone fragment came from the side of a polished stone axe (Pye 1958, 82; Fig 3.).

HN 15, Dorstone (not on SMR) NGR: SO 3325 4168

Found near the Great Llanavon/Cross Lodge long barrow (HN3) - a Group VIIIa polished stone axe, broken and re-chipped at both ends. The likely source of the stone is SW Wales (Pye 1958, 81).

HN 16, Moccas (SMR 08425) NGR: SO 3490 4250
A flint axe head now in Hereford City Museum (acc. no. 9607).

HN 17, Peterchurch (SMR 01017) NGR: SO 3530 3960
From the flint scatter at "Greenway No.2" (see HN 39 below) -.an axe of fine-grained volcanic ash of north Wales or Cumbria (Robinson 1934, 63).

HN 18, Peterchurch (SMR 01132) NGR: SO 3510 3940
From the flint scatter at "Greenway No.1" (see HN 42 below) - a fragment of a polished flint axe used as a knife or scraper (and possibly originating in Lincolnshire or Yorkshire) and a fragment of polished stone, probably from an axe of welded rhyolitic tuff (Brown 1961, 79).

HN 19, St. Margarets (SMR 01518) NGR: SO: 3301 3463
From Marresses Farm - a Group I axe head. At some later date in the Bronze Age an abortive attempt appears to have been made to turn the implement into a perforated axe-hammer (Norwood 1961, 104-5). Hereford City Museum acc. no. 7801. See HB 78.

HN 20, Abbey Dore (SMR 01506) NGR: SO 3920 3180
From south-east of Upper House Barn, Abbey Dore - a polished axe head with the butt snapped off. Now in Hereford City Museum (acc. no. 9196).

HN 21, Orcop (not on SMR) NGR: SO 457 260
Found in the Garway Brook - a partially ground Group VIII stone axe. Probably from SW Wales (Norwood 1963, 349-50, Fig. 2). Hereford City Museum acc. no. 8152.

HN 22, Garway (SMR 06261) NGR: SO 4536 2220
A large fragment of polished stone axe found in 1974 by its current owner (R. Flynn).

Lithic Finds (HN 23-54, Fig. 8)

HN 23, Bredwardine (SMR 01550) NGR: SO 3160 4380
From south of Crafta Webb, Bredwardine on Arthur's Stone Ridge - a light brown side scraper and a small arrowhead which is slightly irregular in outline. Chipping floors and finds burnt flint have been found in the adjacent fields (Brown 1961, 80).

HN 24, Dorstone (SMR 01544) NGR: SO 3090 4390
From S of Cae Mawr Wood, Merbach - a scatter of scrapers, chips and flakes (Robinson 1934, 62).

HN 25, Dorstone (SMR 08329) NGR: SO 3100 4350
From Pen y Moor Farm, Dorstone - a Neolithic leaf-shaped arrowhead The site also produced a Bronze Age spindle whorl. Both now in Hereford City Museum (acc. no. 9445).

HN 26, Dorstone (SMR 01543) NGR: SO 3160 4360
From NW of Arthur's Stone - a scatter of scrapers, chips and flakes from the S central area of field 398, at 900ft (273m)

above OD. Robinson's Site 17 (Robinson 1934, 62; illus. 17).

HN 27, Dorstone (SMR 01548) NGR: SO 3190 4310
From SE of Arthur's Stone, Dorstone - a small, neatly trimmed arrowhead of white flint, a broken serrated blade of light-grey translucent flint, a broken notched blade of similar flint, two fragments of polished stone axes, a small calcined oval scraper and a number of rough scrapers of dark grey flint (Brown 1961, 80). Jenkins (1957, 322) also records the find of a burnt chip from the blade of polished flint axe with a wide facet at the end of the cutting edge at SO 318 432. Pye mentions several other assemblages of Neolithic flints between Dorstone Hill and Arthur's Stone long barrow (HN2). Unfortunately, his descriptions of the location of these sites is so vague as to be virtually useless (Pye 1958, 81).

HN 28, Dorstone (SMR 01542) NGR: SO 3220 4270
Robinson's "Bodcotte No. 2", field 684, 850 ft (258m) above OD. A scattered working floor on W central area of the field with scrapers and chips (Robinson 1934, 62, illus. 16).

HN 29, Dorstone (SMR 01547) NGR: SO 3230 4270
Robinson's "Bodcotte No. 1", field 685, 850 ft (258m) above OD. At the NW end of field, a scatter with Neolithic arrowheads, chips, cores (Robinson 1934, 62, illus. 15).

HN 30, Craswall (SMR 06128) NGR: SO 2740 3820
Close to Robinson's 'Abbey A' site (Robinson 1950, 112-7) - a leaf-shaped arrowhead found in a molehill of light grey flint (Brown 1973, 116).

HN 31, Michaelchurch Escley (SMR 01114) NGR: SO 3100 3820
At Pen-y-parc, field 262, 1,020 ft (310m) above OD - in the S central part of the field, two flint nodules, flakes, knives, chips and cores (Robinson 1934, 62 , illus. 27).

HN 32, Michaelchurch Escley (SMR 01111) NGR: SO 3080 3770
Robinson's "Pucha No. 1", Tanners Place, Michaelchurch Escley, field 220, 1,074 ft (326m) above OD - a working floor in the S central area of the field with Neolithic arrowheads, scrapers, flakes and chips. The site also produced arrowheads of Bronze Age date. A small, very prolific site. The main working floor was in the area where there appears to have been a cutting in steep slope, facing south. Robinson interpreted this as the remains of a hut site (Robinson 1934, 62, illus. 24).

HN 33, Michaelchurch Escley (SMR 01120) NGR: SO 3050 3730
From near Wernderris standing stone (HB 40), Michaelchurch Escley - a few flakes picked up near the stone, together with a fine oval scraper.

HN 34, Michaelchurch Escley (SMR 01116) NGR: SO 3110 3700
From Pentwyn, Michaelchurch Escley, field 348, 1,068 ft (324m) above OD - a scatter of six Neolithic flint flakes and Bronze Age round scraper at the N end of the field approx. 90m from a ploughed-out round barrow (Robinson 1934, 62, illus. 29; Brown 1973, 116).

HN 35, Peterchurch (SMR 08449) NGR: SO 3490 4090
Robinson's "Woodbury No. 1", field 351, 959 ft (291m)
above OD - several small discrete scatters on S slope of the
field with a denser scatter on the highest point. The site
produce Neolithic arrowheads, scrapers and chips (Robinson
1934, 61, illus. 12). See also HM11.

HN 36, Peterchurch (SMR 01546) NGR: SO 3450 4130
Robinson's "Woodbury No.2", Peterchurch, field 354, 906 ft
(275m) above OD - a widespread flint scatter (Robinson
1934, 61, illus. 13). More recent finds include a blade of
cloudy blue patination, a large knife of coarse grey mottled
flint, a fragment of polished flint axe and a small spherical
core. Burnt flints, chips and debitage are common in these
and neighbouring fields at Greenway (Brown 1961, 79). A
round scraper and four flint flakes were discovered nearby
(SO 343 408) between 1965 and 1967 (Brown 1973, 116).

HN 37, Peterchurch (not on SMR) NGR: SO 3530 4040
From Upper Godway - a Neolithic core of rhyolite (Brown
1973, 116).

HN 38, Peterchurch (SMR 01127) NGR: SO 3680 3830
Robinson's "Stockley No. 2", Peterchurch, field 1178, 765ft
(232m) above OD - a diffuse scatter over the SW end of the
field with well worked Neolithic and Bronze Age arrowheads
and knifes (Robinson 1934, 61, illus. 2). More recent finds
(from SO 3670 3860) include a leaf-shaped arrowhead, a
notched blade and a Bronze Age barbed and tanged
arrowhead (Brown 1961, 77). This site is also listed as SMR
01127.

HN 39, Peterchurch (SMR 01017) NGR: SO 3530 3960
From Robinson's "Greenway No.2", N of Oaken Coppice,
Greenway Farm, Peterchurch, field 442, 772 ft (234m) above
OD - a discrete scatter which included three arrowheads (two
of "Long Barrow type"), an axe of fine-grained volcanic ash
of N. Wales or Cumbria, scrapers (one of honey-coloured
flint), flakes and chips (Robinson 1934, 63, illus. 7). This
was identified by Robinson as an occupation area on a small
ridge at the edge of a swamp. More recent finds include one
circular scraper of dark grey translucent flint and one oval
scraper of similar but denser material (Brown 1961, 79). The
SMR records other finds of undiagnostic flint at Greenway at
SO 3540 3950 (SMR 08439) and SO 3540 3950 (SMR
08440).

HN 40, Peterchurch (SMR 01233) NGR: SO 3550 3970
From the Greenway Farm area - a small knife, an oval
scraper, a rough triangular scraper and a triangular flake
which may be an arrowhead (Brown 1961, 79).

HN 41, Peterchurch (SMR 01109) NGR: SO 3400 3700
From "Shegear No. 1", SW of Lords Coppice, Shegear Farm,
Peterchurch - a scatter of chips and flakes with one scraper
(Robinson 1934, 58). More recent finds (at SO 3410 3690)
include a broken dark grey blade and a small calcined scraper
(Brown 1961, 80).

HN 42, Peterchurch (SMR 01132) NGR: SO 3510 3940
Robinson's "Greenway No. 1" - W of Oaken Coppice,
Greenway Farm, Peterchurch, field 443, 772 ft (234m) above
OD - a scatter of flakes and scrapers over the NW corner of

the field (Robinson 1934, 61, illus.6). Other finds (at SO
3510 3950) include a light grey knife, a steep-edged thumb
scraper, a re-worked thin scraper of cloudy blue flint, a
fragment of a polished flint axe used as a knife or scraper
(and possibly originating in Lincolnshire or Yorkshire) and a
fragment of polished stone, probably from an axe of welded
rhyolitic tuff (Brown 1961, 79).

HN 43, Peterchurch (not on SMR) NGR: SO 3490 3880
From the Wellbrook Farm area - the lower portion of a
broken leaf-shaped arrowhead of dark translucent flint
(Brown 1961, 78). See SMR 01530.

HN 44, Peterchurch (SMR 07171) NGR: SO 3620 3840
In Bradley's Wood, Poston, at approx. 225m above OD - six
flints, including a leaf-shaped arrowhead, knife and scrapers,
were found when the Poston Iron Age barrow was excavated
(Marshall 1933b, 32; Robinson 1934, 61, illus. 11).

HN 45, Peterchurch (SMR 01126) NGR: SO 3670 3840
Robinson's "Stockley No.1", Stockley, Peterchurch, field no.
1175, 764 ft (251m) above OD - a very dense scatter of
Neolithic material in the E area of the field and Bronze Age
working floor 30m from W hedge. The site produced
arrowheads, knives, scrapers and chips (Robinson 1934, 61,
illus. 1). An oblong stone circle had formerly existed at the
N end of this field (*loc. cit.*, 63). The site has also produced
a rough knife of grey mottled flint with traces of extensive
use (Brown 1961, 78).

HN 46, Peterchurch (SMR 01494) NGR: SO 3650 3820
From Stockley Hill, Peterchurch - a lozenge-shaped
arrowhead found in 1952 after deep ploughing. Other finds
include a serrated microlith of grey flint and an untrimmed
flake of devitrified rhyolite (Brown 1961, 78).

HN 47, Vowchurch (SMR 07490) NGR: SO 3590 3765
Poston Camp, Lower Park Wood, Vowchurch - excavations
conducted in 1932 (Marshall 1933) revealed evidence
(mainly flint) for Neolithic and Bronze Age occupation of
the hilltop later occupied by the Iron Age hill-fort. Five
flakes, one scraper and two chips were recorded (Antony
1958). For further discussion see HI 2 below.

HN 48, Vowchurch (SMR 01124) NGR: SO 3710 3720
From E of Vowchurch Common - Neolithic flints reported.

HN 49, Vowchurch (SMR 08483) NGR: SO 3720 3720
On Vowchurch Common - a flint working site.

HN 50, Vowchurch (SMR 01532) NGR: SO 3720 3820
On Vowchurch Common - a concentration of implements
and flakes. A flint working site and probable occupation
site.

HN 51, Madley (SMR 06272) NGR: SO 4017 3596
From Brampton Hill, fields 781/782, 500 ft (152m) above
OD - a scatter of flints found during timber felling operations
in 1934-35 (Robinson 1934, 62, illus. 19). The collection
included a chert "spear or lance head of Neolithic Northern
Ireland type" and a scraper "of unusual working and
uncommon flint" (Robinson 1934, 63).

HN 52, Kingstone (SMR 08370) NGR: SO 42 35

From Brampton - a possible Neolithic chert tool.

HN 53, Kentchurch (SMR 06791) NGR: SO 4350 2670
From Llanithog Farm, Kentchurch - Neolithic and Bronze Age flints. Now in Hereford City Museum.

HN 54, Garway (SMR 23402) NGR: SO 4450 2500
From Sun Field, Garway Hill - a small leaf-shaped arrowhead and a quantity of flints were discovered after the field was ploughed in 1992/93. The site also produced 14th century pottery.

9.3 Bronze Age Sites (HB 1-79)

Round Barrows and Cairns (HB 1-26, Fig. 23)

HB 1, Craswall (not on SMR) NGR: SO 2760 3828
On Cefn Hill - Grinsell's "Craswall 1" - a round barrow approx. 16m x 13m by 1m high with a central depression (Grinsell 1993, 308).

HB 2, Craswall (SMR 00159) NGR: SO 2749 3820
On Cefn Hill - Grinsell's "Craswall 2a". Discovered by Gavin Robinson (1950, 115), this is possibly a clearance cairn (Grinsell 1993, 308) or a ruined building (Brown 1972, 315).

HB 3, Craswall (SMR 00160) NGR: SO 2604 3754
A possible barrow on Parc y Meirch, Craswall close to a N hedge. Grinsell's "Craswall 3" (1993, 308). There is a small standing stone some 30m to the NE (SMR 07253) and, in 1950, Robinson saw several large flat slabs lying against the hedge bank which could have been the remains of a wrecked cist (Robinson 1950, 116).

HB 4, Craswall (SMR 06127) NGR: SO 2572 3671
On a prominent knoll (which is the meaning of *Llanoleu*) at the head of the river Monnow, S of Llanoleu, Craswall - a round barrow superimposed upon a kerbed round cairn which has 18 stones still visible. The barrow measures some 10m x 9m and lies off centre to the SW. A lime kiln has also been inserted into the original cairn. The whole site measures approx. 25m x 17m x 1.2m high and is aligned NE-SW along the long axis.

HB 5, Craswall (SMR 11363) NGR: SO 2585 3670
About 100m E of SMR 06127 - a possible round cairn. A slight, roughly circular mound with large stones on the surface. The mound does not appear to have been ploughed.

HB 6, Craswall (SMR 05493) NGR: SO 2994 3520
SE of Trelan Farm, Craswall - a low circular mound about 10 m in dia., over a central red sandstone-lined cist (1.42m x o.74m) aligned approx. N/S along the long axis. Two flint flakes and some fragments of burnt bone were recovered from the spoil when the farmer destroyed the cist with a JCB. There are indications of other ploughed out barrows in the vicinity. Grinsell's "Craswall 2" (Grinsell 1993, 308).

HB 7, Craswall (SMR 13020) NGR: SO 2872 3388
At Upper Coed, Craswall - according to the SMR, aerial photographs (uncited) appear to show the site of a destroyed barrow on a former field boundary.

HB 8, Llanveynoe (SMR 01585) NGR: SO 2798 3231
At Olchon Court, Llanveynoe - two Early Bronze Age cists found in May 1932 during ploughing in a field on the W side of the road to Llanveynoe opposite Beili Bach. The first cist was covered by a capstone and contained a crouched male inhumation (25-30 years of age) with a beaker and a barbed and tanged arrowhead. The second cist , about 1m to the E, lacked its capstone and the contents were poorly preserved - they consisted of traces of another inhumation, charcoal and a beaker containing worked flint. There was no barrow or cairn covering the cists (Marshall 1932, 147). One cist and its contents are now in Hereford City Museum.

HB 9, Llanveynoe (SMR 13056) NGR: SO 2997 3167
Aerial photographs taken in 1973 show a circular cropmark some 350m NW of Llanveynoe church which has been interpreted as the ring ditch of a ploughed-out round barrow.

HB 10, Llanveynoe (SMR 12019) NGR: SO 2986 2870
On Loxidge Tump at approx. 560m above OD, partially transversed at the W by the Offa's Dyke footpath and the Welsh border - an oval cairn, approx. ?m by ?m by 1.8m high, the centre has been robbed out, apparently in antiquity.

HB 11, Llanveynoe (SMR 12020a) NGR: SO 3000 2830
A flat-topped round cairn (c. 17.6m in dia and 1.2m high) with traces of a ditch on the W side about 30m E of the Offa's Dyke footpath and the Welsh border. Grinsell's "Llanveynoe 1"(Grinsell 1993, 309). About 10m to the N of the cairn, a ring of stones (HB 37) some 4.5m in diameter is almost obscured by heather. Grinsell interpreted this as the site of a small cairn, "Llanveynoe 2a" (1993, 309), but Nash argues for its being a small stone circle (Children and Nash 1994, 59).

HB 12, Llanveynoe (not on SMR) NGR: SO 303 280
A cairn with a central pit, approx. 13m in diameter and 1.5m high (Grinsell 1993, 309).

HB 13, Michaelchurch Escley (SMR 01134) NGR: SO 3010 3730 (Fig. 20)
S of Glibes Farm - a round barrow 7m x5m by 1m high. Some 300m to the E stands the Wern Derries standing stone (SMR 01101). Grinsell's "Michaelchurch 1" (*loc. cit.*)

HB 14, Michaelchurch Escley (SMR 07165/6) NGR: SO 3011 3720 (Fig. 20)
S of Glibes Farm - two other mounds almost levelled in the upper end of the field may be the remains of further barrows. Grinsell's "Michaelchurch 2 and 3" (Grinsell 1993, 309).

HB 15, Michaelchurch Escley (SMR 01011) NGR: SO 3108 3703 (Fig. 20)
A ploughed-out barrow 400m NE of Pentwyn Farm, partially excavated but unpublished (Robinson 1934, 57, 62). A photograph of the 1930s shows a low, flat-topped mound carrying a stand of larch and pine (Brown 1972, 315). Grinsell's "Michaelchurch 4" (Grinsell 1993, 309).

HB 16, Michaelchurch Escley (SMR 01010) NGR: SO 3160 3655 (Fig. 20)
At Upper Llanon Farm, Michaelchurch Escley - a barrow was levelled in a farm improvement scheme in 1946. Also listed as SMR 13004. Grinsell's "Michaelchurch 5" (*loc. cit.*). There are no visible remains. Visited 18.5.1999.

HB 17, St. Margarets (SMR 04236) NGR: SO 3185 3667 (Fig. 20)
West of Wern William Farm - a round barrow. Grinsell's "St. Margarets 1" (*loc. cit.*). No remains are now visible. Visited 18.5.1999.

HB 18, Peterchurch (SMR 04235) NGR: SO 3196 3768 (Fig. 20)
S of Urishay Villa - a circular mound to W of hollow way (SMR 04230) which leads down to Urishay Castle. The

barrow is just visible as a slight earthwork in the NE corner of the field. Visited 18.5.1999.

HB 19, Madley (SMR 00395/6, NMR SO 33 NE 19) NGR: SO 3995 3927 (Fig. 25)
On a knoll to the S of Upper Chilstone House at approx. 75m above OD, the SMR records a ploughed-out disc barrow and bell barrow - Grinsell's "Madley 1 and 2" (Grinsell 1993, 309, 312). The disc barrow measured some 23m in diameter with a 3.5m wide bank, the bell barrow c. 10m. Plans at the NMR for England (SO 33 NE 19) show four other, smaller, round barrows to the S and E (Fig. 25).

However, Grinsell considered it unlikely that these features represented "Wessex-type" barrows (*ibid.*, 304) and photographs taken in 1924 show that the "disc barrow" was, in fact, a superbly preserved ring-bank (RCHM 1931, 198; TWNFC 1924-6, pl.4 facing p. xxiii). See HB 35.

Up until the 1950s, the smaller barrows were preserved in pasture, but have since been destroyed. In 1972, the site of the bell barrow was marked by an area of differently coloured soil, that of the ring-bank had been partially destroyed by quarrying and ploughing (Brown 1972, 315). In 1965-7, burnt flint was found in the field (Brown 1973, 116). The entire site has since been completely destroyed.

HB 20, Tyberton (SMR 01515) NGR: SO 3795 3796
A possible damaged barrow on the Vowchurch/Tyberton parish boundary in Rushen Wood. Recent fieldwork has failed to locate the site. Grinsell's "Tyberton 1" (Grinsell 1993, 311).

HB 21, Turnastone (SMR 08478) NGR: SO 3560 3660
At Turnastone - finds of flint associated with a possible barrow which has also been interpreted as a motte (SMR 01467).

HB 22, Vowchurch (SMR 04308) NGR: SO 3670 3504
A barrow SSE of Chanstone Court Farm, Vowchurch. Grinsell's "Vowchurch 2" (Grinsell 1993, 311).

HB 23, Vowchurch (SMR 04298) NGR: SO 3664 3493
A barrow NE of Haybrooks Wood, Vowchurch. Grinsell's "Vowchurch 1" (*loc. cit.*).

HB 24, Abbey Dore (SMR 01504) NGR: SO 3929 3375
S of Dunseal Wood, Abbey Dore - a round barrow, 12m in diameter, 2.2m high on NW side and 0.8m high on SE. The barrow is built on the edge of the escarpment and to the W a hedge curves to follow the course of a vestigial ditch. Grinsell's "Abbey Dore 1" (*ibid.*, 307).

HB 25, Treville (SMR 06809) NGR: SO 4210 3340
In the grounds of Whitfield, Treville - a cist in which was found a Bronze Age arrowhead, now lost.

HB 26, Walterstone (not on SMR) NGR: SO 3384 3482
A possible round barrow represented by a circular mound, 6.3m in diameter and 0.75m high in the centre (RCHME 1931, 248). The monument has been completely ploughed out. Visited 08/06/99.

Rejected Sites

All in **Peterchurch**:

(SMR 04233-8) NGR: SO 3160 3778
A barrow cemetery centred on Urishay Villa and consisting of eight barrows.

(SMR 04233) NGR: SO 3160 3778
One of a group of three mounds W of Urishay Villa.

(SMR 04234) NGR: SO 3160 3785
W of Urishay Villa - a single mound to the N of the group of three.

(SMR 04236) NGR: SO 3185 3667
S of Urishay Villa - another mound to the W of the SMR 04235.

(SMR 04237) NGR: SO 3185 3785
N of Urishay Villa - another circular mound. Part of the barrow cemetery?

(SMR 04238) NGR: SO 3195 3785
E of Urishay Villa - a large circular mound cut by the road to Snodhill. Part of the barrow cemetery? No remains visible. Visited 18.5.1999.

(SMR 04249-51) NGR: SO 306 385
A roughly triangular group of three barrows to the W of Upper Pen y Park.

(SMR 04332) NGR: SO 3370 3740
E of Urishay - the northern section of a round barrow protruding from the southern field boundary.

(SMR 04349) NGR: SO 3200 3857
A possible barrow on the W side of a field to the S of Newhouse Farm, Peterchurch.

(SMR 11261) NGR: SO 3074 4052
A large barrow SE of Whitehouse, Common Bach.

(SMR 11347) NGR: SO 3474 3918
A ploughed-out barrow SE of Mowbatch Farm.

Ring Ditches (HB 27-32, Fig. 23)

HB 27, Clifford (SMR 08269) NGR: SO 2532 4675
W of Sheepcote Farm – a ring-ditch shown on aerial photographs (Grinsell 1993, 313).

HB 28, Clifford (SMR 08407) NGR: SO 248 464
Grinsell's "Clifford a" - air photographs taken in July 1989 show a ring ditch to the N of the village (*loc. cit.*).

HB 29, Clifford (SMR 09904) NGR: SO 2490 4628
Grinsell's "Clifford b" - aerial photographs show a ring ditch to the N of Whitehouse Farm (*loc. cit.*).

HB 30, Peterchurch (SMR 04313) NGR: SO 3253 4042
E of Snodhill Castle - a ring ditch. Grinsell's "Peterchurch a" (*loc. cit.*).

HB 31, Madley (SMR 10406) NGR: SO 4100 3725

Aerial photographs taken in July 1990 show a ring-ditch to the E of Lower Brampton Farm (*ibid.*, 314). Grinsell's "Madley a".

HB 32, Madley (SMR 10405) NGR: SO 4110 3763
NE of Lower Brampton Farm - a ring-ditch shown on aerial photographs (*loc. cit.*). Grinsell's "Madley b".

Stone Circles and Ring-banks (HB 33-37, Fig. 26)

HB 33, Clifford (not on SMR) NGR: SO 2484 4275 (Fig. 25)
Between Hawks Wood and Mouse Castle Wood on a slight spur at approx. 215m above OD with the ground falling in all directions except to the S - a penannular bank approx. 11m in diameter internally with a small gap or entrance on the S side (RCHME 1931, 42). This is a very well-preserved earthen ring-bank with extensive views over the Wye Valley to the N. Its position is not defensively strong, being overlooked to the S by the prominent knoll upon which Mouse Castle stands (SO 2484 4246). Visited 18.5.1999.

HB 34, Peterchurch (SMR 07171) NGR: SO 3620 3840 (Fig. 24)
In Bradley's Wood, Poston, at approx. 225m above OD - a supposedly Iron Age ritual barrow (HI 14). The structure of the barrow was of exceptional interest. The base consisted of a ring-bank of fine soil some 16.5m in diameter and about 1.2m in height. This was then covered with a carefully constructed cairn of small, flat, sandstone slabs tipping steeply inwards (Marshall 1933b, 32). Although Marshall assumed that the cairn's structure represented a single phase of construction, it is possible that an pre-existing ring-bank was incorporated in a later cairn.

HB 35, Madley (SMR 00395/6, NMR SO 33 NE 19) NGR: SO 3995 3927 (Fig. 25)
On a knoll to the S of Upper Chilstone House at approx. 75m above OD, the SMR records a ploughed-out disc barrow and bell barrow - Grinsell's "Madley 1 and 2" (Grinsell 1993, 309, 312). The disc barrow measured some 23m in diameter with a 3.5m wide bank, the bell barrow c. 10m. Plans at the NMR for England show four other, smaller, round barrows to the S and E (Fig. 25). See HB 19.

However, Grinsell considered it unlikely that these features represented "Wessex-type" barrows (*ibid.*, 304) and photographs taken in 1924 show that the "disc barrow" was, in fact, a superbly preserved ring-bank (RCHM 1931, 198; TWNFC 1924-6, pl.4 facing p. xxiii).

Up until the 1950s, the smaller barrows were preserved in pasture, but have since been destroyed. In 1972,.the site of the bell barrow was marked by an area of differently coloured soil, that of the ring-bank had been partially destroyed by quarrying and ploughing (Brown 1972, 315). In 1965-7, burnt flint was found in the field (Brown 1973, 116). The entire site has since been completely destroyed.

HB 36, Peterchurch (SMR 07164) NGR: SO 3661 3648
At Robinson's "Stockley no.1" (HN 45) - an oblong stone circle once existed (1934) at the N end of a field which produced Neolithic and Bronze Age flint scatters (Robinson 1934, 63).

HB 37, Llanveynoe (SMR 12020b) NGR: SO 3000 2830
About 10m to the N of cairn HB 11, a ring of stones some 4.5m in diameter is almost obscured by heather. Grinsell (1993, 309) interpreted this as the site of a small cairn but Nash argues for its being a small stone circle (Children and Nash 1994, 59).

Standing Stones (HB 38-42, Fig. 26)

Only the King Stone at Wern Derries is definitely known to be in its original position.

HB 38, Dorstone (SMR 04203) NGR: SO 3056 4224
Gannols Farm, Dorstone - old red sandstone pillar now serving as a gatepost on the N side of the field entrance and not in its original position, 1.4m high, 0.63 x 0.5m at base, cup marks under the ivy cover. There is a photograph of the stone in the Woolhope *Transactions* for 1924-26 where Alfred Watkins speculates that it may once have stood in the middle of the field (TWNFC 1924-26, 150, Pl. 33; Williams 1966, 253). Visited 18.5.1999.

HB 39, Peterchurch (SMR 01537) NGR: SO 3420 4020
The Willmarsh Stone, E of Willmastone Farm, Peterchurch - a standing stone seems indicated by Taylor's 1786 map of Herefordshire.

HB 40, Michaelchurch Escley (SMR 01101) NGR: SO 3036 3726 (Fig. 20)
The King Stone, Wern Derries, Michaelchurch Escley - a rectangular prism 7'6" (2.28m) high, 20" (0.50m) thick and 30" (0.76m) wide at the base, tapering (TWNFC 1921-23, 287; Williams 1966, 256).

HB 41, Michaelchurch Escley (SMR 00163) NGR: SO 2721 3882
On Cefn Hill, Michaelchurch Escley - a standing stone called Gold Post, moved from its original position before 1930. Williams differs from the SMR's NGR (above) and puts the stone at SO 273 394 and, although a local farmer informed him that the standing stone was moved prior to 1930, he points out (1966, 256) that it is shown in that position on the 6" OS map of 1904. It is certainly not at the NGR given in the SMR (visited 12/03/99). To add to the confusion, Robinson's plan of the Cefn Hill Neolithic and Bronze Age settlements shows the location of the stone at SO 2763 3968 (Robinson 1946, Fig. 1). It is no longer to be seen at any of these three NGR locations, or anywhere else in the vicinity. Visited and searched exhaustively (!) 08/06/99.

HB 42, Craswall (SMR 07253) NGR: SO 2604 3755
At Parc y Meirch, Craswall - approx. 30m SW of SMR 00160 was a weathered stone 0.8m in height and 0.25m in width - possibly a standing stone (Robinson 1950, 116). It has now disappeared. Visited 08/06/99.

Rejected Sites

Dorstone (SMR 00165) NGR: SO 2803 3989
At the edge of a forestry plantation on Vagar Hill near the Michaelchurch Escley boundary - with an OS benchmark cut into it. This is probably medieval. Williams failed to recognise the OS bench mark as such (Williams 1966, 253).

Settlement Sites (HB 43-46, Fig. 19)

HB 43, Dorstone (SMR 07524) NGR: SO 3260 4230
Dorstone Hill Neolithic settlement - excavations began in 1965, a depression was dated by C-14 to the Bronze Age "on the silting of which had been a large fire". Above this was floor level with a post hole. Interpreted as a Bronze Age building. The site also produced Mesolithic, Neolithic, Iron Age and Roman material (see above).

HB 44, Craswall (SMR 00164) NGR: SO 2670 3950
On the N end of Cefn Hill, Craswall (Robinson's "Cefn Hill Site B") - an indeterminate length of dry stone wall and coarse flints which have been interpreted as of Bronze Age date (Robinson 1946, 35). Nearby, on a flat stretch of ground in Dorstone field no. 1102 just W of the Hay-Michaelchurch road is Robinson's "Cefn Hill Site C" which produced chips, scrapers and borers as well as two barbed and tanged arrowheads (Robinson 1946, 36). Robinson interpreted both sites as Bronze Age settlements.

Flint scatters and areas of darkened soil at the nearby "Cefn Hill Site A" (SO 2690 3960) have been interpreted as a Neolithic settlement (HN 9).

HB 45, Craswall (SMR 00162) NGR: SO 2715 3816
On Cefn Hill, Abbey Farm, Craswall (Robinson's Abbey Farm Site "A") - a ploughzone flint scatter discovered in 1950 on a site which had not previously been cultivated. The discrete scatter consisted of a large number of flint flakes, scrapers and chips covering an area of about a quarter of an acre (Robinson 1950, 112). There were also stone "rubbers or hones" and, outside the immediate scatter, only a "few flakes scattered here and there over the ploughed field". Several areas of blackened soil in the area were interpreted as the result of medieval charcoal burning by the monks of Craswall Priory as there were no flints found in association with them (*ibid.*, 113). A piece of grooved sandstone was tentatively identified as a Bronze Age loom-weight (*loc. cit.*). The site also produced Neolithic material (HN 10) and was interpreted as a Neolithic/Bronze Age settlement site.

HB 46, Craswall (SMR 00161) NGR: SO 2621 3783
At Birches Farm, Parc y Meirch, Craswall (Robinson's Birches Farm Site "B") - a flint scatter discovered in 1950 towards the bottom of a slope on fairly flat ground adjoining an area which showed evidence of having been wet or swampy for a considerable period. The site was also marked by a large patch of whitish soil (Robinson 1950, 115). Among the scatter was a very fine Earlier Bronze Age plano-convex flint knife (*ibid.*, 116). More recent finds include cores, an edge-trimmed flake, burnt flints and waste pieces (Brown 1973, 116). Interpreted as a Bronze Age settlement site (Robinson 1950, 117).

Metalwork (HB 47-56, Fig. 30)

HB 47, Dorstone (SMR 01533) NGR: SO 3100 4100
From Dorstone - two Late Bronze Age looped and socketed axes. Now in Hereford City Museum (acc. no. 1308.3 and 1308.5).

HB 48, Michaelchurch Escley (SMR 01100) NGR: SO 3080 3758

From ESE of Tanners Place, Urishay Common, Michaelchurch Escley - a "winged" palstave with stop-ridge found by the owner of Pucha Farm. Loaned to Hereford City Museum (acc. no. 5378). A photograph of the objects appears in TWNFC 1924 (p.150, plate 33) and shows an early unlooped palstave of Savory's MBA I - Needham's Acton Park 1 - the very end of the Early Bronze Age c. 1650-1400 cal. B. C.

HB 49, Turnastone (SMR 01123) NGR: SO 3500 3600
From Turnastone - a Late Bronze Age looped, socketed axe with splayed blade. Now in Hereford City Museum (acc. no. 1308.6).

HB 50, Vowchurch (SMR 01461) NGR: SO 3600 3600
From Vowchurch - a Late Bronze Age looped socketed axe. Now in Hereford City Museum (acc. no. 1308.4). Wrongly described on the SMR as a Middle Bronze Age palstave.

HB 51, Vowchurch (SMR 08485) NGR: SO 3730 3570
From Vowchurch, found "in field on west side of Eaton between it and the road" - two Middle Bronze Age palstaves. Now in Hereford City Museum (acc. no. 1308.1-2).

HB 52, Vowchurch (SMR 01468) NGR: SO 3700 3570
From a cutting in the road at Chanstone Mill, Vowchurch - a Middle Bronze Age looped and socketed spearhead with leaf-shaped head and central rib. Hereford City Museum acc. no. 1309. The SMR wrongly described the find-spot as "Chanstone Hill".

HB 53, St. Margarets (SMR 01502) NGR: SO 3590 3300
From Park Wood, St. Margarets, about 1km S of the embankment cross in St. Margaret's - several bronze spear ferrules discovered during ploughing. Late Bronze Age (Stanford 1991, 33). Current whereabouts unknown - information supplied by Hereford City Museum.

HB 54, Madley (SMR 12089) NGR: SO 4179 3788
From S of Madley - a hoard of twelve Late Bronze Age socketed axes discovered in 1982. The hoard includes five South Wales axes, three "Croxton type" axes, one of Llanarth type (see MB 43), two collared axes with twin ribs and one fragment. Now in Hereford City Museum - not accessioned (National Museum of Wales Lab. Nos. 84.1679-90).

Doubtful Sites

HB 55, Eaton Bishop (SMR 06821) NGR: SO 4447 3899
From near Stony Street, Eaton Bishop - two bronze axeheads supposedly deposited at Hereford City Museum. Current whereabouts unknown.

HB 56, Eaton Bishop (SMR 06280) NGR: SO 4500 3800
From the bank of a brook E of Eaton Bishop - a hoard iron and copper objects were found in 1815 where the bank of a brook E of Eaton Bishop had collapsed. Many items had become rusted together and could not be identified. The hoard included several copper ornaments, a flint arrowhead, battle axes. Several arrowheads were preserved, but many other items including spearheads, battle axes, iron hoops 3-4" in diameter, rims of pots and cauldrons and massive rings of various dimensions were destroyed.

Lithic Finds (HB 57-79, Fig. 19)

HB 57, Dorstone (SMR 08329) NGR: SO 3100 4350
From Pen y Moor Farm, Dorstone - a Bronze Age spindle whorl. The site also produced a Neolithic leaf-shaped arrowhead. Both now in Hereford City Museum (acc. no. 9445).

HB 58, Bredwardine (SMR 01549) NGR: SO 3127 4354
From NW of Arthur's Stone, Dorstone - an almost complete barbed and tanged arrowhead of white flint, a small broken blade with a battered back and a roughly trimmed, broken scraper 3.3cm across (Brown 1961, 80 - where the NGR is given as SO 313 436).

HB 59, Dorstone (SMR 01547) NGR: SO 3250 4270
From Arthur's Stone Ridge, Dorstone - a barbed and tanged arrowhead of grey flint with one barb missing, another broken arrowhead and a small, broken knife of mottled flint carefully trimmed along the working edge (Brown 1961, 80). The site also produced Mesolithic material (see above).

HB 60, Dorstone (SMR 04772) NGR: SO 3270 4210
From Dorstone Hill - an end scraper.

HB 61, Dorstone (SMR 04207) NGR: SO 2925 4088
From W of Penlan Farm, Dorstone - a barbed and tanged arrowhead reported to Hereford City Museum.

HB 62, Dorstone (SMR 01267) NGR: SO 2740 4010
Flint chippings and two Bronze Age arrowheads.

HB 63, Michaelchurch (SMR 01114) NGR: SO 3100 3820 (Fig. 20)
From Pen-y-parc Farm, field 262, 1,020 ft (310m) above OD, from the S central part of the field - two flint nodules, flakes, knives, chips and cores, (Robinson 1934, 62, illus. 27).

HB 64, Michaelchurch Escley (SMR 01111) NGR: SO 3080 3770 (Fig. 20)
Robinson's "Pucha No. 1", Tanners Place, field 220, 1,074 ft (326m) above OD - a working floor in the S central area of the field with arrowheads of Bronze Age date. A small, very prolific site. The main working floor was in the area where there appears to have been a cutting in steep slope, facing south. Robinson interpreted this as the remains of a hut site (Robinson 1934, 62, illus. 24). The site also produced Neolithic material.

HB 65, Michaelchurch Escley (SMR 01120) NGR: SO 3036 3726 (Fig. 20)
From near the Wernderries standing stone (SMR 01101) - a fine oval scraper some 3cm across and a few flint flakes (Brown 1061, 81).

HB 66, Michaelchurch Escley (SMR 01112) NGR: SO 3090 3730 (Fig. 20)
Robinson's "Pucha No. 2", N of Ivy House, field 296, 1,068 ft (324m) above OD - a scatter which produced barbed and tanged arrowheads and a bronze axehead (Robinson 1934, 62, illus. 25). This is probably the winged palstave recorded in SMR 01100.

HB 67, Michaelchurch Escley (SMR 01116) NGR: SO 3110 3700 (Fig. 20)
From Pentwyn Farm, field 348, 1,068 ft (324m) above OD, about 90m from a round barrow - a scatter of Neolithic and Bronze Age flint on the N side of the field (Robinson 1934, 62, illus. 29). The site also produced a Bronze Age round scraper (Brown 1973, 116).

HB 68, Michaelchurch Escley (SMR 01119) NGR: SO 3090 3690 (Fig. 20)
From S of Ivy House, Michaelchurch Escley - a plano-convex knife of grey flint, an end scraper of translucent orange flint not common in the Golden Valley, a carefully trimmed oval scraper of grey flint, a number of less regular scrapers and a large, rough scraper 6cm x 3.7cm. This field also produced waste pieces and burnt flints (Brown 1961, 81).

HB 69, Michaelchurch Escley (SMR 08418) NGR: SO 3190 3460
From Michaelchurch Escley - an Early Bronze Age stone adze.

HB 70, Peterchurch (SMR 01102) NGR: SO 3030 3940
From Snodhill, Peterchurch - a barbed and tanged arrowhead.

HB 71, Peterchurch (SMR 01546/08449) NGR: SO 3450 4130
Robinson's "Woodbury No.2", field 354, 906 ft (275m) above OD - a widespread flint scatter in NE corner of the field (Robinson 1934, 61, illus. 13). More recent finds include a blade of cloudy blue patination, a large knife of coarse grey mottled flint, a fragment of polished flint axe and a small spherical core. Burnt flints, chips and debitage are common in these and neighbouring fields at Greenway (Brown 1961, 79). A round scraper and four flint flakes were discovered nearby (SO 343 408) between 1965 and 1967 (Brown 1973, 116).

HB 72, Peterchurch (SMR 01018) NGR: SO 3500 3960
Robinson's "Greenway No. 3", field 444, 780 ft (237m) above OD, centre of field - one Early Bronze Age arrow, scrapers, chips and flakes (Robinson 1934, 61, illus. 8).

HB 73, Peterchurch (SMR 01126) NGR: SO 3670 3840
Robinson's "Stockley no. 1", field no. 1175, 764 ft (232m) above OD, Neolithic material in the E area of the field, Bronze age working floor 30m from W hedge. A very prolific site, arrows, knives, scrapers and chips (Robinson 1934, 61, illus. 1). Until its removal in 1934, an oblong stone circle existed at the N end of this field (*ibid.*, 63).
More recent finds include a hollow scraper or spokeshave of devitrified rhyolite and a rough knife of mottled grey flint with traces of extensive use along the working edge (Brown 1961, 78).

HB 74, Peterchurch (SMR 08448) NGR: SO 3630 3820
From Wellbrook Park, Peterchurch - a Bronze Age whetstone. Part of the R. S. G. Robinson Collection at Hereford City Museum (acc. no. 7172)

HB 75, Peterchurch (SMR O1127) NGR: SO 3680 3830
Robinson's "Stockley No. 2", field 1178, 765ft (232m) above OD - scattered over SW end of field, well-worked Neolithic

and Bronze Age implements, arrows and knives (Robinson 1934, 61, illus. 2). More recent finds include a leaf-shaped arrowhead, a notched blade and a Bronze Age barbed and tanged arrowhead (Brown 1961, 77).

HB 76, Vowchurch (SMR 07490) NGR: SO 3590 3765
Bronze Age flints from Poston Camp (see HN 47 and HI 2).

HB 77, Vowchurch (SMR 01128) NGR: SO 3720 3800
From NW of Kiln Wood, Hill Farm, Vowchurch - Robinson's "Hill Farm", field 113, 737 ft. (224m) above OD, a scatter of good quality Bronze Age flints in the S central area of the field (Robinson 1934, 61). This site is about 800m S of those on Stockley Hill and has commanding views down the Grey Valley though none over either the Golden Valley or that of the Wye. Among the finds were a well-worked knife, an arrowhead and a very minute circular scraper (Robinson 1934, 57). The densest area of flints was some 20m from the highest point of the field.

HB 78, St. Margarets (SMR 01518) NGR: SO: 3301 3463
From Marresses Farm - a Later Neolithic Group I axe head. At some later date in the Bronze Age an abortive attempt appears to have been made to turn the implement into a perforated axe-hammer (Norwood 1961, 104-5). Hereford City Museum acc. no. 7801. Wrongly described on the SMR as a battle-axe. See HN 19.

HB 79, Kentchurch (SMR 06791) NGR: SO 4350 2670
From Llanithog Farm, Kentchurch - Neolithic and Bronze Age flints. Now in Hereford City Museum.

9.5 Iron Age (HI 1-14)

Hill-forts (HI 1-7, Fig. 33)

HI 1, Dorstone (SMR 01552, SAM 27512) NGR: SO 3271 4216 (Fig. 35)
A univallate promontory hill-fort on the SE tip of the spur forming the highest portion of Dorstone Hill and divided from the remainder of the plateau by a straight rampart and ditch approx. 55m in length. The rampart is 5.0m wide at the base and stands about 2.0m above the bottom of the ditch. On average, the ditch is 2.5m wide and 0.5m deep. There is no trace of a counterscarp. The enclosure covers is roughly triangular in plan, some 59m by 82m, and covers 0.2ha. The NE slope has been artificially steepened to enhance the defences (Kay 1963).

HI 2, Vowchurch (SMR 01462) NGR: SO 3590 3756 (Fig. 35, 36)
Poston Camp, Lower Park Wood - a small promontory hill-fort of approx. 2.2ha from which the ground falls away steeply on all sides except the N which is defended by a bank and ditch. The site is known locally as "The Rounds" (RCHME 1931, 245). It is possible that the original entrance was situated at the E end of the rampart and there was some evidence of internal quarry scoops. At the W of the site, the rampart continued about half-way along the W scarp before gradually fading out and there may have been another original gateway some half-way along its length (Marshall 1933, 27).

The site was excavated in the Autumn of 1932 (Marshall 1933a, 27) and again in 1958 (Antony 1958). The earlier investigations produced flint evidence of Neolithic and Bronze Age occupation of the hilltop and Romano-British occupation was also attested. Antony pointed out similarities between the material from Poston (especially the "duck-stamped" pottery) and that from Bredon Hill, Worcs., and from the other Herefordshire hill-fort sites of Sutton Walls and Aconbury which has been dated by C-14 to the period c.390 B. C. to c.250 B. C. (Children and Nash 1994, 111). Antony accepted an Iron Age date and a funerary purpose for a barrow close to the hill-fort (see HI 14).

The excavation trench at the E end of the rampart produced soft pale red ware and gritty black ware which were compared to Roman pottery from Ariconium (Marshall 1933a, 28). Trenches to the W produce a blue melon-shaped pendant of Roman date. The rammed floor of a hut produced charcoal, animal teeth and antler. The pottery from this feature included grey-fumed ware with grooved decoration a little way below the rim which Marshall dated to c. 100AD. A bronze brooch was also dated to the period 80 to 120 AD (*loc. cit.*). Another hut-floor below this feature produced the very friable remains of a large flat-bottomed vessel of black-gritted ware. It was evident that the excavations had produced two successive occupation sites, the most recent dating to c. 100 AD (*ibid.*, 29).

HI 3, Madley (SMR 01463) NGR: SO 3877 3677
Timberline Camp - a univallate enclosure of about 2 ha. The rampart is well preserved all around the circumference and stands on average at a height of 1.5m with a ditch about 0.5m deep on the W,N and E sides. There is on entrance to the NE.

The camp was the subject of excavation in 1934 and again in 1950. The 1934 investigations discovered what may have been the remains of an internal stone revetment for the rampart near the entrance. The defences were sectioned - the rampart stood some 5.7m high while the ditch measured some 7.6m across at the top. In the silt infill of the ditch was found the tip of a spearhead.

HI 4, Llanveynoe (Brecon Beacons PRN 5012) NGR: SO 2968 2956 (Fig. 32)
A bivallate promontory hill-fort at a height of 500m above OD on a spectacular spur of rock to east of Black Darren (W. Daren Ddu). The site is small (some 56m by 12m) and defined by two rock-cut ditches and a fragmentary bank. Surveyed 28.4.99.

HI 5, Walterstone (SMR 01586) NGR: SO 3489 2507 (Fig. 36)
Walterstone Camp (also known as Coed y Grafell) - a well-preserved multi-vallate hill-fort - one of the five major hill-forts which guard the south-eastern approaches to the Black Mountains. A roughly circular enclosure of about 4 ha., with three concentric ramparts and ditches to the NW and SW and a single rampart to the E. There are currently three entrances, though the more northerly of the pair on the NE side is likely to be the original one (RCHME 1931, 248).

HI 6, Eaton Bishop (SMR 00907) NGR: SO 4540 3930 (Fig. 36)
Eaton Camp - a bivallate promontory hill fort on the S bank of the Wye at the mouth of the Cage Brook. The fort is roughly triangular in form and covers c. 7 ha. Steep natural slopes form the only defences on the N and SE sides. The western defences, however, are massive, with the inner bank rising to some 5m in height. There are several modern breaches in the defences, but the original entrance probably stood at the NW corner. At the E tip of the fort is a mound which may have formed an element in the original defensive layout (RCHME 1931, 62).

HI 7, Credenhill NGR: SO 450 446 (Fig. 34)
The largest hill-fort in Herefordshire, Credenhill Camp was partly excavated by Stanford in 1963 (Stanford 1970). The site is on a steep hill, well-suited to defence and encloses some 20ha. Two entrances, probably with guard-chambers, survive. Excavation was restricted to an area behind the rampart just S of the E gate. Stanford interpreted the four-post structures he found there as houses and estimated a total population of some 4,000 people - in effect, the political capital of the region. It is now thought that these features are more likely to be granaries. The construction of the fort was dated to c. 390 B. C. (Hogg 1975, 184-185; Children and Nash 1994, 87-89).

Smaller Defended Settlements (HI 8-11, Fig. 33)

HI 8, Craswall (SMR 00157) NGR: SO 2668 3720
From Parc y Meirch, Craswall - the upper stone of a rotary quern of Iron Age type (described in the SMR entry as "Iron Age B Wessex type"). Now in Hereford City Museum (acc. no. 7415).

HI 9, Vowchurch (not on SMR) NGR: SO 363 362

The upper stone of another sandstone rotary quern. Found 1.5km SSE of Poston hill-fort (Norwood 1961, 103-4). At Twyn y Gaer, the introduction of rotary querns such as this and HI 8 has been dated to the period c. 200 B. C. (Probert 1976, 118).

HI 10, Kenchester (SMR 07250) NGR: SO 4460 4260
Field Barn Farm, Brockhall, Kenchester - excavations on a suspected Romano-British temple revealed Iron Age occupation underlying Roman-British buildings. The Iron Age phase consisted of one (possibly two) round houses surrounded by a ditch. The site produced much pottery of late Iron Age date, together with furnace fragments and two crucibles.

HI 11, Garway (SMR 6251) NGR: SO 4423 2492 (Figs. 35, 45)
A well-preserved sub-rectangular, univallate enclosure (approx. 50m by 50m and 0.25ha in area) on the E facing ridge of Garway Hill. On the W and E sides, the ramparts still stand to approx. 3m in height with well-defined ditches, the N and S defences are slighter (approx. 2m high) and no ditch is visible on the S side. The E side is slightly convex. The defences are breached in six places by modern tracks but only that in the E side appears to be original. The site has outstanding views throughout the E.

Stray Finds (HI 12-13, Fig. 33)

HI 12, Madley (SMR 12090) NGR:SO 4185 3743
A Dobunnic gold stater found at Stone Street, Madley in 1981.

HI 13, Kenchester (SMR 08368) NGR: SO 440 428
Gold staters from the site of Magnis - the Roman town of Kenchester. Now in private hands.

Barrows (HI 14, Fig. 33)

HI 14, Peterchurch (SMR 07171) NGR: SO 3620 3840 (Fig. 24)
In Bradley's Wood - an Iron Age barrow excavated in 1932 (Marshall 1933b, 30-35) The site slopes slightly towards the N and has extensive views to the NW towards the Black Mountains. Prior to excavation the mound was some 21m in diameter and 2.30m high. A trench through the centre of the mound failed to find any sign of a central burial, but did produce the remains of nine hearths, five flints and five pieces of pottery (*ibid.*, 31). The flints included an Earlier Neolithic leaf-shaped arrowhead which may was originally thought to have been brought to the site with the fine soil which formed the base of the mound (*ibid.*, 33). At the base of the mound were found two pieces of pottery which Marshall dated to the period c. 50-100 A. D. (*loc. cit.*) and upon which his assignment of the mound to the Iron Age rested.

The structure of the mound was of exceptional interest. The base consisted of a ring-bank of fine soil some 16.5m in diameter and about 1.2m in height. This was then covered with a carefully constructed cairn of small, flat, sandstone slabs tipping steeply inwards (*ibid.*, 32). Although Marshall assumed that the cairn's structure represented a single phase

of construction, it is possible that an earlier ring-bank was incorporated in a later cairn.

Antony suggested an Iron Age date and a funerary purpose for this site. However, the excavation of a similar feature at Croft Ambrey demonstrated ritual use (but not burials) throughout the late Iron Age and Romano-British periods (Stanford 1974, 132-143). In about 75 A. D. a raised ceremonial floor was constructed at Croft Ambrey into which were dug several fire-pits. Also found were numerous fragments of the bones of sheep, goats and cattle together with much broken pottery. This has been taken as evidence of ritual animal sacrifice and feasting (Children and Nash 1994, 95). Marshall's excavation of the Poston mound in 1933 uncovered several hearths similar to those at Croft Ambrey (Marshall 1933b, 30-35) and its seems likely that it fulfilled a similar function.

Appendix: Aerial Photographs

The following aerial photographs were consulted during the compilation of this gazetteer:

1, National Monuments Record of Wales

72/257/040-49
72/257/075-79
72/257/065-69
72/326/049-51
72/326/076-91
72/326/177-79
72/353/680-81
73/089/066-66
73/089/093-94
73/089/115-16
73/089/119
73/089/150-51
73/089/162-63
73/089/164-65
73/089/206-08
73/089/281
75/037/071
75/317/605-08

2, National Monuments Record of England

Llanveynoe
427/1066/UK/1652/2181-86
427/1066/UK/1652/3181-86
SO 2832/1 NMR 15063/22
SO 2832/2 NMR 15063/23
SO 2832/3 NMR 15063/24
SO 2833/1 NMR 15063/25
SO 2833/1 NMR 15063/26

Peterchurch
427/1066/UK/1652/4291-97
427/1066/UK/1652/5291-96
2170/543/2339/0455-56

Clodock
427/1066/UK/1652/1175-79
427/1066/UK/1652/2071-75
427/1066/UK/1652/4176-80
427/1066/UK/1652/5176-80
SO 3228/1 CAP 7669/66
SO 3229/1 NMR 4848/01
SO 3229/2 NMR 4848/02
SO 3229/3 NMR 15062/29
SO 3229/4 NMR 15062/30
SO 3229/5 NMR 15062/31
SO 3229/6 NMR 15062/32

Bibliography

Arch. Camb. - *Archaeologia Cambrensis*
AW - *Archaeology in Wales*
BBCS - *Bulletin of the Board of Celtic Studies*
Mon. Antiq. - *Monmouthshire Antiquary*
PPS - *Proceedings of the Prehistoric Society*
TWNFC - *Transactions of the Woolhope Naturalist Field Club*

Antony, I. E. 1958. *The Iron Age Camp at Poston, Herefordshire* (Hereford: The Woolhope Club).

Ashton, N. and David., A. 1994. *Stories in Stone* (London: Lithic Studies Society Occasional Papers No. 4).

Babbidge, A. 1977. 'Reconnaissance excavations at Coed y Bwnydd, Betws Newydd, 1969-1971', *Mon. Antiq.* Vol. III, Pts. 3-4 (1977), 159-178.

Barnatt, J. 1989. *The Stone Circles of Britain* (BAR British Ser. 215 i and ii, Oxford).

Barrett, J. C. 1994. *Fragments from Antiquity: An Archaeology of Social Life in Britain, 2900-1200 B. C.* (Oxford: Blackwell).

Bewley, R. 1994. *Prehistoric Settlements* (London: Batsford)

Boon, G. C. and Lewis, J. M. 1976 (eds.) *Welsh Antiquity, essays presented to H. N. Savory* (Cardiff, National Museum of Wales).

Bradley, R. 1984. *The Social Foundations of Prehistoric Britain* (London: Longman.

Bradley, R. 1987. 'Flint technology and the character of Neolithic settlement' in Brown and Edmonds 1987, 181-185.

Bradley, R. 1993. *Altering the Earth* (Edinburgh: Soc. of Antiquaries of Scotland)

Bradley, R. 1998. *The Significance of Monuments* (London and New York: Routledge)

Bradley R. and Edmonds, M. 1993. *Interpreting the Axe Trade* (Cambridge: University Press).

Bradley, R. and Gardiner, J. 1984. (eds.) *Neolithic Studies*, BAR Brit. Ser. 133 (Oxford)

Britnell, W. J. and Savory, H. N. 1984. *Gwernvale and Penywyrlod: Two Neolithic Long Cairns in the Black Mountains of Brecknock* (Cambrian Archaeological Monographs No. 2).

Brown, A. 1991. 'Structured deposition and technological change among the flaked stone artefacts from Cranborne Chase' in Barret, J.C. et. al. 1991. *Papers on the Prehistoric Archaeology of Cranborne Chase* (Oxford: Oxbow Monograph 11), 101-33.

Brown, A. E. 1961. 'Records of surface finds in made in Herefordshire, 1951-60', TWNFC 37 (1961), 77-91.

Brown, A. E. 1972. 'Round barrows in Herefordshire', TWNFC 40 (1972), 315-317.

Brown, A. E. 1973. 'More flint and stone implements from Herefordshire', TWNFC 41 (1973), 115-117.

Brown, A. G. and Edmonds, M. R. 1987. (eds.) *Lithic Analysis and Later British Prehistory* (Oxford: BAR 162).

Burgess, C. B. 1963. 'A socketed axe from Llanarth, Mon.', *Mon. Antiq.* Vol. I, Pt. III (1963), 20-22.

Burgess, C. B. 1980. 'The Bronze Age in Wales' in Taylor 1980, 243-286.

Burl, A. 1976. *The Stone Circles of the British Isles* (London: Yale University Press)

Burl, A. 1979. *Prehistoric Avebury* (New Haven and London: Yale University Press).

Burns, E. K. 1995. 'The prehistory collection at Abergavenny Museum: a catalogue', *Gwent Local History* 79 (Autumn 1995), 41-47.

Case, H. 1993. 'Beakers: deconstruction and after', PPS 59 (1993), 241-268.

Caseldine, A. 1990. *Environmental Archaeology in Wales* (Cadw and St. David's College, University of Wales, Lampeter).

Chappell, S. 1987. *Stone Axe Morphology and Distribution in Neolithic Britain*, BAR Brit. Ser. 177, i and ii.

Children G. and Nash, G. 1994. *Prehistoric Sites of Herefordshire* (Little Logaston: Logaston Press).

Children G. and Nash, G. 1996. *Prehistoric Sites of Monmouthshire* (Little Logaston: Logaston Press).

Clarke, D. L. 1970. *Beaker Pottery of Great Britain and Ireland*, Vols. 1 and 2 (Cambridge: University Press).

Clarke, D. V., Gowie, T. G. and Foxon, A. 1985. *Symbols of Power at the Time of Stonehenge* (Edinburgh: HMSO and National Museum of Antiquities of Scotland).

Clay, P. 1998. 'Neolithic/Bronze Age pit circles and their environs at Oakham, Rutland', PPS 64 (1998), 293-331.

Clough T. H. McK. and Cummins, W. A. 1988. *Stone Axe Studies* Vol. 2 (CBA Research Report 69)).

Cohen, I. 1952a. 'Barrow near Peterchurch', TWNFC 34 (1952), 31.

Cohen, I. 1952b. 'Lozenge-shaped flint arrowhead from Poston, Peterchurch', TWNFC 34 (1952), 36.

Condit, T. and Simpson, D. 1998. 'Irish hengiform enclosures and related monuments: a review' in Gibson and Simpson 1998, 45-61.

Corcoran, J. X. W. P. 1969. 'The Cotswold-Severn Group' in Powell et al. 1969., 13-104.

Crampton, C. B. and Webley, D. 1966. 'A Section through the Mynydd Troed Long Barrow, Brecknock', BBCS 22, 71-77.

Crawford, O. G. S. 1925. *The Long Barrows of the Cotswolds* (Gloucester: John Bellows).

Cunliffe, B. 1991. *Iron Age Communities in Britain* (London: Routledge and Kegan Paul, 3rd ed.).

Cunliffe, B. 1993. *Danebury* (London: Batsford/English Heritage).

Darvill, T. C. 1979. 'Court cairns, passage graves and social change in Ireland', *Man* (ns) 14, 311-327.

Darvill, T. C. 1982. *The Megalithic Chambered Tombs of the Severn-Cotswold Region* (Highworth: Vorda).

Darvill, T. C. 1987. *Prehistoric Britain* (London: Batsford).

Davies, W. 1979. *The Llandaff Charters* (NLW, Aberystwyth).

Dorling, P. 1990. 'Hatterall Hill', AW 30 (1990), 52.

Dorling, P. 1991. 'Hatterall Hill', AW 31 (1991), 21.

Drewett, P. L. 1975. 'The excavation of an oval burial mound of the third millennium B. C. at Alfriston, East Sussex, 1974', PPS 41, 119-152.

Dumville, D. N., 1986. 'The Historical Value of the Historia Brittonum', *Arthurian Literature* IV, (1986), pp.21/2.

Dunn, C. J. 1970. 'Hatterall Hill', AW 10 (1970), 12.

Edmonds, M. 1995. *Stone Tools and Society* (London: Batsford).

Edmonds, M. and Thomas, J. 1987. 'The Archers: an everyday story of country folk' in Brown and Edmonds 1987, 187-199.

Evans, J. G. *et al.* 1975. *The Effect of Man on the Landscape of the Highland Zone* (CBA Research Reports 11).

Evans, J. G. and Rhŷs, J. 1893 (eds.) *The Text of the Book of Llan Dâv* (NLW, Aberystwyth facsimile edition 1979)

Ford, S. et al. 1984. 'Flint-working in the Metal Age', *Oxford Journal of Archaeology* 3, 157-173.

Ford, S. 1987a. 'Chronological and functional aspects of flint assemblages' in Brown and Edmonds 1987, 67-85.

Ford, S. 1987b. 'Flint scatters and prehistoric settlement patterns in south Oxfordshire and east Berkshire' in Brown and Edmonds 1987, 101-135.

Foster, I. Ll. and Alcock, L. 1963. *Culture and Environment* (London: Routledge and Kegan Paul).

Gardiner, J. 1987. 'Tales of the unexpected: approaches to the assessment and interpretation of museum flint collections', in Brown and Edmonds 1987, 49-65.

Garton, D. *et. al.* 1989. 'Newton Cliffs; a flint working and settlement site in the Trent Valley' in Philips 1989, 81-180.

Gelling, M. 1988. *Signposts to the Past* (Phillimore, Chichester, repr. 1992)

Gibson, A. 1995 .'First impressions: a review of Peterborough Ware in Wales' in Kinnes and Varndell 1995, 23-40.

Gibson, A. and Simpson, D. 1998. *Prehistoric Ritual and Religion* (Stroud: Sutton).

Gibson, A. and Wood, A. 1990. *Prehistoric Pottery for the Archaeologist* (Leicester: University Press).

Graslund, B. 1994. 'Prehistoric soul beliefs in northern Europe', PPS 60, 15-26.

Green, H. S. 1980. *The Flint Arrowheads of the British Isles*, BAR Brit. Ser. 80 (Oxford).

Griffiths, W. E. 1960. 'The excavation of stone circles near Penmaenmawr, North Wales', PPS 26, 303-339.

Grimes, W. F. 1939. 'The excavation of Ty-Isaf Long Cairn, Brecknock', PPS 5 (1939), 119-142.

Grimes, W. F. 1951. *The Prehistory of Wales* (Cardiff: National Museum of Wales)

Grimes, W. F. 1963. 'The stone circles and related monuments of Wales' in Foster and Alcock, 1963, 93-152.

Grinsell, L. V. 1993. 'Herefordshire barrows', TWNFC 47 (1993), 299-317.

Guilbert, G. 1976. 'Moel y Gaer (Rhosesmor) 1972-1973: an area excavation in the interior' in Harding 1976, 301-317.

Harding, D. W. 1976. *Hill-forts - Later Prehistoric Earthworks in Britain and Ireland* (London: Academic Press).

Harding, A. F. and Lee, G. E. 1987. *Henge Monuments and Related Sites of Great Britain* (BAR British Ser. 175, Oxford).

Haselgrove, C. 1985. 'Inference from ploughsoil artefact samples' in Haselgrove *et. al.* 1985, 7-29.

Haselgrove, C. *et al.* 1985. (eds.) *Archaeology from the Ploughsoil* (Sheffield: Dept. of Archaeology and Prehistory, University of Sheffield).

Healy, F. 1987. 'Prediction or Prejudice? The relationship between field survey and excavation' in Brown and Edmonds 1987, 9-17.

Hemp, W. J. 1935. 'Arthur's Stone, Dorstone, Herefordshire', *Arch. Camb.* 90 (1935), 288-292.

Hodder, I. 1990. *The Domestication of Europe* (Oxford: Blackwell).

Hogg, A. H. A. 1973. 'Hill-forts and Herefordshire', TWNFC 41 (1973), 14-22.

Hogg, A. H. A. 1975. *Hill-Forts of Britain* (London: Hart-Davis).

Holgate, R. 1985. 'Identifying Neolithic settlements in Britain: the role of field survey in the interpretation of lithic scatters' in Haselgrove, C. *et al.* 1985, 51-57.

Houlder, C. H. 1965. 'Dorstone Hill', AW 5 (1965), 10.

Jacobi, R.M. 1980b. 'The Early Holocene Settlement of Wales' in Taylor 1980, 131-206.

Jarrett, M. G. and Wrathmell, S. 1981. *Whitton: An Iron Age and Roman Farmstead in South Glamorgan* (Cardiff: University of Wales Press).

Jones, P. .M. 1972. 'Garn Wen', AW 12 (1972), 18.

Jones, P. .M. 1976a. 'Garn Wen', AW 16 (1976), 17.

Jones, P. .M. 1976b. 'Black Darren', AW 16 (1976), 25.

Jones, P. .M. 1976c. 'Hatterall Hill', AW 16 (1976), 25.

Jones, P. .M. 1978a. 'Cwm Bwchell (sic)', AW 18 (1978), 40.

Jones, P. .M. 1978b. 'Craig Ddu', AW 18 (1978), 40.

Jones, P. .M. 1978c. 'Loxidge Tump', AW 18 (1978), 40.

Jones, P. .M. 1978d. 'Hatterall Ridge', AW 18 (1978), 40.

Jones, P. .M. 1978e. 'Pen y Gadair Fawr', AW 18 (1978), 60.

Jones, P. .M. 1979. 'The Darren', AW 19 (1979), 9.

Jones, P. M. 1980. ' Bâl Mawr', AW 20 (1980), 20.

Jones, P. .M. 1981. 'Cross Ash', AW 21 (1981), 30.

Jones, P. .M., and Palmer, K. 1983. 'Hatterall Ridge', AW 23 (1983), 24.

Jones, P. .M., and Palmer, K. 1992. 'Hatterall Hill', AW 32 (1992), 49.

Jones, P. .M., and Palmer, K. and Tucker 1978. 'Hatterall Hill', AW 18 (1978), 40.

Jones P. M., Tucker, B. and Palmer, K. 1980. 'Craig Ddu', AW 20 (1980), 34- 35.

Jenkins, R. J. 1957. 'Flint artifacts and other material found in the Kington area during 1956 and 1957', TWNFC 35 (1957), 320-327.

Kay, R. E. 1963. 'Three unrecorded earthworks from south-west Herefordshire', TWNFC 39 (1963).

Kay, R. E. 1984. 'Pentwyn Hill-fort', TWNFC 44, Part III, 315-320.

Kinnes, I. and Varndell, G. 1995. *Unbaked Urns of Rudely Shape: Essays on British and Irish pottery for Ian Longworth* (Oxford: Oxbow Monograph 55).

de Laet. S. 1976. (ed.) *Acculturation and Continuity in Atlantic Europe* (Briges: de Tempel).

Leslie, J. V. L. 1962. 'The Camp, Tir y Mynach', AW 2 (1962), 5.

Lillie, M. C. 1991. *Bronze Age Gwent* (University of Nottingham unpublished dissertation), 56.

Lloyd Jones, M. 1984. *Society and Settlement in Wales and the Marches 500 B. C. to A. D. 1000*, BAR Brit. Ser. 121, i and ii (Oxford).

Lynch, F. 1975. 'The impact of landscape on prehistoric man' in Evans et al. 1975, 124-7. Evans, J. G. *et al.* 1975. *The Effect of Man on the Landscape of the Highland Zone* (CBA Research Reports 11).

Lynch, F. 1993. *Excavations in the Brenig Valley* (Cambrian Monographs 5, Bangor).

Lynch, F. and Burgess, C. 1972 (eds.) *Prehistoric Man in Wales and the West* (Adams and Dart, Bath).

O' Kelly, M. J. 1989. *Early Ireland: an Introduction to Irish Prehistory* (Cambridge: CUP).

Makepeace, G. 1996. 'Ysgyryd Fawr/The Skirrid', AW 36 (1996), 66-68.

Makepeace, G. 1997a. 'Llanelli', AW 37 (1997), 58.

Makepeace, G. 1997b. 'Llantilio Crossenny', AW 37 (1997), 58.

Makepeace, G. 1997c. 'Abergavenny, Sugar Loaf', AW 37 (1997), 57.

Manning, W. H. 1981. *Report on the Excavations at Usk 1965-1976: The Fortress Excavations 1968-1971* (Cardiff: Board of Celtic Studies).

Marshall, G. 1932. 'Report on the discovery of two Bronze Age cists in the Olchon Valley, Herefordshire', TWNFC (1932), 147-153.

Marshall, G. 1933a. 'Lower Park Wood Camp, Poston, in the parish of Vowchurch, and some remarks on the Iron Age in Herefordshire', TWNFC (1933), 21-29.

Marshall, G. 1933b. 'Report on the excavation of a prehistoric mound in the parish of Peterchurch, Herefordshire', TWNFC (1933), 30-35.

Marshall, E. C. and Murphy, K. 1991. 'The excavation of two Bronze Age round cairns with associated standing stones in Dyfed: Parc Maen and Aber Camddwr II', *Arch. Camb.* CXL, 28-76.

Mein, A.G. 1989. 'Tregare', AW 29 (1989), 48.

Mein, A.G. 1990. 'White Castle Farm', AW 30 (1990), 52.

Mellars, P. 1976. 'Settlement patterns and industrial variability in the British Mesolithic', in Sieveking *et al.* 1976, 375-399.

Morris, J., (1980) (ed.) *Nennius, British History and the Welsh Annals* (Phillimore, London and Chichester).

Musson, C. R. 1976. 'Excavations at the Breiddin 1969-1973' in Harding 1976, 293-302.

Myers, A. 1987. 'All shot to pieces? Inter-assemblage variability, lithic analysis and Mesolithic assemblage 'types'; some preliminary observations' in Brown and Edmonds 1987, 137-153.

Nash, G. 1997. 'Monumentality and the landscape: the possible symbolic and political distribution of long chambered tombs around the Black Mountains, central Wales' in Nash, G. 1997. (ed.), *Semiotics of Landscape: Archaeology of Mind*, BAR Brit. Ser. 661, 17-30.

Nash-Williams, V.E. 1933. 'An early Iron Age hill-fort at Llanmelin, near Caerwent, Monmouthshire', *Arch. Camb.*, LXXXVIII (1933), 237-346.

Nash-Williams, V. E. 1939. 'An early Iron Age coastal camp at Sudbrook, Monmouthshire', *Arch. Camb.*, XCIV (1939), 42-79.

Needham, S. 1996. 'Chronology and periodisation in the British Bronze Age', *Acta Archaeologia* 67 (1996), 121-140.

Norwood, J. F. L. 1957. 'Prehistoric accessions to Hereford Museum, 1957', TWNFC 35 (1957), 316-320.

Norwood, J. F. L. 1959. 'Prehistoric accessions to Hereford Museum, 1958-59', TWNFC 36 (1959), 233-237.

Norwood, J. F. L. 1961. 'Prehistoric accessions to Hereford Museum, 1960-61', TWNFC 37, Pt. I (1961), 102-107.

Norwood, J. F. L. 1963. 'Prehistoric accessions to Hereford Museum, 1962-63', TWNFC 37, Pt. III (1963), 345-349.

Palmer, K. 1980. 'Black Mountains', AW 20 (1980), 33-34.

Palmer, K. and Jones, P. M. 1980. 'Ysgyryd Fawr', AW 20 (1980), 34.

Palmer, K. and Tucker, B. 1978. 'Twyn y Gaer', AW 18 (1978), 40.

Palmer, K. and Tucker, B. 1978. 'Bâl Bach', AW 18 (1978), 40.

Parker Pearson, M. 1993. *Bronze Age Britain* (London: Batsford/English Heritage).

Philips, P. 1989. (ed.) *Archaeology and Landscape Studies* (Oxford: BAR 208).

Piggott, S. 1962. *The West Kennet Long Barrow* (London).

Powell, T. E. G. *et al.* 1969. *Megalithic Enquiries in the West of Britain* (Liverpool: University Press).

Pitts, M. W. and Jacobi, R. M. 1979. 'Some aspects of change in flaked stone industries of the Mesolithic and Neolithic in southern Britain', *Journal of Archaeological Science* 6 (1979), 163-177.

Price, M. D. R. 1981. Palynological Studies on the Black Mountains, South Wales, *unpublished Ph.D. thesis*, University of London.

Probert, L. A. *et al.* 1968-69. 'Excavations at Abergavenny 1962-69, I, Prehistoric and Roman Finds', *Mon. Antiq.*, Vol. II, Part IV (1968069), 163-198.

Probert, L. A. 1976. 'Twyn y Gaer hill-fort, Gwent: an interim assessment' in Boon and Lewis 1976, 105-120.

Pye, W. R. 1958. 'Report on prehistoric finds in north-west Herefordshire', TWNFC 36 (1958), 80-83.

Pye, W. R. 1967. 'Dorstone Hill, Dorstone', AW 7 (1967), 8.

Pye, W. R. 1968. 'Dorstone Hill, Dorstone', AW 8 (1968), 8-9.

Pye, W.R. 1969. 'Dorstone Hill', AW 9 (1969), 11.

RCAHMW 1976. *An Inventory of the Ancient Monuments in Glamorgan, Vol. 1 Part 1: The Stone and Bronze Ages* (Cardiff: HMSO).

RCAHMW 1986. *An Inventory of the Ancient Monuments in Brecknock (Brycheiniog), Part ii: Hill-forts and Roman Remains* (Cardiff: HMSO).

RCAHMW 1997. *An Inventory of the Ancient Monuments in Brecknock (Brycheiniog), Part i: Later Prehistoric Monuments and Unenclosed Settlements to 1000 A. D.* (Aberystwyth: RCAHMW).

RCHME 1931. *An Inventory of the Historical Monuments in Herefordshire, Vol. I - South West* (London: HMSO).

Rees, S. 1992. *A Guide to Ancient and Historic Wales: Dyfed* (London: HMSO)

Renfrew, C. 1973a. *Social Archaeology* (Southampton: University Press).

Renfrew, C. 1973b. 'Monuments, mobilisation and social organisation in Neolithic Wessex' in Renfrew 1973c, 539-558.

Renfrew, C. 1973c. (ed.) *The Explanation of Culture Change: Models in Prehistory* (London: Duckworth).

Renfrew, C. 1976. 'Megaliths, territories and population' in de Laet 1976, 198-220.

Richards, J. 1990. *The Stonehenge Environs Project* (London: Historic Buildings and Monuments Commission).

Richardson, R. E. 1992. 'Iron Age and Romano-British farmland in the Herefordshire area', TWNFC 47 (1992), 144-161.

Robinson, R. S. G. 1934. 'Flint workers and flint users in the Golden Valley', TWNFC (1934), 54-63.

Robinson, R. S. G. 1936. 'Recent discoveries along the Greenway', TWNFC (1936), 47-49.

Robinson, R. S. G. 1946. 'The prehistoric occupation of Cefn Hill near Craswall', TWNFC 32 (1946), 32-37.

Robinson, R. S. G. 1950. 'Notes on Bronze Age settlements on Abbey Farm, Craswall', TWNFC 33 (1950), 113-117.

Roese, H. E. 1978. 'Recent field observations on Neolithic and Bronze Age monuments in south-east Wales', BBCS 28 (1978), 129-135.

Roese, H. E. 1980. 'Some aspects of topographical locations of Neolithic and Bronze Age monuments in Wales: I Menhirs', BBCS 28 (1980), 645-655.

Roese, H. E. 1981a. 'Some aspects of topographical locations of Neolithic and Bronze Age monuments in Wales: II Henges and Circles', BBCS 29 (1981), 164-170.

Roese, H. E. 1981b. 'Some aspects of topographical locations of Neolithic and Bronze Age monuments in Wales: III Round Cairns and Round Barrows', BBCS 29 (1981), 575-587.

Roese, H. E. 1981c. 'Some aspects of topographical locations of Neolithic and Bronze Age monuments in Wales: IV Chambered Tombs and Burial Chambers', BBCS 29 (1981), 765-775.

Savile, A. 1990. *Hazleton North* (London: Historic Buildings and Monuments Commission).

Savory, H. N. 1963. 'The personality of the Southern Marches of Wales in the Neolithic and Early Bronze Age' in Foster and Alcock 1963, 25-52.

Savory, H. N. 1971. 'Prehistoric Brecknock', *Brycheiniog* 15 (1971), 3-22.

Savory, H. N. 1976. 'Welsh hill-forts: a reappraisal of recent research', in Harding 1976, 237-291.

Savory, H. N. 1980a. *Guide Catalogue of the Bronze Age Collections* (Cardiff: National Museum of Wales).

Savory, H. N. 1980b. 'The Neolithic in Wales', in Taylor 1980, 207-232.

Schofield, A.J. 1987. 'Putting lithics to the test: non-site analysis and the Neolithic settlement of southern England', *Oxford Journal of Archaeology* 6, 269-86.

Schofield, A.J. 1991a. (ed.) *Interpreting Artefact Scatters. Contributions to Ploughzone Archaeology* (Oxford: Oxbow Monograph 4).

Schofield, A.J. 1991b. 'Artefact distributions as activity areas: examples from south-eastern England' in Schofield, A.J. 1991a., 117-28.

Schofield, A. J. 1994. 'Looking back with regret; looking forward with optimism: making more of surface lithic scatter sites' in Ashton and David 1994, 90-98.

Sherratt, A. 1990. 'The genesis of megaliths: monumentality, ethnicity and social complexity in Neolithic north-west Europe' in Sherratt 1997, 333-353.

Sherratt, A. 1995. 'Instruments of conversion? The role of megaliths in the Mesolithic-Neolithic transition' in Sherratt 1997, 354-371.

Sherratt, A. 1997. *Economy and Society in Prehistoric Europe: Changing Perspectives* (Edinburgh: University Press).

Sieveking, G. de G., Longworth, I. H. and Wilson, K. E. 1976. *Problems in Economic and Social Archaeology* (London: Duckworth).

Stanford, S. C. 1970. 'Credenhill Camp, Herefordshire', *Archaeological Journal* 127 (1970), 82-129.

Stanford, S. C. 1972. 'The function and population of hill-forts in the Central Marches' in Lynch and Burgess 1972, 307-319.

Stanford, S. C. 1974. *Croft Ambrey* (Hereford: The Woolhope Club).

Stanford, S. C. 1981. *Midsummer Hill: An Iron Age Hill-fort on the Malverns* (Hereford: The Woolhope Club).

Stanford, S. C. 1991. *The Archaeology of the Welsh Marches* (Ludlow: S. C. Stanford)

Stockley, J. 1998. *The Hill-forts of the Woolhope Dome, Herefordshire* (University of Bristol unpublished MA dissertation).

Taylor, J.A. 1980. (ed.) *Culture and Environment in Prehistoric Wales*, BAR Brit. Ser. 76 (Oxford).

Tingle, M. 1987. 'Inferential limits and surface scatters: the case of the Maddle Farm and Vale of the White Horse fieldwalking survey' in Brown and Edmonds 1987, 87-99.

Thom, A. 1967. *Megalithic Sites in Britain* (Oxford).

Thomas, J. 1988. 'The social significance of Cotswold-Severn burial sites', *Man* 23 (1988), 540-559.

Thorpe, I. J. 1984. 'Ritual, power and ideology: a reconstruction of Earlier Neolithic rituals in Wessex' in Bradley and Gardiner 1984, 41-60.

Tilley, C. 1994. *A Phenomenology of Landscape: Places, Paths and Monuments* (Oxford: Berg).

Trett, B. and Hudson, R. 1989. 'Newport Museum - recent acquisitions', AW 29 (1989), 48.

Trett, B. and Hudson, R. 1990. 'Newport Museum - recent acquisitions', AW 30 (1990), 52.

Trett, B. and Hudson, R. 1991. 'Newport Museum - recent acquisitions', AW 31 (1990), 21-22.

Warrilow, W., Owen, G. and Britnell , W. J. 1986. 'Eight ring-ditches at Four Crosses, Llandysilio, Powys, 1981-85', PPS 52 (1986), 53-88.

Webley, D. P. 1958. 'A "cairn cemetery" and Secondary Neolithic Dwelling on Cefn Cilsanws, Vaynor (Brecs.)', BBCS 18, 79-88.

Webley, D. P. 1976. 'How the west was won: prehistoric land-use in the Southern Marches', in Boon and Lewis 1976, 19-35.

Wheeler, R. E. M. 1925. *Prehistoric and Roman Wales* (Oxford: Clarendon Press).

Wheeler, R.E.M. and Wheeler, T.V. 1932. *Report on the Excavation of the Prehistoric, Roman and Post-Roman Site in Lydney Park, Gloucestershire* (Society of Antiquaries Research Report no. 9).

Whittle, A. W. R. 1977. *The Earlier Neolithic of Southern England and its Continental Background*, BAR Brit. Ser. 35 (Oxford).

Whittle, A. W. R. 1991. 'Wayland's Smithy, Oxfordshire: excavations at the Neolithic tomb in 1962-63 by R. J. C. Atkinson and S. Piggott', PPS 57(2), 61-101.

Whittle, A. W. R. 1996. *Europe in the Neolithic: the Creation of New Worlds* (Cambridge: University Press).

Whittle, E. 1992. *A Guide to Ancient and Historic Wales: Glamorgan and Gwent* (London: HMSO)

Williams, G. 1988. *The Standing Stones of Wales and South-West England*, BAR Brit. Ser. 197 (Oxford).

Williams, J. G. 1966. 'Herefordshire's prehistoric standing stones', TWNFC 38 (1966), 255-256.

Williams, R. 1990. *People of the Black Mountains: I The Beginning* (London: Palladin).

Wymer, J. J. 1977. *Gazetteer of Mesolithic Sites in England and Wales* (CBA Research Report 20).